ASSESSING ORGANIZATIONAL COMMUNICATION

THE GUILFORD COMMUNICATION SERIES

Recent Volumes

Assessing Organizational Communication

STRATEGIC COMMUNICATION AUDITS

CAL W. DOWNS
ALLYSON D. ADRIAN

THE GUILFORD PRESS
New York   London

© 2004 The Guilford Press
A Division of Guilford Publications, Inc.
72 Spring Street, New York, NY 10012
www.guilford.com

Printed in the United States of America

This book is printed on acid-free paper.

Last digit is print number: 9 8 7 6 5 4 3 2 1

Library of Congress Cataloging-in-Publication Data
Downs, Cal W., 1936–
    Assessing organizational communication: strategic communication audits / Cal W. Downs,
Allyson D. Adrian.
        p. cm. — (The Guilford communication series)
    Completely rev. ed. of and successor to: Communication audits / Cal W. Downs. c1988.
    Includes bibliographical references and indexes.
    ISBN 1-59385-010-7 (pbk: alk. paper)
    1. Communication in organizations—Auditing.   2. Management audit.   3. Communication in
management.   4. Intercultural communication.   5. Organizational effectiveness—Evaluation.
I. Title: Strategic communication audits.   II. Adrian, Allyson D.   III. Downs, Cal W., 1936–
Communication audits.   IV. Title.   V. Series.
    HD30.3.D68 2004
    658.4′5—dc22

                                                                          2004003132

Preface

Teaching and consulting in organizational communication have been immensely rewarding to us. The blending of the academic orientation toward theory and the consulting orientation toward utility and practicality has been challenging, gratifying, and humbling. Thousands of books and articles have been published to "explain" how communication is supposed to work in organizations, but our work in many organizations has taught us how inadequate most of the generalizations are. That is why we try to avoid exact formulas for assessments and interpretation of data. We emphasize to students that the ability to analyze is one of the most important skills they can learn, but doing it well requires creativity, an effort to move out of the academic box, and a great enthusiasm for new organizational experiences.

The purpose of this book is to explain different means of analysis, from which the reader is free to choose what will work best in a given situation. No attempt is made to rank-order them, and we encourage people to use applicable bits of each as well as to develop new technologies.

As you read this book, keep in mind that the aim is not to provide formulas for the analysis or auditing of organizations. The primary aim is to acquaint you with some tools of the trade, to describe the basic strategy of the art, and to challenge you to improve upon them.

Acknowledgments

My growth has been the product of collaboration with many people. One of my exciting growth periods was during the development of the ICA audit procedures, and I am deeply indebted to many colleagues: Gerry Goldhaber, Tom Porter, Don Schwartz, Phil Salem, Peter Hamilton, Sue DeWine, Bill Ticehurst, Howard Greenbaum, Anita James, Susan Hellwegg, and Ray Falcione. In a sense, they are the old guard. Now there are many younger colleagues who have continued to teach me lessons about analysis. Particularly, I owe a great deal to former graduate students with whom I have worked who stimulated me to grow in new ways: Phillip Clampitt, Angie Laird Brenton, Al Hydeman, Gerald Driskill, Ana Jensen, Di Wuthnow, Federico Varona, Robert Chandler, John McGrath, Darren Lawson, John Gribas, Tammie Potvin, David Cook, James Patterson, and many others. Finally, I must also acknowledge the contributions of the many managers in organizations with whom I have worked. Jack Light, Chuck Curtis, Doug Newberry, Dan Osinski, Sherry Schaub, Jeannette Terry, Mofid Allossi, Kip Rosner, Clyde Wills, David Zhong, David Green, and Ed Klumpp are a few who deserve special recognition. I have grown and refined my thinking because of them.

—C. W. D.

I too owe a great debt to the people listed above. They have been my teachers, mentors, and fellow students. They have made my study of organizations infinitely more challenging and enjoyable. To their names I would add those of my colleagues in the communication area at the McDonough School of Business at Georgetown University: Annette Shelby and Lamar Reinsch. They opened up a new world of ideas to me about communication in organizations. Likewise, Michael Fitzgerald crystallized for me the importance of strategic conversations in everyday communication. Several students have contributed to my understanding of the communicative needs of people in the 21st century: Alisa Tugberk, Aleksander Terzic, Ece Altay, Sara Kim, and Jeremy Kestler have helped me focus on communication in contexts in the United States and the world. Finally, a special thanks goes to my assistant, Maria Luisa Maggiolo, for her help on the manuscript and her willingness to debate ideas over a good cup of coffee. May the learning continue.

—A. D. A.

Contents

1

Communication Audits as Organizational Development

Cal Downs's internal communication audit allowed us to identify critical breaks in our communications chain. We have incorporated these data into our strategic plan, and now we can track the improved ability of our departments to communicate with one another.
—CHARLES L. CURTIS, CEO, Advertising Company

The approach to the communication audit, particularly the well-studied use of communication factors, gave a much more diagnostic approach than many alternative surveys. We feel very confident in going forward with the base of information that we now have as a result.
—HUGH STUART-BUTTLE, Corporate Communications Director, United Kingdom

Communication problems in the organization are not unlike the progressive development of a headache. If the initial bodily cues are ignored or not monitored, the full throb will hit. The result is much more time and effort lost in trying to correct the unbearable condition than would have been needed to prevent the situation in the first place. The communication audit can provide that initial sensoring or monitoring for the organization that will allow for a preventative stance regarding communication problems rather than the typical corrective stance. —HOWARD GREENBAUM AND NOEL WHITE, Professors

The audit process served as a catalyst for organizational change by bringing us face-to-face with issues only randomly perceived before. The result provided a framework for specific action steps such as: • the investment of increased attention and energy in the planning function at all levels of the organization; • an increased focus on the skills of giving performance feedback and recognizing excellence in staff training.
—JEANNETTE TERRY, Director of Staff Development, Seminar Company

Our management team has studied the results of the audit to address several of the key issues that were brought to our attention. Efforts will be directed to maintain the areas of strength and to improve upon a select number of weaknesses. I thought it was a favorable experience.
—STEPHEN R. SCHUCHART, Vice-president, Savings and Loan Company

At every level—interpersonal, organizational, and international—people depend on effective communication, and they expect that their problems will be solved by good communication. When a married couple petitions for a divorce, observers often assume they must have had a communication problem. When employees initiate a work slowdown or strike, outside observers may blame such actions on a lack of communication between workers and management. And when readers learn that international superpowers have broken off negotiations, they often wonder why the negotiators could not communicate better. But as these examples illustrate, a common tendency is to take communication for granted until there is some problem. This predisposition has led to some terrible mistakes. No one needs to convince most organizational members of the importance of communication: they know it intuitively; they experience its results daily; they have faith in what it can accomplish. But we find that many organizational members are still stuck with the habitual behavior of not paying attention to communication until something goes awry. Such concentration on problems may be typical human nature, but such behavior cannot be the basis for excellent organizational development.

To overcome the tendency to pay attention to communication only after a problem arises, we advocate in this book that organizational processes need periodic monitoring. Organizational members need a realistic determination of which organizational processes are operating effectively as well as where potential problems are developing. Although management guru Warren Bennis (1969) described this need graphically many years ago, organizational cycles are still very apparent:

> Organizational systems, like other organisms, evolve and have a life cycle. They have a dawn and, quite often in recent years, a sudden old age or stagnation periods. Given the pace of events and the turbulent environment, organizations confront tremendous problems if decline is not inevitable. Essentially, this means that organizational systems must renew themselves continuously if they are to survive in this society. (p. 37)

The dynamism of national economies sometimes compresses the length of time in the cycles so that things change even more rapidly today than when Bennis made his statement. A combination of downsizing, reengineering, deregulation, rapid technological innovations, employee mobility, international competition, wars, attacks by terrorists, and independence of the workforce have produced dynamic environments in which organizations try to survive and prosper. These changes also have created an awareness of the tremendous importance of internal organizational communication to any organization's attempts to remain effective.

At the most fundamental level, organizations need to monitor how well employees communicate because the organization's very survival often depends on workers' abilities to exchange and coordinate information. No one claims that lack of communication is the only reason for organizational problems. For example, good internal communication would not have kept the airlines from suffering a decline in passengers after 9-11. The psychological impact of that disaster on travelers and business operations was unpredictable. Nevertheless, Hargie and Tourish (2000) boldly claim that *many* organizational difficulties are a result of poor internal communication policies. That sounds straightforward; however, organizational contexts and environments significantly influence the success of organizational communication.

Globalization offers a good case study. Globalization demands that people from different national cultures work together, sharing information and interacting in ways that are not common in some cultures. Intercultural seminars by both Downs and Adrian have reinforced the fact that what is taught as standard communication procedures in U.S. schools of business simply does not work in other cultures. So what would one expect to happen when people from different cultures work together using very different prescriptions about what will make them effective? The necessity to adapt to others makes sense but is also often resisted. For example, many Americans believe they are most effective when they are frank and to the point, but this frank behavior may be considered very rude by people from other cultures. Recently we worked in a company in which 17 different languages were spoken on one floor. With such cultural mixes, there was a predictable opportunity for communication problems to arise and a need to assess how well people were communicating internally. We can predict that there might be communication problems, but we cannot predict exactly what those problems will be. A communication audit can clarify the situation.

COMMUNICATION IN THE WORK ORGANIZATION

Although many people accept the concept of communication as being important to organizational effectiveness, they often oversimplify its role, considering communication to be a mere message exchange or a simple technique that, if followed, can automatically mold a person into an effective communicator. Some people also treat communication as a manipulative tool: if you communicate "just right," the receiver will have no alternative but to do what you want. These approaches to communication are not helpful because they overlook the essential nature of the communication process.

Communication is one of the most interesting organizational phenomena to investigate precisely because it is so complex and multifaceted. An understanding of this complexity forms the basis for a practical communication audit. From the beginning of an audit, communication should be thought of as an ongoing, dynamic process—a description that is intended to differentiate it from a static, linear, finite phenomenon. Popularized in the communication literature by Berlo in 1960, the term "process" conveys the general ideas that (1) many components interact together, (2) the outcomes of these interactions are determined by some unspecified contingencies, and (3) these interactions do not have a finite beginning or end. In other words, every communication is rooted in both a historical and a current situational context. Therefore, to understand any current communication interaction, one may need to understand both its history and the impact of noncommunication variables on the situation.

In one of the earliest models, Lasswell (1948/1971) described the communication process as "who says what through what channels to whom and with what impact" (p. 37). Shannon and Weaver (1949) made major contributions in developing a model of communication, outlined in Figure 1.1. Berlo (1960) emphasized many of the same concepts in his famous SMCR model, in which sources encoded *messages* and sent them

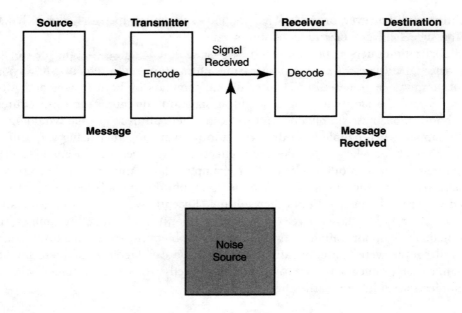

FIGURE 1.1. Shannon and Weaver model.

through channels to be decoded by receivers, who then responded with feedback to the sources. Building on Berlo, the Downs model of communication pictured in Figure 1.2 visually depicts each person as both a sender and a receiver; the two people maintain an ongoing interaction with one another as well as with others. But communication is rarely limited to the exchange between just two people; a total environmental context is very important. The Downs model tries to show the general dynamic context in which any given message exchange may be viewed. The ways, for example, that Persons 1 and 2 in the Downs model communicate will be seriously affected if we put them in an organizational context so that one is the boss of the other. Furthermore, Persons 1 and 2 are receiving and sending messages to lots of other people as well. Interactions are shaped by cultural determinants, legal requirements, economic conditions, what kind of security people feel they have, and the necessity to compete with other organizations. In the study of organizational communication, we could easily substitute "Unit 1" and "Unit 2" for "Person 1" and "Person 2" and highlight the fact that organizational coordination is also affected by the total environmental context.

The models call attention to the unique processes of encoding (deciding what and how to communicate) and decoding (interpreting messages) inherent in each individual. It is important to know that the messages sent throughout organizations are not necessarily the ones received, because the original messages are filtered through the motivations, listening habits, and perceptions of their receivers. This *filtering* phenomenon is not merely a capricious notion by which a person or unit decides what to pay attention to or how to interpret a message. The filter is the essence of a person's total frame of reference. To understand that we must be somewhat aware of all the environmental constraints affecting a person or unit. For example, in audits it is often useful to probe how key managers filter. In doing so, one can begin to understand how choices are made about communicating.

Probing the filtering phenomenon can also show how communication is related to noncommunication variables such as costs, competitors, goals, and images of organizational values. Sometimes communication is linked inside a person's head to some very unexpected variables. Although it is important to audit the filtering of key people in the organization, filtering occurs at an organizational level as well. This too should be audited. Different levels of management will have access to different messages, as will different units in the organization. Such differences often have profound ramifications for the coordination and control of the organization.

Another important subprocess of communication is *feedback*, which refers to the behavioral responses to messages. In the model presented in Figure 1.2, the letters A and D refer to times when people monitor their own messages. They hear what they say and read what they write, often correcting themselves. The D–E–F continuum represents responses to messages by other people. It is this feedback loop that develops two-way communication, which has been demonstrated to be more effective and more satisfying than one-way communication. The letters G and H refer to the fact that most organizational communication takes place among many people in some kind of organizational network. Therefore, filtering involves many different interpretations. One does not receive just one feedback message, but many feedback messages, some of which will not be in agreement. Organizational communication is a challenge.

Many sophisticated organizations acknowledge that there are many dimensions to communication at work. Different organizational scholars often choose to focus on different aspects of these communication processes that they deem important. Developing focal areas for communication audits is discussed in great detail in Chapter 4. For example, they may focus on the substance of messages, the richness of the media, the relationships among the communicators, the credibility of the communicators, or the approaches to resolving conflict. Each of these can be important.

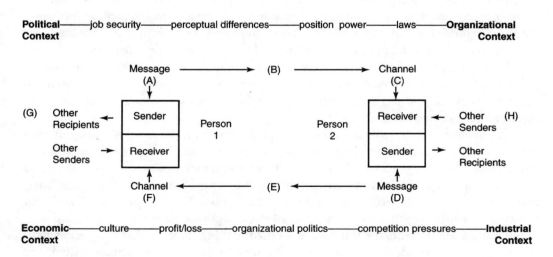

FIGURE 1.2. Downs total environment communication model.

Auditors also commonly pay attention to how communication processes can be linked to organizational results such as commitment to the organization, job satisfaction among employees, productivity, the effectiveness of implementing a change, and financial stability. How does it impact the proverbial "bottom line?" For instance, Finnegan (2000) linked commitment to agreement with organizational values that should be communicated by top management. Employees who are more satisfied with top management's communication are more likely to commit to the organization (Potvin, 1991; Varona, 1996; Adrian, 2001). Similarly, employees who are satisfied with (1) personal feedback (Downs, 1988; Potvin, 1991; Smidts, Pruyn, & van Riel, 2001; Varona, 1996), (2) supervisor communication (Downs, 1988; Putti, Aryee, & Phua, 1990), or (3) organizational information (Downs, 1988; Smidts et al., 2001) identify more with their organizations.

Research consistently supports the link between communication and job satisfaction (Hilgerman, 1998; Orpen, 1997; Pincus, 1986; Ticehurst & Ross-Smith, 1992). Indeed, Clampitt and Downs (1993) found that the benefits of good internal communication included greater productivity, less absenteeism, improved quality of goods and services, fewer strikes, reduced costs, and increased levels of innovation. And if those were not compelling reasons in and of themselves, more people are acknowledging the role that quality internal communication plays in supporting positive organizational change (Ford & Ford, 1995; Lewis & Seibold, 1998) and innovation (Albrecht & Hall, 1991; Ruppel & Harrington, 2000).

NATURE OF COMMUNICATION ASSESSMENTS

For many people in the United States, the word "audit" elicits fear or irritation because of its association with the Internal Revenue Service. Basically, however, an audit is merely a process of exploring, examining, monitoring, and evaluating something. Accountants audit financial records, physicians audit patient health, professors audit student learning progress, and managers review and audit employee levels of performance. In other words, the auditing process is one with which most people are familiar. The idea of conducting a communication audit may be new to many organizations, but it follows a long tradition of management trying to obtain feedback about the current state of the organization. Many organizations are now eager to improve their internal communication (Hargie & Tourish, 2000). Likewise, many managers see the need to conduct regular communication audits.

A communication audit takes a communication perspective on the organization. It puts people's tasks and interactions into the context of a complex set of interactions that the participants may perceive differently. When we conduct a communication audit, we assume that how workers communicate messages determines how they work and interact with each other. We do not take a formulaic approach, for example, "Say X and your problems vanish." We do say, "Your audience's perceptions of communication matter." Communication provides the framework for getting things done, rather than being just a side concern. We conduct each audit with a process perspective on communication, and that, in turn, enables us to relate communication to other organizational processes. Therefore, communication audits differ from other assessments only in that they focus primarily on communication. Chapters 5–12 review special methodologies that are applicable to communication audits.

CHARACTERISTICS OF COMMUNICATION ASSESSMENTS

A communication assessment, like all others, should possess the following characteristics: (1)independence, (2) professionalism, (3) diagnostic thoroughness, (4) skilled evaluation, (5) tailored design, and (6) current time frame.

Independence

The investigation should be conducted by *independent assessors* with training that qualifies them to make the investigation. In other words, neither organizations nor individuals should be allowed to review themselves because they would have such a vested interest in the results that the results would be suspect. The need for independence was certainly emphasized in the Enron scandals of 2002 and the resulting demise of Anderson Consulting. Although an assessment can be conducted by outside professionals or by in-house experts, the element of professional independence is critical to its success. In our experiences, outside independent auditors can collect information that employees simply would not reveal to an insider. In a 2003 audit of one organization we found results that were contrary to those revealed by an internal questionnaire processed by the company's CEO. During the data collection period workers repeatedly expressed worry to us that someone from the organization might see their answers. Their reactions indicated that they did not feel as free to answer the CEO's questionnaire as they felt with ours. Our very independence gave us credibility because we promised confidentiality.

Professionalism

To be credible and accurate, the investigation needs to be conducted by *professionals* who understand the intricacies of organizational dynamics and who also have expertise both in the analysis of communication and in the general processes of consultation. Filley (1985, p. 3) describes a good consultant as having (1) the ability to diagnose problems accurately, (2) the ability to serve as a facilitator or catalyst, (3) the knowledge of and skill with consulting processes, (4) sensitivity in using change processes, and (5) the ability to give people the experience of success. To these, we add (6) a willingness to grow and learn from the experience and (7) a dedication to the critical review of one's own theories. Auditors must continually fight against a doctrinaire attitude that is held despite evidence to the contrary.

Diagnostic Thoroughness

An assessment is a diagnostic *process* that collects important data to be used in constructing a realistic description of the actual organization. It is what Clegg, Hardy, and Nord (1996) call "mapping the terrain." It answers the questions "What characterizes this organization?", "What does it do well?", and "What needs improving?" The diagnostic design should provide for systematic observations to be made about all areas of communication that are considered important.

Skill in diagnosis is critical to obtaining a realistic, usable view of the organization's strengths and weaknesses. Furthermore, unless the auditor makes a skilled diagnosis, his or her proposals for change will undoubtedly be inappropriate. Because a common tendency for many researchers and consultants is to define problems according to the solutions that they have available, it is very important that the initial diagnosis not be bound just by whatever solutions an auditor would like to implement. When auditors allow themselves to be limited this way, their whole effort may become biased—and consequently unrealistic. Their judgments should be conceptually sound, precise, accurate, and relevant to the purpose of the audit.

Skilled Evaluation

One reason for conducting the diagnosis is to make judgments about communication within an organization. Implied in every assessment is a comparison of *what is* to *what ought to be*. What are *your* criteria for judging whether or not a particular organization is effective? Evaluation requires the identification of some criteria to be used in judging the adequacy of current communication. These criteria may be based on (1) standards generated by the organization or a professional organization such as the Occupational Safety and Health Administration (OSHA), (2) pet theories of the auditors, (3) purposes announced by management, (4) benchmark comparisons with other successful organizations, (5) internal comparisons over time, (6) current popular notions of management or leadership, or (7) objectives—and sometimes the performance levels of competitors—against which the organization can be judged.

Having credible criteria for effectiveness needs to be emphasized. While anyone may collect information about communication in the organization, it takes persons with special expertise and insights to determine what kinds of information will be helpful and then to make practical, usable sense of that information to identify strengths and weaknesses. For example, Dunham and Smith (1979) claim that "the most frequent mistake that managers make is to interpret a relative score in absolute terms, that is, without reference to some comparative standard" (p. 71). In other words, what does it really mean if 30% of employees say they do not get enough feedback? If 70% say they get enough feedback, does that mean the feedback communication channels are okay? Is that percentage too low or too high? How can a manager use that information? *Observations must always be put into some context historically, organizationally, industrially, or economically.* The process of putting things in context is necessary to make an evaluative judgment.

Credible auditors will have developed norms or a body of knowledge against which they can interpret the data obtained in an assessment. From where do these norms come? Consultant A may specialize in banks, developing an expertise that gives him or her special comparative insights about any new bank to be examined. Consultant B may investigate a variety of organizations within a midwestern city. Although these organizations are all different, Consultant B may become so familiar with the characteristics of the city that his or her estimates are based on knowledge of the kind of employees working there. Both types of insights are practical and invaluable. Although the standards for effective communication vary from situation to situation, the entire assessment is founded on the existence of some evaluative criteria. In one case, we audited the same organization many times, and, as a result, developed a historical context for the evaluation that other auditors could not furnish. Soon we will audit this organization for the 10th time, investigating the same aspects of communication so we can evaluate the company against its developmental past.

Tailored Design

Both the audit methodologies and the criteria for evaluation must be tailored to the specific organization. Each organization has some unique features; therefore, auditors may not easily take the procedures used in Organization X and use them again in Organization Y. A good motto is "Adapt, don't adopt." This is not to say that one cannot profit from experiences in auditing other organizations, *for not all audits start from square one.* Ideally, there should be some tailoring in the form of new or different questions or wording, or perhaps there must be adaptation of other audit procedures. For example, network studies, reviewed in Chapter 11, may be useful in some contexts and not in others. Furthermore, in small organizations, an auditor may rely on interviews more than is possible in larger organizations. When we assess governmental service organizations, the organizational dynamics are often different from those in private profit-oriented organizations. Therefore, we may need to ask different questions and recognize some key differences in the way communication works in those different types of organizations. Such adaptations are what we mean by "tailoring."

Uniqueness of design is more likely to yield very practical results for a particular organization. However, with the growth of Internet usage in the 2000s, an auditor will continually face the problem that some managers feel that they can go to the Web and download some questionnaires to use. These can be inexpensive and easy to administer. However, such general questionnaires may often generate information that is not very usable or very applicable to that organization. Therefore, when making a case for an audit to the organization, you should emphasize the necessity of tailoring the audit to its needs.

In recognition of the need to tailor audit procedures to a particular audit, Chapters 5–12 cover in detail important alternative methods available for an audit. It is not expected that auditors would use all of these methods for a particular audit. These descriptions are made so that they can make reasonable choices by weighing the benefits and limitations of each. Some data-gathering techniques that can contribute to creating a unique audit include questionnaires, confidential interviews, observations, critical incidents, communication diaries, content analysis of messages, focus groups, and network studies. Downs, DeWine, and Greenbaum (1994) provide an overview of many measures of organizational communication, each of which looks at a particular part of communication (Rubin, Palmgreen, & Sypher, 1994). Usually a combination of these is desirable to avoid inadequacies that can occur from overreliance on one instrument. Adaptation to the organization may require using a "cafeteria approach" to find the methodologies that would be most useful in a specific organization. Generally, some methodological *triangulation* is likely to give a more complete picture of the organization. "Triangulation" refers to the collecting of data about the same phenomena using several different methods or approaches to data collection. For example, in a 2001 audit of a governmental organization, the qualitative data we obtained in interviews and the quantitative data we obtained from questionnaires yielded seemingly contradictory data about employee perceptions of training opportunities in the organization. These differences had to be reconciled. In this case, the final observations were different than would have been possible had we used either only a questionnaire or only interviews and had we not become aware of the conflicts in the data. A more complete discussion of resolving apparent conflicts in data takes place in the discussion of analysis in Chapter 13.

Current Time Frame

Even though an assessment usually involves weeks of study, it still takes a time-bound snapshot of an organization over a particular time period. The assessment can be useful and practical, but generalizations to be made from it may be limited to that particular time frame because of the dynamic environments in which many organizations work. Since organizational circumstances are generally in a gradual but constant state of change, auditors must keep changes in time in mind. Constant change is the reason why financial records are checked periodically. The communication patterns in organizations are not static either. They too need to be audited periodically to keep the information current. The fact that we audited one police department five times in 7 years enabled us to plot out the changes over that period by constructing a timeline of environmental things influencing the department's internal operations. Some aspects of communication improved. However, one particular aspect of communication continued to be a problem even though we had made a recommendation to improve it. We eventually discovered that a union contract and a civil service rule prevented doing anything about that particular problem.

MANAGEMENT RATIONALE FOR ASSESSMENTS

If comprehensive communication audits possess the characteristics described above, the assessments provide the following functional benefits:

1. Strategic planning is facilitated.
2. Verification of perceptions promote realistic appraisals.
3. New data are generated.
4. A unique feedback loop is constructed,
5. Benchmarking allows effective comparisons.
6. Organizational members are sensitized to communication.
7. Training is enhanced.
8. Member participation fulfills a need to influence their organizations.

These functional benefits have a real impact on the organizational outcomes of degree of organizational commitment, job satisfaction, and productivity, and even finances.

Strategic Planning Benefit

"Strategic planning" normally refers to the processes by which organizational goals and the special tactics for achieving those goals are formulated by management and implemented throughout the organization. Michael Porter (1996) defines *strategy* as the basic positioning that guides the structuring and tactical operations of the organization. Generic strategies include costs, leadership, differentiation, and focus. To him, "strategic positioning means performing different activities from rivals' or performing similar activities in different ways" (p. 62).

Even the decision to undergo an assessment of communication can be a strategic decision, often reflecting a very definite leadership orientation. Savvy organizations use the results of communication audits strategically (J. Smythe, personal communication, 1997). Communication audits provide both (1) a picture of how employees view the organization and (2) a picture of how the organizational management relates its goals and strategic vision to its employees. Do they know, for example, information about costs or do they know how their organization is different from their competitors? In essence, participants estimate whether the current communication culture at the organization is consistent with their perceptions of where the organization plans to go in the future. This information provides powerful feedback to integrate into a strategic plan.

Since organizational strategies need to be communicated in the organization, the success with which strategic information is communicated can be pinpointed by an audit. One advertising agency incorporated the communication assessment as part of its corporate strategy and tied the results directly to improvements found in audits from previous years. They called it the "Downs effect." One of the critical areas we examined was the degree to which employees understood the strategic intent of the agency. Upper management had devised a number of ways to publicize the intent, and we were able to measure the degree to which they had succeeded.

One of the most strategic benefits of any communication assessment is to develop an awareness of paradigm shifts that are molding the organizational culture. Often waves of change taking place within the national culture impact the way the organization is developing. These changes often can be gleaned from people's comments about their organizations. If decentralization becomes a part of the cultural psyche, then workers expect more decentralization at work. Clark and Clegg (1998) provide an excellent backdrop for tracing some of these paradigm shifts. Their work is particularly helpful for auditors to use to understand the general paradigm shifts happening in the culture that also influence what is happening inside the company.

Verification Benefit

All organizational members have perceptions about the way the organization works and judgments about whether or not it operates effectively. We have found through many audits that these perceptions vary tremendously within a given organization. Yet all members behave on the basis of their perceptions. Consequently, one of the great benefits of an audit is to substantiate or refine members' perceptions. When perceptions are verified, guesswork about the organization is replaced with valid information. "To verify" is to check the accuracy of perceptions.

> Most managers believe they acquire a considerable amount of knowledge about worker attitudes and opinions through formal and informal interaction with their employees. Undeniably, this sort of unstructured observational testing does provide a good deal of valid information. Unfortunately, it can also provide a good deal of distorted information. The personal observations of a manager are greatly limited by his or her interpersonal sensitivity and by possible preoccupation with other responsibilities. In addition, the workers' dependence upon their managers for continued employment and income can inhibit or disguise their real feelings. . . . Indeed, this is one of the major insights achieved by managers who have participated as interviewers on survey teams in many organizations. (Dunham & Smith, 1979, p. 10)

As suggested above, perception plays a key role in shaping the way people communicate in organizations. The truth of the matter is that most perceptions are oriented to validate one's own vested interests and experiences. One member's perceptions will rarely be shared completely by all members; therefore, they would consider those perceptions as merely partially true and sometimes dead wrong. For example, the way that a manager perceives an organizational chart is not necessarily the way the nonmanagement employees perceive it. Consider the following examples. Odiorne discovered that when both bosses and subordinates were asked to describe the subordinates' jobs, they disagreed on an average of 25% of the things they mentioned (Filley, 1978, p. 74). We still find that when bosses are asked to list the kinds of problems they thought their subordinates encountered, their list contains items that are quite different than the items on the list made by the subordinates. And we recently found in a 2003 audit of a government department that 36% of the organizational members felt that their supervisors did not understand their problems or offer good guidance on handling them. This 36% represents a minority opinion to be balanced by the fact that over 50% felt their supervisors did understand their problems. Still, a minority percentage of this size has a meaningful impact on the organization.

These results are not unusual, and they reinforce the need to verify management perceptions. What one finds most of the time is that there are several very different impressions of the same organization. Consider the differences reflected in the following actual results of an audit designed to address the issue: Our intranet is an important communication tool for accomplishing my work.

Strongly agree	9
Agree	14
Somewhat agree	22
Somewhat disagree	22
Disagree	19
Strongly disagree	10

People with different perspectives, in different positions, and at different geographical locations look very differently at the "same" organization and how it operates. Furthermore, perceptions of how people communicate are often inadequate. The organizational chart, for example, is a fixture in many organizations. To some extent, the chart identifies authority and communication lines, and it is assumed that it represents who talks with whom. Not surprisingly, many communication assessments have demonstrated that the actual communication networks seldom look exactly like the organizational charts and often do not resemble them at all. Furthermore, the pervasive informal channels through which people accomplish much of their work generally are omitted altogether.

In the absence of reliable or substantiated information, people make assumptions about the organization and why things happen as they do. For example, during an audit of the reservation system of a major airline, we discovered that the ticket agents were harried by frequent fare changes, and especially by the fact that sometimes fares would change without the agents' knowledge. They blamed their supervisors for not keeping them informed, and their resentments were quite strong. Of course, the agents believed that their supervisors had the information they needed and were just not passing it on to them; they could not imagine that the supervisors too lacked this vital information. The assessment revealed, however, that the supervisors were not being provided with the information on time either. In fact, once corporate headquarters changed fares, it took 3 days before the changes were put into the computer. For 3 days every ticket issued was incorrect, and this caused extra work for the ticket agents to correct. Naturally, they were very resentful. Aside from implementing changes that sped up the sharing of information, the audit revealed to the ticket agents that their previous evaluations of their supervisors had not been entirely correct. Publicizing these results had a direct impact on the working relationships between supervisors and subordinates.

We have met many sensitive, skillful managers who have had fairly good intuitive understandings of their organizations. Even some of them have been surprised by audit findings because their employees had not been completely open in revealing their feelings to them. The challenge facing the assessor is to determine how the various differences in perceptions should be interpreted in order to capture the more accurate portrayal of the organization. Perhaps a very basic benefit of any communication audit, then, is that all parties—management and employees alike—can check, validate, and amend their perceptions about their organization and its members—including themselves. A skillful auditor will then be able to help the managers integrate the results into a consideration of basic strategies in the organization.

Data-Generating Benefit

An important function of communication audits is that they generate new information that verify employee perceptions and help the organization strategically. In most instances, these audits generate information that can not be obtained in any other way. This data generation facilitates the diagnostic function described earlier in this chapter. The new data in the assessment gives management the new information it needs to plan organizational development.

Assessments forecast problems and highlight strengths. An important goal of an assessment is to identify strengths that need to be reinforced and weaknesses that must be corrected. Although a proper audit identifies strengths, it also pinpoints those areas in which aspects of communication need some repair before they actually break down. One problem often identified is the desire for information that some workers believe to be needed but not received. For example, upper management in a public utility developed a system for feeding information to managers with the expectation that they would in turn pass it on to the employees reporting to them. The system was designed in this way to reinforce the role of managers as providers of information. The audit identified major problems caused by those managers who did not transfer the information because they felt that retaining the information gave them more power. The whole system had to be changed. In a 2002 audit of a police department, we discovered how some middle managers had become gatekeepers of information by not passing on information that upper management had communicated to them. Consequently, people were blaming upper management. Upon hearing about the transfer of one individual from one department to another, and learning that wherever this person went communication problems accompanied him, one very astute auditor observed:

> "I had thought that most of the problems were coming from the upper managers and their inability to do their jobs and get along with other people. But suddenly I understood something else. I had been blaming the top manager for 90% of the problem. But I had to change my view. . . . A person in a subordinate, but gatekeeping position, can undermine the best efforts at communication."

In this sense, both audits enabled upper management to do a better job of planning and controlling operations by selecting a different channel for distribution of some kinds of information.

Assessments also yield information that explains or predicts critical organizational events such as dissatisfaction, lapses in productivity, breakdowns in interunit coordination, union activity, turnover, poor teamwork, and lack of commitment. For example, when upper management in a large production company became aware of tremendous dissatisfaction in one unit that was beginning to hamper coordination and productivity, an audit revealed two primary sources of the reactive behavior. One communication source was traced to a executive manager's comments at a specific department meeting so that nearly all the draftsmen felt he had "insulted" them. Reactions by the draftsmen interfered with team coordination of all work. The second source of the problem was a structural space problem that was less easy to change. When audit information gave managers information that could be used in analyzing the root of these two problems, they were able to influence the effects of the head manager's comment, but they were unable to develop an immediate fix to the spacing problem.

Even when top management knows that employees are feeling a certain way, they still may not understand *why* they feel that way. *Diagnosis of the "why" may be as important as identifying the "what."* For example, in 2001 there was great economic anxiety of many companies in the United States. One client knew that employees were feeling insecure about their jobs. Consequently, we audited the organization every 3 months and mapped out why this was occurring by taking employee verbatim comments and analyzing the content of their comments in terms of common themes expressed. In some instances, some managers were surprised at the high level of job insecurity and the reasons causing it.

Finally, assessments may diagnose areas of concern before they become serious problems. Unfortunately, many organizations fail to exploit the *predictive value* of audits by using them only to diagnose a problem after it has emerged. It is also possible to use surveys to *prevent* such problems. For example, early detection of employee dissatisfaction with company policies could facilitate a careful evaluation and restructuring of these policies in hope of having a constructive impact on employees. If an audit identifies important employee concerns at a relatively early stage, the results allow management to work toward maintaining organizational "well-being" rather than fighting to remove "illness" (Dunham & Smith, 1979, p. 44).

Feedback Benefit

As the previous examples illustrate, audits may become important components in a feedback loop as new information is generated to verify perceptions and apply to the development of organizational strategies. Communication (input) is designed to produce certain effects (output). Like the thermostat on a furnace, the audit feeds back some measure of performance so that adjustments can be made if the output is not exactly what was wanted. The audit can offer a comprehensive review of many general patterns of communication in the organization, or it may examine only specific programs of interest to management. For example, we have used audits (1) to develop new communication training programs, (2) to assess how changes in telephone equipment and usage could save money, (3) to test the impact of a new performance review system as a communication vehicle, (4) to provide information about the structure of an organization that could be used to restructure it, (5) to determine the effectiveness of printed communications so they could be improved, and (6) to detect employee support for strategic thrusts by management. In regard to the support for strategic thrusts, five top managers of a company in Great Britain were very surprised when they learned that each of their three main strategies had the support of only one-third of the workers. Such feedback about communication effectiveness can have important ramifications for developing the communication systems in the organization.

Benchmark Benefit

An early 1983 survey of Fortune 500 companies discovered that 45% had conducted some form of communication audit. *These included some full-fledged analyses as well as short attitude surveys.* The basic rationale given for this practice was that "the evaluative process offered a benchmark for the progress and future of corporate programs" (Greenbaum, Hellwegg, & Falcione, 1983, p. 5). The results of initial assessments are often used as benchmarks against which later assessments will be compared. We have found this to be one of the most salient features of the auditing process. Companies like to be able to plot out where they are going. One of the best ways of gauging their effectiveness is to be able to compare their progress with where they have been. Figure 1.3 illustrates how an organization can measure its progress through audits.

In the 2000s the idea of organizational culture has become popular again, and benchmarking is a way of watching the development of the culture. Three of our clients

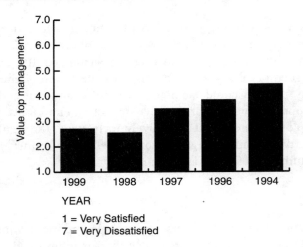

FIGURE 1.3. Historical comparison of communication with top management.

in the 2000s have worked this benchmarking process into their overall organization strategy. They judge where they are by the progress made from where they have been.

Communication Benefit

The mere fact that an assessment takes place communicates to the workforce that the organization has a strong commitment to effective communication. The recognition of that commitment not only builds goodwill but also sensitizes people to good organizational and communication practices. The audit process is seen as an important communication vehicle in itself, particularly for upward communication. The fact that management is sponsoring an audit indicates that the organization is determined to make communication more effective. Therefore, the assessment benefits communicative practices merely by focusing attention on them. Anyone familiar with the "Hawthorne effect" recognizes that people generally respond positively when attention is paid to them. A communication assessment implicitly demands "Don't take communication for granted."

In our experiences, participation in an assessment becomes a motivator for improved communication performance even while the auditing is taking place. Assessments pinpoint beneficial ways to change behaviors so that communication becomes more effective. Some ideas come from the auditors, but most assessments also enlist suggestions from those being reviewed. In some sense, the participants become a direct communication link between managers and other employees. Suggestions from organizational members are invaluable. Brooks, Callicoat, and Siegerdt (1979) surveyed several organizations that had conducted communication audits. They concluded that most organizations adopted positive changes in their communication practices as a result of the audit:

> Structural changes included new, revised, or eliminated divisions, work units, job specifications, policy manuals, standard operating procedure, committees, committee membership,

and "open door" policies. Changes in communication methods involved added, revised or eliminated schedules and formats of existing communication facilities, feedback spans, periodic and incident reports, newsletters, bulletin boards, internal office memos, group planning sessions, top management visits, meetings and presentations with employees, and employee recognition ceremonies and banquets. Training changes added or revised existing training programs to include workshops on communication practices and processes, orientation training . . . skill interviews, and skill training. (p. 9)

These outcomes support the idea that communication assessments can be effective communication channels that yield pragmatic results just because they focus on communication. Of course, no one change is a panacea for all time to come; communication dynamics change with changes in the organization. That is why we recommend periodic feedback from regular monitoring of the organizational communication.

Training Benefit

The inherent training benefit of a communication assessment may easily be overlooked. Such training happens in three ways.

First, the principal educational benefit is likely to be experienced by those managers who are involved in the planning or the follow-up stages. Exploring communication practices provides them with an opportunity to develop skills and attain insights into the whole communication process. By participating in the assessment, one's awareness of communication is sharpened, and often one becomes sensitized to interact with others more thoughtfully. We have found it particularly useful in making organizational members aware of how what they do in their units impacts other departments in terms of task interdependence. Without some teamwork, some important work may be delayed or thwarted. We found this to be true in a manufacturing plant when two managers whose work was task-interdependent had not talked together in 2 years even though lack of coordination was a recognized problem. They finally started to problem-solve during a feedback session on audit results.

Second, comparisons across specific units allow management to pinpoint where specific strengths or problems occur. Publicizing the good points trains others in how to perform better: training for the weak parts integrates the units as part of a cohesive whole. When one unit in a police department was recognized as being particularly outstanding, one of the officers suggested that maybe they should examine it in order to determine why it was so successful and what other units could do to have the same effects.

Third, audit reports often become a needs analysis for training. We often are able to recommend that organizations develop training programs to overcome some difficulties. Additionally, the very data reported from the audit offers exceptional substance for developing formal training programs. A 1999 audit of a police department and a 2001 audit of a garage door manufacturer became the foundations for development of special training packages for their organizations. One trainer, an expert policeman himself who headed an international organization, was able to work the findings from the audit to reinforce the basic leadership ideas that he wanted to present. The trainer in the manufacturing plant was also focusing on leadership and linked management development directly to the communication results of the audit in that plant.

Participation Benefit

In many modern Western societies, a communication audit is a useful forum for employee participation to make a difference in their organization. Suggestions from the subordinates are considered. Organizational members often say things to the auditors that they would not say to their bosses. Thus employees have opportunities to be heard and to shape their organizations. In one organization that we regularly audit, managers' bonuses are directly linked to their subordinates' evaluations of their communication in the audit. In that way, employees have a significant voice in shaping the manner in which their superiors communicate with them. This influence is very real. In one instance, the problems were so great that the supervisor was terminated; in another instance, a manager was transferred. Therefore, a receptive management can be influenced when employees are given a confidential voice through an audit.

CONTRIBUTIONS OF THE AUDITING PROCESS TO THE AUDITOR

Early in this chapter we emphasized that auditors need to be willing to grow and must fight against doctrinaire attitudes. Audits are one of the best research tools to help develop theories about how organizations work. No two are exactly alike, and those differences provide great fodder for theorizing. Jim Collins (2001) testifies to this approach as the basis for his best-selling book *Good to Great*. He said, "It is important to understand that we developed all of the concepts in this book by making empirical deductions directly from the data. We did not begin this project with a theory to test or prove" (p. 10). It is the wise auditor who thrills over new learning. So get ready to have fun and grow while producing practical results that improve companies.

CONCLUSION

Managing an assessment from start to finish is a growth experience that is also fun, invigorating, and creative. Every organization is different, and the auditors' sense of discovery compensates for their hard work. Textbook answers rarely apply, so the auditors are left with a sense of creative problem solving. Moreover, the generally enthusiastic response of managers is rewarding itself. For us, the audits have generated a greater understanding of, and sensitivity to, the realities with which organizations must deal. Because of the challenges and the opportunities for growth, however, assessments require planning and a lot of hard work—some of it tiring and mundane.

Now that we have established the value of the assessment process, in succeeding chapters we will explore the aspects of communication that should be examined and how the audit should be implemented. Chapter 2 emphasizes the necessity of comprehensive planning and outlines basic considerations for that planning. The discussion is general because every assessment operates a little differently, varying with the type of organization, the focus wanted by management, the tools available to the auditor, the size of the organization, and the time and money available for the audit. Basically, however, there are six phases to an audit: (1) initiation, (2) planning, (3) diagnosis or fact finding, (4) analysis, (5) evaluation, and (6) feedback.

Phases 1 and 2 are important to the success of any assessment because they provide the general orientation. Phase 3, diagnosis, covered in Chapter 4, points out the important areas that need to be investigated. Phase 4, analysis, is discussed in Chapters 5–12. These chapters focus on methodologies that might be useful to the auditor. Phase 5, evaluation, is described in Chapter 13. This phase is perhaps the most important one in the entire process because it is here that the analytic data are made meaningful to both auditors and managers. Phase 6, feedback, covered in Chapter 14, is the goal of the audit. It is during this phase that the organization finally discovers the usefulness of the audit. Information is provided to launch whatever adaptations the organization needs in order to make improvements.

Finally, auditors have a tremendous opportunity to make practical contributions to the development of any organization. We are proud to say that communication audits have proven beneficial not only in U.S. companies, but in companies around the world (Lee & Chen, 1996; Hargie & Tourish, 2000; Ticehurst & Ross-Smith, 1992). We have personally participated in audits in more than a dozen countries and anticipate opportunities to continue to apply communication assessment methods in many more. When the proper cultural adjustments are made, communication assessments provide unique insights into managing in the era of globalization.

2

Initiating and Planning
an Assessment

Not everyone understands the same thing when we say, "We're going to do a communication audit." Nor does everyone have the same ideal for the auditor–client relationship. Planning is necessary to orient both the auditor and the client to the assessment project. The auditor needs to know the client's needs; both parties need to define the boundaries of the communication audit. Careful planning helps both sides manage expectations about the audit process.

PHASE 1: INITIATION

Assessments can be initiated either by the consultant or by the client. Some auditors market their services just as they would market training programs—for example, through advertisements or personal contacts. In many cases, however, the clients make the initial contact because they are looking for help with a problem generally considered to be in the area of communication. Once the contact has been made, the goal is to determine whether or not the assessment technology is suitable for the organization's purpose. The ethical auditor must pursue these deliberations with the realization that sometimes he or she should refuse the assignment because of lack of expertise or because of the unsuitability of certain goals. However, if there does seem to be a fit between auditor and client, the guidelines discussed in the following sections will complete the initiation phase.

Meet with Key People

The first phase of every audit ought to include several preliminary meetings with key representatives from the organization. More than one meeting is desirable because the ideas of both auditors and clients can go through an incubation period. Basically, these meetings should accomplish five things:

1. Accommodate the client's purposes.
2. Achieve consensus about the project.
3. Define the scope of the assessment.
4. Familiarize the assessment team with the organization.
5. Familiarize management with the assessment procedure.

Accommodate the Client's Purposes

An assessment can be time-consuming and expensive, so the decision to conduct one should not be taken lightly. We must emphasize that there is no one purpose for an audit, and each client may have a special objective in mind. For example, one manager at a manufacturing plant wanted to treat the assessment as a basic attitude survey; another manager wanted to test a particular communication system; a new police chief wanted to familiarize himself with the strengths and weaknesses of his new organization; and still another manager wanted an audit to serve as the basis for some training in teamwork. We set up these assessments differently because of their different purposes. While the auditor should have the expertise to design a general assessment, the client's objectives need to guide the specific assessment design.

Achieve Consensus about the Project

One problem auditors sometimes encounter is that influential members of the client organization have different goals for the assessment. For example, a corporate manager retained Downs to audit a plant with the express purpose of developing a new communication system. Downs assumed that all managers knew about, and agreed upon, the basic purposes of the assessment. However, midway through the analysis he realized that the plant manager always talked about training as the end result; in fact, he always changed the subject when talk centered on a new communication system. Eventually, Downs had to face the issue of differences in purposes, but the differences were never really reconciled. This example demonstrates the necessity of clearly identifying the client's objectives at the very beginning of the assessment process and securing agreement with them. The purposes then determine the scope of the assessment.

Define the Scope of the Assessment

Since communication is a broad concept, the focal points for an assessment are virtually limitless. Therefore, its scope needs to be clearly defined. Some assessments, for example, are designed to be comprehensive analyses of an entire organization. Others limit themselves to a particular communication unit in the organization. Some focus on internal communication only; others include external communication with clients. Finally, some audits focus primarily on communication networks, while others evaluate the kind and number of messages exchanged. In other words, the scope is determined by what the organization values most at the time and by where management thinks problems can be uncovered. It may be desirable to fashion a broad format in general, but also to conduct an in-depth examination of issues of special concern. Of course, defining an assessment's scope has political ramifications because auditing or investigating any aspect of a work unit can be threatening to those people being investigated.

Familiarize the Assessment Team with the Organization

All organizations are not alike. And one must be careful *not* to assume that the descriptions of organizations found in academic textbooks necessarily describe any particular organization. While investigative techniques can be fairly standardized, a general survey of the company is needed before starting to plan the actual mechanics of the assessment. It is helpful, for example, to have people describe both the structure of the organization and some of its key players. A physical tour of the facilities gives an overview of the work processes, the employees, and the general climate. Finally, the organization's printed reports, brochures, and statements of values provide useful indicators of what is important to the organization. Of particular importance would be a thorough understanding of both the task processes and key financial data. A practical way to assess how much you know about the organization is to try to develop a comprehensive description of it. After sketching out the description, examine it closely to see if there are any obvious gaps.

Familiarize Management with the Assessment Procedure

Be prepared to summarize how an assessment is conducted and how it can benefit the organization. Refer to previously satisfied clients and then walk the prospective clients through a typical methodology from a previous assessment. Without violating client confidentiality, you can *camouflage* parts of a previous audit report to demonstrate the kind of information that can be generated. Once the decision to conduct the assessment is finalized, there are numerous details to be decided concerning how auditor and client will relate to one another. Thus the auditor moves into Phase 2, the planning stage.

PHASE 2: PLANNING

Just as an organization needs to identify its strategies, auditors need a basic roadmap for what they are trying to accomplish. Some degree of planning will be necessary to avoid unexpected pitfalls along the way. Based on our experiences, the following are crucial to the successful implementation of most audits: (1) finances, (2) expectations about final report, (3) the nature of auditor–client relationships, (4) liaison format with the organization, (5) identification of major focal areas, (6) appropriateness of audit techniques, (7) selection of respondents, (8) time sequence, (9) publicity about the audit, and (10) documentation of audit arrangements.

Make Financial Arrangements

There are many costs involved in an assessment other than just the employees' time. These include telephone calls, postage, computer time for analysis, secretarial help, duplication expenses, travel costs, and charges for supplies. These costs are not always predictable; managing an assessment involves managing a budget. It must be determined who will pay for expenses, when, and how. Furthermore, one needs to work out in advance exactly what the consulting costs are going to be and whether to charge by the project, by the day, or by the hour. The latter gives greater flexibility.

Decide the Nature of the Final Report

From the outset it should be clear as to what information is going to be provided to whom. Normally, the main emphasis is on comprehensive oral and written reports for management.

An alternative approach is to meet with individual managers and give them oral and written reports about their units. In some cases, managers have asked the auditor to be present as they discuss the audit in a meeting with their units.

A third possibility is to prepare a written report of one to two pages to be circulated to all employees. During the audit process, employees typically ask what is going to happen to the information gathered. If they have participated in other surveys and have never seen their results, that lessens their motivation to participate now. In fact, in her survey of the uses of information collected in attitude surveys, Davis (1986) found that organizations typically do not use or report in detail the results of their surveys. Therefore, the promise of a report can be a positive motivator for individuals to participate in the assessment. Consequently, when employees ask about the possibility of seeing a report, you want to be able to answer "yes" or "no" *truthfully*, but you can only do this if you have made the agreement in advance. Any report to employees should not be too detailed. Moreover, management should have the opportunity to review the report and to make changes. An assessment is designed to help solve problems, not to create them by reporting information that should not be widely circulated.

Clarify the Auditor–Client Relationship

How the auditors and the clients are to work together is one of the most important decisions to be made. And because there exists a variety of consulting styles, this relationship needs to be clarified early. How much is management to be involved in implementing the assessment? What expectations does management have about focusing the efforts of the auditors? What kinds of discussions are to take place between managers and auditors during the analysis and evaluation phases? Basically, there are three approaches that can be used (Goldhaber, 1979).

A *purchase model* occurs when the client organization diagnoses a specific problem and contacts the auditors to solve it. In such an instance, the managers decide where the focus of the assessment shall be and then may leave the other decisions to the auditors.

For example, managers in one organization decided that they had a teamwork problem, contacted us, and then had nothing to say about the audit until we gave them the final evaluation. After the audit, a teamwork seminar was presented, and the relationship was terminated. In this case, the involvement of management throughout the process was minimal.

A *medical model* occurs when the client organization (the patient) describes the symptoms and asks the auditors (the doctor) to diagnose the problem. Usually the auditors are expected to determine what is wrong and to suggest remedies. Again, in this model, management leaves the auditors alone. As an example, one of our clients believed that the employees needed to be more involved in and to contribute more creativity to their jobs. Therefore, an assessment was conducted with the specific purposes of identifying obstacles to job involvement and designing a new model of employee participation.

A *process model* demands that auditors and clients work jointly on all phases of the audit. They plan together, they discuss the analysis together, and they discuss ways of implementing new procedures together. One major assumption behind this approach is that no outside auditors can ever completely understand the nuances of the organization in the way that its employees do. Therefore, the auditors function as important resource advisers, but managers must be the doers. They are ultimately responsible for all decisions and their implementation.

As an auditor, one may have a preference in regard to how to operate. Nevertheless, one must clarify this preference and win acceptance for the approach from management. We learned a valuable lesson about this issue through a failure. We were hired to do a second project for a company because the first project had been very successful. Management had liked the analytic process we had previously used. Consequently, we started the second project by assuming that the guidelines were the same. However, we soon learned that that assumption was incorrect. We were dealing with a different plant manager. When we wanted to discuss preliminary findings, he was uneasy. When we asked for his input on directions to explore, he was vague and would change the subject. Actually, he wanted us to present solutions, and our credibility actually suffered when we ourselves did not make outright decisions. Furthermore, this situation was complicated by the fact that we were being paid by a top-level manager who had one set of expectations, but we had to work with a plant manager who had a different set of expectations. He was expecting a medical model while we were trying to use a process model.

Arrange Liaison with the Organization

Every audit requires a great deal of coordination within the organization itself. Therefore, it is useful to have a liaison employee or committee of employees to handle these details. Such people are invaluable because they publicize the audit, win support for it, schedule interviews, arrange conferences, and dispense questionnaires. Furthermore, it is useful to have a person (or persons) designated to be the contact(s) when problems occur. One of our best liaison experiences occurred during the assessment of a university. A committee of approximately 20 people functioned well in assisting in the entire design and follow-up of the audit. Most often, however, we only deal with one or two individuals. Since much of the coordinating work is clerical, a good secretary or assistant can be helpful.

The relationship with the liaison individual(s) is crucial to the success of the assessment. It is imperative to explain the purpose and procedures of the assessment thoroughly to this person. Watch for signs of lack of support and try to counter them. Once a liaison manager assigned much of the coordination to an assistant who obviously was fearful of the project. She created obstacles by developing unnecessarily complicated schedules, not assigning enough interview rooms, insisting that she talk to only one member of the audit team, and informing us that certain key people could not be interviewed. We circumvented these problems by going around her to her boss, so the assessment did not suffer. But when she volunteered to dispense the questionnaires, we politely made other arrangements because we feared the impact her negative attitude might have on the respondents.

The liaison individual does not have final say in what is done. We are currently working with a client that has a very supportive liaison individual, but the boss has changed his mind about what should be done several times. Therefore, we keep the network open to meeting with him regularly too.

Determine Focal Areas

Although the general purpose of an assessment may be to find out the organization's strengths and weaknesses, there are some specified focal points in communication. Some of these will be worked out in advance with management. Selection of focal areas is discussed in detail in Chapter 4. However, you may ask the following valuable questions:

1. What do you need to know for the analysis?
2. What would you like to know?
3. What information is it possible to get?
4. What are your priorities? Management's priorities?
5. What information will most benefit the organization when it is fed back?

The focal points of the assessment will shape the choice of instruments, which is the next step.

Select Assessment Techniques

Each of the following research techniques has proven to be a reliable form of auditing communication: (1) observations, (2) interviews, (3) questionnaires, (4) critical incidents, (5) network analysis, (6) content analysis, (7) focus groups, and (8) communication diaries. Each has special utilities that make it somewhat different from the others; these unique features are depicted in Table 2.1. Why not use them all? There is, of course, a point of diminishing returns in collecting information. After a while no new ground is being explored because the auditor keeps discovering the same information. Furthermore, there are limits to time and financial resources. Each technique will be analyzed in detail in later chapters, and the question of choosing which is appropriate

TABLE 2.1. Potential Audit Technologies

Observations

Time:	Variable
Cost:	Relatively inexpensive cost of observing environment and task processes
Yield:	Data from people processes
Disruption:	Little if it remains unobtrusive

Interviews

Time:	30–60 minutes
Cost:	Expensive; must pay interviewers; must pay workers for interview time
Yield:	Coverage of many topics; probing allows in-depth answers
Disruption:	Time away from job

Questionnaires

Time:	20–30 minutes
Cost:	Relatively inexpensive; principal costs are general overview of many employees' time and analytic time of aspects of the auditor
Yield:	Standardized data about many topics; qualitative 20–30 minutes
Disruption:	Minimal; mass-produced questionnaires can be filled out at will

Critical incidents

Time:	Usually built in as part of a questionnaire or interview
Cost:	Relatively inexpensive
Yield:	Specific examples of communication, but many refuse to give them
Disruption:	Little

Network analysis

Time:	20–30 minutes
Costs:	Paid time to employees for filling out forms; very inexpensive to analyze with computer software
Yield:	Structural information; interaction networks
Disruption	30 minutes for filling out questionnaire

Content analysis

Time:	None
Costs:	Expensive; takes worker time to write; auditor needs many hours to code and analyze content
Yield:	Kind of information processed throughout the organization; evaluation of channels
Disruption:	None

Focus groups

Time:	2 hours each
Costs:	Pay for facilitators, participants, and facilities
Yield:	Quantitative data plus inexpensive in-depth information revealed in discussion
Disruption:	Little as is usually scheduled in nonwork times.

Communication diaries

Time:	Time-intensive
Costs:	Worker requires time to report everything
Yield:	Comprehensive message reports
Disruption:	Frequent interruptions of daily work

under what circumstances will be answered at that time. At this point, however, we offer three general recommendations in making choices among them.

First, use multiple techniques when possible. This process is called *triangulation,* which is the collection of data about the same organizational phenomena using at least two different methods. From the viewpoint of pure academic research, one criticism of audits is that the validity of the findings is questionable when only one instrument is used. Situations differ, of course, as do the purposes of audits. For more limited projects, we have relied on only one technique—generally the interview—and the results have worked out well. However, for more elaborate audits, data derived from at least two techniques are desirable. The more measures used to collect data, the more reliable are the data; they supplement one another so that the consistency of findings can be tested. For example, questionnaires provide important numerical information that can be analyzed statistically, whereas interviews provide qualitative data that are rich in terms of in-depth explanations of responses. By supplementing one with the other, auditors can ensure that their estimates of the organization are likely to be realistic.

Second, focus on actual behaviors as well as perceptions. Since employees behave according to the ways they perceive situations, it is useful to tap their perceptions. Nevertheless, we find many instances when employee perceptions are not consistent with the facts (perhaps a communication problem in itself) or when the perceptions among employees vary widely. That is why interviews, content analysis, critical incidents, or observations may be good supplements to questionnaires. Also, multiple techniques are useful since subjects respond differently to different ways of collecting information. There are nearly always problems with reconciling seemingly contradictory information.

Third, collection of data through electronic means is increasingly promising. Having audited the same organization many times, we have discovered two things about the process. First, more people respond to electronic questionnaires than to traditional paper questionnaires. Apparently, the computer is so commonplace that people feel comfortable using it. Second, the responses to open-ended questions contain more depth when the questionnaire is electronic. Respondents seem to be more willing to type out an answer than to write one by hand. The differences are phenomenal.

Choose the Employees to Be Audited

In small organizations of less than 200 people, all employees can be canvassed, but collecting data from a more limited sample is perfectly acceptable. The decision to sample or to canvass employees depends on a number of factors.

First, cost is a primary consideration. It is less expensive to sample than to collect data from everyone.

Second, the choice of audit technique is important, since more people can be observed or be surveyed by questionnaires than can be interviewed. However, some standard techniques for compiling a communication network often demand that each employee be audited; failure to do so leaves gaps in the network. If multiple methods are used, canvassing can be used with some while sampling is used with others. For example, it is common to give questionnaires to everyone but to interview only a small number.

Third, expectations by the employees are a concern. Any sampling may leave out people who wish to participate while selecting others who, feeling they have been targeted for some negative reason, may be uncooperative. One way to avoid either circumstance is to include everyone.

Ultimately, the decision to canvass or to sample may be most affected by how management wants to use the data. If it is to be used as a catalyst for action, canvassing the employees is helpful. We are currently conducting an audit of every person in a plant that employs 429 across three shifts because management wants everyone to know they are involved. It should be remembered that a sample does not necessarily give less information than a canvass. If reliable procedures are used in its selection, a sample permits an auditor to generalize about the entire organization while auditing only a portion of the workers. The following guidelines may be helpful in deciding who should be included.

1. *Stratified sampling is necessary* for the data to be truly representative of all dimensions of the organization. "Stratification" simply means that employees are included from every level, every work unit, and every shift. The essence of representativeness is that you will get the same information by taking a sample that typifies the organization as you will by auditing everyone.

2. *Avoid making the sample too small.* While there are no guaranteed formulas for deciding exactly how many people should represent the organization, it is better to have too many people than too few. Some guidance may be obtained from a table developed by Krejcie and Morgan (1970) to estimate the approximate sample size from a given population. This is reproduced in Table 2.2. There is nothing magical about these numbers but they do demonstrate how large a sample is needed to generalize to a given size of organization.

3. *Include all key people.* Some people are in a position to give more of an overview of the organization; make certain all these people are included. Although it would be a mistake to audit only the key people, we have found that their insights are crucial to creating a fair assessment of the organization.

4. *Do not overlook part-time employees.* Organizations seem to be hiring more and more people for less-than-full-time work. Since they significantly impact organizational communication, part-time workers should be included.

Forecast the Time Sequence

Most audits are conducted over a period of several weeks, often making coordination difficult. Therefore, it is helpful to set up a checklist of procedures with target dates. Such targets not only help the auditors keep on track, but they also give the clients a sense of progress. Operating without such a plan creates a lack of definition for many clients, who experience anxiety wondering when and if things are going to happen. Time is a factor in other ways too. Employees take time away from their jobs to participate, and this needs to be coordinated well in advance to minimize the audit's interference with regular work. Furthermore, schedules must allow enough time for participation to be meaningful.

TABLE 2.2. Determining Sample Size from a Given Population

N	S	N	S	N	S
10	10	220	140	1,200	294
15	14	230	144	1,300	297
20	19	240	148	1,400	302
25	24	250	152	1,500	306
30	28	260	155	1,600	310
35	32	270	159	1,700	313
40	36	280	162	1,800	317
45	40	290	165	1,900	320
50	44	300	169	2,000	322
55	48	320	175	2,200	327
60	52	340	181	2,400	331
65	56	360	186	2,600	335
70	59	380	191	2,800	338
75	63	400	196	3,000	341
80	66	420	201	3,500	346
85	70	440	205	4,000	351
90	73	460	210	4,500	354
95	76	480	214	5,000	357
100	80	500	217	6,000	361
110	86	550	226	7,000	364
120	92	600	234	8,000	367
130	97	650	212	9,000	368
140	103	700	248	10,000	370
150	108	750	254	15,000	375
160	113	800	260	20,000	377
170	118	850	265	30,000	379
180	123	900	269	40,000	380
190	127	950	271	50,000	381
200	132	1,000	278	75,000	382
210	136	1,100	285	100,000	384

Note. N, population size; *S*, sample size.

Time schedules also have to be arranged around space requirements, workloads, and important key events. Forecasting key events that may affect the audit is very helpful. Some things we have encountered that compete with the audit are personnel changes, recent attitude surveys, reorganization, productivity campaigns, and vacation schedules during the summer.

Publicize the Assessment before It Happens

The last step in planning is to determine how to let employees know about the project. An aspect of organizational communication that is often criticized is the lack of timely information about new things. Since the assessment is a major communication in itself, every effort should be made to publicize it in advance. The publicity should cover who is conducting it, a simple overview of some of the procedures, and why it is being done.

To give the audit legitimacy, we have found it useful to employ a minimum of three forms of publicity. First, a member of management and an auditor should explain the audit to all managers and supervisors in meetings. This gives the project management's blessing, allows the auditor to answer questions, and equips the supervisors to answer any questions from their subordinates. Second, a top manager should send a letter or memo to all employees announcing and supporting the project. Third, an announcement should be featured in the organization's printed media to keep people informed while securing their support. Furthermore, the announcement should be couched in terms that will allay fears and present a feeling of urgency. Most people are receptive to the possibility of improving communications.

In some ways, the publicity campaign is the most critical aspect of the assessment. It sets expectations, it secures cooperation, and it provides a good example of communication. This process must not be neglected. Without it, participation will suffer or interviewers will have to spend valuable time explaining the audit to the interviewees.

Furthermore, the publicity campaign may also help one gauge the effectiveness of communication systems in the organization. *In fact, auditors need to monitor the publicity campaign as an important message in the organization.* An example will explain what we mean and demonstrate the importance of the publicity campaign. Once we were auditing a hospital with more than 700 employees. Hospitals are interesting in that they are open 24 hours a day, 7 days a week, so it is challenging to contact all the employees. We went through the three publicity stages listed above. Managers were genuinely supportive of the effort and had sent out messages to their staff about the audit. But 6 weeks into the audit we found ourselves interviewing employees who had never heard about the communication audit or who we were. It turned out that some of the managers had only communicated to their staff about the communication audit using electronic mail—and there were only two computers per workstation. We quickly saw that, given the current resources, electronic mail was not the way to communicate with everyone in the organization.

In that particular situation, even though they had not heard about the communication audit in advance, employees were still open to talking about internal communication; however, sometimes the results are not so positive. Another time we were auditing a public health agency distributed across seven geographic locations. There was one particular location where the interviewees were quite reserved in their responses. One man in particular tensed up when we asked him, "Tell us about your job." We later discovered that the managers at that location had not sent out the messages about our communication audit. In light of some turmoil in the organization, the grapevine at that location had circulated rumors that layoffs were coming and that "people" were coming in to assess who was "deadwood." Naturally, when we arrived and started asking people to describe their jobs to us, they were frightened. At that point, it did not matter that we said at the beginning of the interview process, "Hi, we're here as part of a communication assessment. . . ." Employees already expected and believed us to be doing something else.

These examples demonstrate the necessity of doing a good job of publicizing the communication audit. When employees have partial or even no information about the purpose of the audit, they are more likely to resist participating in it. If one wants to set an example of good communication and good tone, it is important to follow through with the publicity campaign in ways that demonstrate healthy communication practices. In one sense, this may be the first chance we have to convince people that we can actually improve communication at work!

Formalize Audit Arrangements

The initiation and planning stages of managing an audit rely heavily on oral discussion. However, after auditors and clients have explored the issues and have agreed on the elements of the audit, agreements often need to be documented. One way to do this is to sign a formal contract. An example of a formal contract is given in Table 2.3. The benefit of a contract is that it spells out exactly what the responsibilities of each party will be during the audit. On the other hand, some consultants use letters to document the arrangements. A sample letter is included in Table 2.4. Notice that it sets out the consultants' expectations and requirements after prior meetings with managers. Some consultants have conducted audits merely on the basis of oral exchanges, and this can work well. However, specificity of detail and documentation for future reference are important. Generally, the arrangements should be formalized in writing.

A MATTER OF PERSPECTIVE

The entry to an organization is almost always through management. This is a fact of life. They control who comes into the organization. Nevertheless, Hargie and Tourish (2000) note, "Organisations are increasingly becoming viewed as partnership arrangements, in which the principles of coalition building are the key to success. But employees cannot buy into ideas that they neither know nor understand" (p. 4). Indeed in our own experience and from reports of the experiences of others (Clampitt & Berk, 2000; Hargie & Tourish, 2000) we know that many people in organizations are excited at the prospect of improving communication. Occasionally we meet with those who see the need to improve communication, but simply cannot face what that task requires. Adrian was once told by an executive at a rapidly growing communications firm, "We know our communication is bad here; we just don't want to know how bad it is."

We find, though, that organizations are systems of human interaction. Employees want to be respected and involved at work. Often when employees resist organizational change, the resistance can be traced to how the change was introduced rather than to the nature of the change itself (Turnbull & Wass, 1998). Clampitt (2001) notes that even when employees are negatively affected by a change, how the organization communicates the news dramatically affects whether employees view the change as legitimate. Lewis and Seibold (1998) characterize managing change as a matter of managing communication. And that means communicating with employees in respectful ways that give them voice. Quirke (1995) emphasizes the idea that new communication objectives should include stimulating thinking, participation, networking, and "the expansion of what all employees believe is possible" (p. 77). *We view communication audits as a powerful integrative tool in helping managers and employees meet their rights and obligations to communicate with each other.*

TABLE 2.3. Sample Contract for Apex Organization

1. Management responsibility and personnel

   The Communication Audit of Apex will be directed by Dr. Cal W. Downs and Dr. Allyson D. Adrian. The audit team will consist of Mary Doe, Harry Poe, and Pat Washington. They will work with a liaison group, designated by management, in the planning, administration, interpretation, and follow-up of the communication assessment.

2. Audit procedures

   a. Thirty employees will be interviewed during the initial stages of the audit. Those interviewed will be selected by the auditors to represent every aspect of the organization.
   b. All employees will be surveyed by a questionnaire. Included on the questionnaire will be information about communication relationships, information exchange, networks, outputs, channels of communication, and suggestions for improving the organization.
   c. A second round of interviews will include 30 interviews. This will be conducted after the questionnaire data has been analyzed in order to probe for significant findings.

3. Audit timetable

   a. March 15–20
      First round of interviews to be completed.
   b. April 8–17
      Questionnaires will be administered and analyzed.
   c. May 1–15
      Second round of interviews to be completed.
   d. June 2
      A report will be presented orally and in writing to management.
   e. June 12
      A two-page report will be circulated to all employees.

4. Audit budget

   A breakdown for the cost of the audit is as follows:
   a. Director's salary
   b. Staff salaries
   c. Other expenses: computer time, supplies, postage, binding of report, travel and sustenance, and miscellaneous expenses.

   Payment should be made in two equal installments. The first is due on _____, and the second is due on _____. In addition to these expenses, Apex is committed to publicizing the assessment, reproducing all instruments, printing all reports, supplying space and facilities for administering the audit instruments, supplying organizational outcome data to be used in the analysis, supplying a liaison committee, distributing the final report, and collecting printed documents appropriate to the communication analysis.

5. Audit products

   Apex will receive a formal printed report and thorough oral presentation of it on _____. This report will include (a) a description of all procedures, (b) a summary of major findings, and (c) recommendations for future actions to improve communication.

TABLE 2.4. Sample Letter Formalizing Audit Arrangements

April 9, 2004

Ms. Jane Smith
Apex Corporation
151 Junction Avenue
Los Angeles, California 95131

Dear Ms. Smith:

It was good to talk with you on Monday. As I mentioned, I prefer to start working with a company by interviewing most or all of the people in it. Where the number is great, I generally have individual interviews with managers and group interviews with some of the employees. In large organizations I also like to give everyone a questionnaire. If there are fewer people, I use individual interviews with everyone. The interviews do three things. First, they acquaint me with the organization's structure and communication processes. Second, they acquaint me with the people, demonstrating to them that I can be helpful and trusted. Finally, they give me people's perceptions about the strengths of the organization and obstacles to their performance and satisfaction. The questionnaires give information that can be used to cross-validate the interview information.

After collecting the information I prepare and present a report to you in written and verbal form. It is an important document since it serves as the basis for our plans for change. I like to arrange a 2-hour meeting for us to discuss the findings.

I am enclosing a draft memo that you may want to revise and distribute to your employees. I am also scheduling May 10 and 11 to be with your company. Depending on our further discussions in Los Angeles this week, we may want to use the first day for individual interviews and the second for group meetings.

I would like to be able to tell those interviewed that they will receive a report, either verbally or in writing. Also, it should be made clear to people that I am not there to make judgments or to evaluate individuals.

My charges for this work are _____ a day plus expenses. If you have any questions please call me at my office (913) 843-0752.

I look forward to seeing you in Los Angeles.

Sincerely,

Allyson D. Adrian, PhD
Consultant

AC:re

Perspective also means determining what your professional standards are and how they will be used. A reviewer of this book asked, "How does an auditor maintain professional standards in the face of management requests that may run against them? For example, what if the manager wants the auditor to recommend people to be laid off?" On the one hand, we would never do anything that would violate our personal code of ethics, and our clients pick that up quickly. *We appreciate the management role, but we are neither suspicious of it nor intimidated by it.* Consequently, we have never had a request to compromise our integrity and what we do. On the other hand, Downs has supervised a number of audit trainees who did not want to report data if it might get someone "in trouble." That is equally unprofessional. If an audit reveals that some people are not performing well or that there are dysfunctional areas of the organization, these weaknesses must be reported if one is to give an accurate assessment. And while we might not recommend that certain individuals be laid off (that is a management prerogative), we have certainly given information that has been the catalyst for changes in assignment, abolition of positions, and even changes in personnel. It is never unprofessional to "tell it like it is." It is woefully unprofessional either to bend your assessment to a management whim or to avoid dealing with unpleasant assessments related to specific people.

Of course, there is always the possibility that someone may be asked to compromise his or her professional standards. If and when that occurs, the auditor is faced with a very important professional and personal decision.

AN IMPORTANT OPPORTUNITY

Auditors often have a research component in their assessments. There may be specific questions that they wish answered, not for the improvement of the organization, but for the refinement of their own theories. The Downs–Hazen Communication Satisfaction Questionnaire, discussed in Chapter 8, was partially developed this way. Similarly, Rogers (1995) has employed many types of assessment tools in historical explorations of the diffusion of innovations. Cumulatively, such audits have been worthwhile in developing research tools that try to discover the keys to effective organizational communication. For example, summarizing the results across several audits, Goldhaber and Rogers (1979, pp. 16–17) concluded that communication behavior was *strongly* related to job tenure, organizational tenure, and age. The demographics that were moderately related to communication behavior included education, supervisory status, communication training, and the number of people with whom one communicated.

For the last 12 years, we have explored in numerous cultures how communication processes affect organizational commitment, and we have found major differences in the predictors of commitment based on type of organization and on the culture in which it operates (see Downs, Adrian, & Ticehurst, 2002). Such a research component gives the auditors additional insights into organizations over time. And this insight then becomes invaluable to interpreting data from new organizations.

We have found that many organizational representatives are excited about this and have, indeed, wanted to cooperate. Twice, the presidents of companies we audited wanted to be coauthors of papers we were writing.

However, there is one caution. An auditor is a professional doing a job for a company. That is the first objective. Do not let the research component betray that objective.

CONCLUSION

Planning a communication audit sets the stage for its successful completion. The client and the auditor collaborate on the plans in order to establish how the auditor will meet the client's needs and to define the audit's boundaries. Clarifying expectations about the scope of the audit and what will actually happen proves invaluable when the audit team starts working. Do not rush through or gloss over the planning stage: it provides auditors with opportunities to explain what they do, the value they bring to the company, and their expectations about coordinating the process.

3

Conducting Team Audits

David Cook
James Patterson
Cal W. Downs

Consultants often conduct communication audits alone or in pairs; graduate communication classes, however, generally take a team approach to auditing. Since managing an audit team presents some unique challenges, we focus this chapter on team collaboration when making communication audits. Actually, these teams become regular work units, with all the pitfalls that befall any other work organization. Graduate students often remark that the audit class taught them more about *interpersonal dynamics* than they had learned in any other situation. Most people are eager to carry a significant part of the load; others are not. Some want to treat it as just another class project; others will adopt the professionalism of a consultant. Some enjoy going out to conduct interviews at midnight, but there will always be some who do not want to interfere with their own schedules. Some are exceedingly conscientious; others have been known to do almost anything to avoid an inconvenience—even making up some of the data. The following discussion is designed to facilitate the smooth operation of an audit team.

BASIC CONSIDERATIONS

Most readers have already participated in some form of "team." Some will have been successful; other team efforts will have been painful. The word "team" as it applies to communication audits implies individual members coordinating their work together toward a common goal. In a team audit, the common goal is predetermined: a valid review of the client organization. How the team performs in relation to this goal is the single most important measure of the team's success.

Being client-focused means putting aside individual differences, working together to provide the best possible service for the client, and utilizing each individual's own special qualities to produce a superior communication audit. To function as a team, audit members must work together in one place, which is not as easy as it sounds. The team audit will fail if individual members think they can work independently of one another, or if they are very competitive with one another, or if they think they can piece the audit together at the end. Being a team means working together in the strictest sense—maximizing communication, coordination, and collaboration—to produce something greater than the sum of any individual effort. Our goal in this chapter is to discuss various techniques and to offer tips that may aid the team in conducting audits, to provide team members with many alternatives to conducting and analyzing audit data, to let them decide what best fits their specific audit team. We have organized this chapter around the steps of the audit process previously outlined in Chapters 1 and 2. Figure 3.1 provides a summary of the issues facing teams as they undertake the audit process.

Initiation Phase
Focus efforts inward
Create a vision for the team
↓

Planning Phase
Designate team roles
Develop schedules
Publicize team to organization
Create mechanisms for collaboration
↓

Focus Areas
Assign areas of focus
Determine primary and secondary roles
Establish collaborative norms
↓

Data Collection Phase
Determine interview teams
Outline data collection guidelines
↓

Interpretation Phase
Organize information
Synthesize all members' perceptions
Verify all data for accuracy and reliability
↓

Final Report Phase
Determine standards for writing report
Verify final report
Develop plan for report presentation
↓

Shared Review of Audit Processes

FIGURE 3.1. Audit team processes.

INITIATION PHASE

Focus Efforts Inward

It is important that the audit team be *intact* prior to entering the organization. Merely *assuming* that group members will "eventually work well together" once the process gets underway benefits neither the client nor the audit team. The workload builds too fast for that. Become familiar with audit team members; learn each other's strengths and weaknesses; and build a unified whole working toward a common goal prior to entry into the organization. The focus here should be on how team members are different from one another rather than on who is more skilled, knowledgeable, or qualified to conduct the audit. Audit teams should ask, "What unique qualities, skills, and expertise does each individual member bring to the audit?"

One element to focus on at this early stage is individual member's communication styles. Basing his work on Jungian psychology, Downs (2000) identified four communication styles that affect how individuals in groups interact and behave. These communication styles are intuitors, doers, thinkers, and feelers. Understanding each other's communication style may help generate a better plan of action for conducting the audit. Doers, for example, may be more effective when given audit tasks such as conducting statistical analyses and scheduling, while feelers may be more effective when given relational tasks such as communicating with key individuals within the organization and conducting interviews.

To understand the organization, audit teams must be familiar with its own history and styles of communicating, and how these elements may impact the audit process.

Create a Vision for the Team

It is not uncommon for team members to hold different perspectives on organizations, to follow different agendas in the audit process, and to have different priorities regarding audit outcomes. This diversity is characteristic of any consulting group or any academic class. In a recent audit of an advertising agency by a graduate class, two group members made it clear that their goal was to receive graduate credit for the project. Moreover, they were not willing to produce work that was not clearly outlined on the course syllabus. In another audit, several members insisted that the audit end automatically when the academic term ended, even though interviews with key organizational members could not be scheduled because of seasonal vacations and the assessment was not finished. Since most organizations seeking communication audits do not fall under the academic umbrella, such attitudes are counterproductive to the audit process and demonstrate a lack of accountability and professionalism. Fortunately, in both instances, other members of the teams adopted a more professional attitude and finished the projects eagerly.

The skillful audit team creates a team vision that is client-focused. A client-centered vision is based on a simple standard: to provide superior service to the client organization. This type of vision helps transcend unproductive conflict and personality clashes. Indeed, communication experts emphasize that resolving conflict begins with finding common ground between competing parties. In the case of a communication audit, the common ground is always already there: the client organization.

PLANNING PHASE

Designate Team Roles

During the planning phase, develop guidelines as a "game plan" for working with one another and the organization. The first priority is to develop individual roles within the team. Three specific roles should spearhead the planning phase of the audit.

First, the group should appoint a *contact person* who will serve as the liaison to the organization. Ideally, there would be a similar contact person from within the organization. The contact person must be both flexible and readily available. Since organization members will have all kinds of questions about the audit, the contact person should clarify concerns, while taking advantage of these communications to publicize the benefits of the project.

A *scheduler* also needs to be designated to develop the interview plan. This involves organizing interviewer "free time" schedules first, and then matching them with available times for organization members. For example, during one audit several interviews were canceled literally minutes before the interviewers were to arrive at the business. Because the scheduler had worked closely with the organizational liaison individual in making the appointments, he was able to move quickly to rearrange several schedules to accommodate the changes.

Finally, a *coordinator* must be selected to be in charge of the entire operation. The coordinator oversees the project and must be knowledgeable concerning current events.

A contact person, a scheduler, and a coordinator are essential to the success of the project. While the rest of the team may not have designated roles, it is essential that they inform one another both formally and informally on recent findings. Much of the learning takes place by individuals who take the initiative to be interested or curious and share openly with others.

The key function of assigning the three suggested roles is to increase accountability, while not diffusing the responsibility across too many team members. When these roles are absent, it is easy for key issues to get lost in the shuffle. Similarly, when too many roles are appointed, it is easy for key responsibilities to be forgotten.

Publicize the Audit Team to the Organization

Another priority is to publicize the audit team to the organization. Once the audit begins, team members may be walking throughout the organization to do interviews, make copies, or meet with employees. They will feel more comfortable and have more success when employees understand why they are there. When the organization publicizes the audit, it shows the employees that company management is backing the project. Advance publicity also allows interviewers to spend less time building their own credibility and more time gaining information to benefit the process.

An audit team may publicize itself to the business in several ways. They may provide summary resumes to the key management team and perhaps to workers through interoffice mail or attached to a company newsletter. Other possibilities may be to have management introduce the team during a monthly meeting or have the CEO mention the audit on employee voice mail. Finally, the audit team may produce an open letter to employees that validates the audit team's credibility and explains the audit process. A sample letter is presented in Table 3.1.

Create Mechanisms for Collaboration

Designate a medium through which team members can openly collaborate and discuss findings. An *electronic mail* (e-mail) account is an excellent way to communicate to the entire team at any hour of the day. Make sure it has the capability to send and receive distribution lists to every member simultaneously. Not only is this a quick way for the team to communicate, it also can be used as a record of perceptions, assumptions, and findings when it comes time to write the final report.

Use a "*filing cabinet*" to store all artifacts from the audit. It may include company newsletters, training schedules, organization charts, job descriptions, or communications between the coordinator and the organization. Place the filing cabinet in a central location where all members have access to it.

Negotiate *meeting times* for the team. Conducting an audit requires more time spent together than a typical graduate class; it is unlikely that the challenges of the audit will be met if the team tries to limit meetings to normal class periods.

Assign Areas of Focus

Individuals in an assessment team often have particular interests and research skills that determine how they want to participate on the team. For example, a person may want to focus primarily on upward communication processes or coordination among departments. Sometimes, the team member may make focal decisions because of a preference for one kind of data over another. Letting people select what they want to explore can be highly motivating as teams develop expertise in certain areas. However, the team should keep an individual's contribution in a team perspective since sometimes the individual's reports have to be reconciled in order to get a meaningful view of the organization. Furthermore, it is useful for each individual to be involved in multiple focus areas so that he or she can maintain an overall organizational perspective.

Determine Primary and Secondary Roles

Audit members should expect to get involved with all aspects of the audit; however, teams often designate primary and secondary roles for each member according to that person's special interests and expertise. For instance, teams often focus energy on two areas: quantitative and qualitative data collection methods. For example, if a team member's primary role is quantitative analysis, efforts should focus on writing items for the questionnaire and determining how and when it may be administered. A secondary role may be to read a rough draft of the interview guide. The audit has multiple phases; team members should have the flexibility to participate in both the quantitative and the qualitative sides of the audit, though perhaps at different stages. One member may enjoy creating surveys in an initial stage, but want a chance to learn content analysis during the data interpretation phase. In that case, the person would work with others on the quan-

TABLE 3.1. Sample Letter of Introduction to the Organization

Open Letter to Pine Hills Police Department Employees

Dear Pine Hills Police Department Employees:

We are currently conducting a communication audit of your organization. The following letter addresses specific questions or concerns you may have regarding the audit process.

The Audit Team

Our audit team consist of six PhD students enrolled in business and communication programs at the University of Kansas. The current project partially fulfills graduate requirements for our selected programs of study. Audit team members have been employed in a variety of organizations, have taught numerous business and communication courses at the college level, and have participated in several communication audits of various organizations. The project is currently being conducted in conjunction with Communication Management, Inc, a professional communication consulting firm. Dr. Cal W. Downs, president of Communication Management, Inc., currently supervises the audit.

The Communication Audit

Ask most employees about the problems they have in their organizations and most will say "communication." Communication audits are designed to help organizations develop and refine the strategic management of communication, people, technologies, and information. Many people erroneously assume that communication audits are designed only to detect problems. In truth, communication audits assess both an organization's strengths and its weaknesses. In addition to detecting problems, audit instruments also tell organizations what they are doing right.

The Survey Instrument

In the next couple of days, you will be asked to fill out a survey that assesses various communication aspects of your work. Interview data and Pine Hills information were used to adapt the Down's Standardized Survey to fit your organization. The Down's Survey has been widely tested for reliability and validity. In addition, adaptations of the instrument have proven effective in a wide variety of organizations: manufacturing plants, airlines, hospitals, agencies, retail companies, automobile industries, and the military.

The success of the instrument, however, depends on receiving feedback from you. We personally guarantee that your answers will be strictly confidential and that no data will be used which could possibly identify an individual respondent. In addition, we will provide a synopsis of the survey results to every employee in the organization.

The survey takes approximately 30 minutes to fill out. Please take the time to fill out the survey and return it in the self-addressed stamped envelope provided. Your input is vital to the success of the Pine Hills Police Department.

Sincerely,

KU AUDIT TEAM

titative side for the initial phase, but would not be locked in to performing the quantitative analysis. Table 3.2 lists various team roles.

Members may work primarily in one of these areas during the focal phase; however, they may want to switch during the data collection or interpretation phase.

Establish Collaborative Norms

Collaborative norms enhance understanding and learning about the organization. A common problem arises when team members see the organization only in terms of those areas or methods they are assigned to or interested in understanding. If not controlled, this "tunnel vision" can cause individual members to misinterpret their perceptions because they are seeing only a fraction of the organization. By setting up norms of collaboration, group processes encourage open dialogues and resist groupthink.

For example, we worked on an audit team where everyone was concerned with the high amount of turnover in the organization. (After distributing the survey we found this company was losing about one-third of its workforce every 3 years.) It was not until one member suggested that management may *want* "fresh" people with "new ideas" that the team openly considered turnover in a positive way. To our surprise, the CEO said he liked turnover for similar reasons. We learned that even intelligent teams may have the tendency to make logical decisions without considering all sides of the story. Better yet, we began to appreciate everyone's opinion, no matter how unusual, in analyzing and interpreting our findings.

DATA COLLECTION PHASE

Generally, communication audits will employ a diverse repertoire of data collection procedures that broadly fall into two camps: quantitative and qualitative methods. *Resist the temptation to have group members work solely in one or the other area.* Each team member should take a large, primary role in one type of collection procedure and a smaller, secondary role in the other. Generally, team members who are involved in both types of data collection procedures make better interpretations by synthesizing all the data, and they produce richer, more detailed final reports. In addition, they are less likely to gloss over contradictions between the two types of data.

Systematize the Quantitative Data Collection

The following guidelines may be helpful in collecting quantitative data as a team. We hope they will help you avoid some problems. In one team, for example, an auditor completely revamped the data format without telling the other team members; the result was chaos. On another occasion, the team detected some sloppy errors of encoding because some team members were not very careful and did not particularly care that things were not done correctly. In this instance, the principal team coordinators spent many, many hours checking each individual number five different times. In other words, team members who are not conscientious make extra work for others.

TABLE 3.2. Team Audit Roles

Initiation phase

Team players
Every member is beginning to work together as a team. This involves identifying strengths and weaknesses and understanding that everyone will take on different roles throughout the audit process.

Investigators
Gathers as much information about the organization as possible. The entire audit team becomes investigators as they try to familiarize themselves with the organization.

Planning phase

Contact person
Serves as liaison between audit team and organization. All communications between the audit team and the organization should go through the contact person.

Coordinator
Oversees the entire audit. Must be knowledgeable of current events including changes, organizational contacts, and scheduling concerns.

Scheduler
Organizes the interview schedules for the audit team and coordinates interview times with organization members.

Focal phase

Primary
Team members are assigned to either quantitative or qualitative roles as their principal focus of research.

Secondary
After deciding on their primary focus, team members should have a minor role in the remaining focus area (either quantitative or qualitative).

Data collection phase

Secretary
In charge of managing central filing cabinet where data files are stored.

Data coders
Coordinate incoming interviews and input survey findings into central statistical database.

Statisticians
Run and analyze statistical tests on quantitative data.

Interview coders
Collect and summarize interview transcripts. This includes identifying quotes from organization personnel.

Interpretation phase

Focus group
Team works together to analyze and interpret audit findings. Involves synthesizing perceptions from both quantitative and qualitative data.

(continued)

TABLE 3.2. *(continued)*

Final report phase

Writers
Organize findings and write sections of final report.

Editor
Reviews written sections. Makes sure grammar, writing style, and format is consistent and correct.

Chart generator
Creates charts and tables for report.

Speakers
Present report and summarizes findings. Suggest recommendations and addresses comments and questions from organization members.

Supporters
Direct efforts toward helping the speakers be as effective as possible. This may involve making overheads or pulling out representative quotes to be used in the presentation. They also may elaborate on questions asked during the presentation or comment on ideas that have been overlooked.

---

1. *Create a central location for coding data.* Using a central location for entering data limits the number of disks and files used. Multiple disks cause problems when corrections need to be made in the data set. Often some data disks get corrected while others do not. Or worse, some disks contain certain corrections while some disks contain others. Update disks continually.

2. *Use a limited number of data coders.* Using a limited number of data coders increases accountability, and it also reduces error rate. In addition, limiting the number of data coders means more individuals will be available to verify the data once it is coded.

3. *Determine guidelines for coding data.* Will missing data be coded numerically or left blank? How will nominal data be coded? What number should be entered when more than one is circled? Addressing questions such as these before data coding begins will save time and energy that can be spent elsewhere.

4. *Verify the data.* Data can be verified either during the process or post hoc. One process involves two coders entering data, one who actually enters the data and another who calls out the numbers and watches to make sure the actual numbers are being entered. After the data are entered, the data can be verified by running a frequency distribution on all the variables. While the frequency distribution will not verify errors that fall in the scale range, it can be used to eliminate double numbers, to detect numbers that fall outside the scale, and to verify that missing data are properly coded. Verification is also possible by encoding the data twice and running a computer check between the two sets of data.

5. *Conduct tests only after data have been completely verified.* Resist the temptation to analyze immediately. If even one number is incorrect in the data coding, the statistical tests can be invalid. In addition, making sure the data are correct before proceeding eliminates unnecessary printing, duplicating work, and much frustration.

6. *Print two copies of the output.* Place one copy of the final output in a binder and

use it as a verification resource only. In this regard, no pages should *ever* be removed from the binder. Take the second copy and divide the output into sections that can be disseminated to members who will write the final report. Using different colored high-lighters, highlight all results that are statistically significant with one color and all results that are interesting, but not statistically significant, with the other. Using two pocket folders, place each output section on one side and a blank, formatted diskette and final report guidelines on the other (see the Final Report section of this chapter).

Summarize Qualitative Data

Qualitative data may include interview summaries, answers to open-ended questions, and observations. The following guidelines may be helpful in making sense of the qualitative data as a team.

1. *Develop interview teams.* One team member should be taking notes while the other member is asking questions. By having a note taker, the interviewer has more freedom to think about questions and probe important issues.

2. *Type written summaries immediately after the interview.* Both interview team members should be involved with typing and verifying the transcripts. Type them up immediately so important details are not forgotten. Each interview write-up should then be made available to all other members of the team.

3. *Determine how the data will be synthesized.* Main ideas need to be summarized, and representative comments from the interviews should be picked out. For example, if the organization has a poor orientation program, a statement about a new employee's experiences may be beneficial when interpreting the data and writing the final report. Interpretations will be made in the next phase based on these summaries. Make sure all ideas are thoroughly flushed out.

INTERPRETATION PHASE

The key to most successful audits lies in interpretation. Making interpretations of the vast amount of data collected during an audit sounds easier than it is, especially when more than one individual is involved. In many cases, making interpretations of the data in a group context is more difficult because members must effectively manage competing perspectives, radically different interpretations, and individuals who think they know the "truth" about the organization.

Poorly managed audit teams usually fall victim to either groupthink or destructive conflict. *Groupthink* refers to the tendency of groups to think alike. Because interpretations of the data come late in the audit process, some members may accept other member's interpretations of the data simply because they are exhausted. In addition, conflict often arises when audit members base their interpretations only on the "slice" of the organization where they have focused their data collection efforts. Some of the following considerations may help in making interpretations of the data.

1. *Communicate like crazy.* Continuous communication is crucial to the audit process. Without forming iron-clad judgments, individuals should begin discussing and investigating possible interpretations of the information throughout the entire process. In a recent audit, for example, numerous themes emerged regarding the organization's recent attempt to implement a reengineering program, yet none seemed to explain its failure. One interviewee commented to an interviewer that the reengineering effort failed because the process required only one representative from each department. While the comment had not been echoed in his other interviews, the interviewer mentioned the comment to other interviewers who, in turn, sought to verify the information. Indeed, auditors found that since the organization had a high turnover rate, these single members were often new to the industry and not well trained in their job duties. Therefore, there were problems in execution of their jobs.

2. *Use focus groups to synthesize team interpretations* (see Chapter 12). Conducting two or three focus groups during the latter half of the audit provides a powerful mechanism for collaboration. Focus groups may be used with subgroups or with the entire audit team. They may be formal or informal. Formal focus groups include a clear agenda with team members synthesizing their own interpretations prior to the focus group session. A discussion leader directs the group across a wide range of issues related to the organization. Informal focus groups are usually unstructured and involve individuals sharing information and interpretations on a smaller issue of the audit.

3. *Triangulate all data.* The team should compare all the data collected, look for complimentary types of information, and note any discrepancies between the two. Synthesizing the qualitative and the quantitative data can be a powerful tool for analyzing the organization and explaining the results to the client.

4. *Test your assumptions.* One's assumptions are excellent fodder for discussion. Two examples illustrate the value of this. First, an assumption often made is that all people are good individuals and that these good people want to solve problems, want to resolve conflict equitably, and want excellence in communication. Nothing is further from reality. Those assumptions do not fit everyone in the organization. Yet we have seen some auditors agonize over whether to report data or make recommendations that might cause difficulties for a given organization member.

A second assumption is made by the auditors who think that they equip people to overcome difficulties by presenting information on active listening, open communication, win–win conflict resolutions, diversity, or sensitivity training, or set up off-site meetings to work through problems. Two things are wrong with this: (1) clients are left to their own devices about how to apply such information; (2) auditors often do not have a way of dealing with people who want conflict or who are basically unprincipled. In other words, these two assumptions miscast the world.

FINAL REPORT PHASE

The final report is visible testimony of the amount of work and effort exerted by the audit team. Yet writing a report by committee can be exasperating. If you have ever written a paper with someone else, you can imagine how difficult it is to manage three, four, or more writers who bring to the final report their own styles of writing, language use, and mechanical preferences. Successful final report procedures employ clear standards of writing, involve extensive verification, and produce organized, effective team presentation.

Agree on Standards for Writing the Final Report

Avoid the temptation to cut-and-paste the final report together. Careful planning before the final report is written can make the difference between a masterpiece and a Frankenstein monster. Here are several guidelines to consider when planning the final report.

1. *Determine verb tense.* The audit team faces many decisions about writing the report. For instance, will the team write the report in the past or the present tense? Will it use active or passive voice? The standard for U.S. business writing today is to use active, concise verb tenses. For instance, one would not say "It was found that employees were satisfied with communication from top management." That sentence uses passive voice, thus making it unclear who did "the finding." Rather, one could use the more concise statement " We found that employees. . . ." Even better, go with the more concise "Top management satisfies employees."

2. *Determine how the results will be reported.* Some consultants prefer to spell out statistical expressions, such as average, mean, and number of responses, while others prefer statistical symbols such as X or N. Still others prefer to write in terms of percentages rather than averages. It is important that the report explains the results consistently, and takes into account the knowledge level or preference of the client organization.

3. *Make wise language choices.* Audit teams must remember that their audience will typically consist of individuals who are not accustomed to academic lingo. For example, reporting something as "statistically significant at the .001 confidence level" may have very little meaning to the client organization. In addition, organizations may object to certain word usages.

4. *Organize consistently.* Adopting a consistent form of organization increases readability and enhances clarity. Generally, most audit reports are organized around variables or departments of the organization. For example, Downs and his associates generally organize their final reports around the communication factors from his *Communication Satisfaction Questionnaire*. Each factor section includes an introduction, an overall review of the factor findings, results by departments, results by tenure, and results by manager versus nonmanager status. Determining the format for the final report beforehand saves time in the final phase of the audit.

5. *Generate charts.* Most organizations use business charts daily. Charts can help the client organization understand the final report. They are an essential part of the organization of the report.

Develop a Plan for Report Presentation

While organization members may have seen a copy of the final report, the presentation may be the first time they have *considered* the findings of the audit. For this reason, the team must spend considerable time planning a professional presentation that will highlight important findings and recommendations.

1. *The presentation must impress the client with its benefits.* Consider some of the same questions asked during the initiation phase. What type of presentation best serves the organization? If the primary purpose of the audit was to serve as an academic learning tool, the final report is an excellent opportunity for students to gain experience in front of an attentive "business" audience. In this case, it seems appropriate to have every team member play a role in the presentation of the audit findings. On the other hand, in dealing with clients as a consultant, the needs of the organization are the number-one priority, and the team should have its most experienced and effective speakers present the final report.

2. *Assign specific roles for the presentation.* At times during the audit certain members take "front-stage roles," while others are better suited for "behind-the-scenes" responsibilities. The presentation of the audit findings is no exception. Simply put, the team should select its most effective presenters to make the best impression on the organization. Even if multiple speakers present, one person needs to be the primary coordinator or master of ceremonies in order to make sure there are smooth transitions between them. For example, the first speaker may give an introduction outlining the audit process. The second and third speakers may share the conclusions. A final speaker may complete the presentation by discussing the recommendations.

3. *Deal with client questions.* The most important part of the report may be the discussion that takes place during and after the actual presentation of the report. One cannot really anticipate all possible questions, but one can be certain that the report will pique the interest of the organization members. They will want to know more and to seek justifications for the report's conclusions. The discussion should be loose enough for all members to participate in the discussion. It is even good form for one member to defer to another to embellish an answer to a question.

SPECIAL INSTRUCTIONS FOR AUDIT CLASSES

The audit class is very different from the average college course. Rarely does the entire focus and learning of a class hinge on the overall attitude and participation of every class member. For this reason, the average class must develop into a team ready to meet the challenges that face them. Some of the more important guidelines for the team to remember are:

1. *Be client-focused.* The organization's interests are the primary concern in decision making.

2. *Share roles and responsibilities.* Team members have different strengths and weaknesses. Everyone should be able to help the team out in unique ways. Tap into these differences to make the team as effective as possible.

3. *Be professional.* Whether the audit is an academic or a consulting project, the professional audit team ultimately realizes the client will measure them by the final product.

4. *Do not expect to be able to conduct an audit using just regular class times.* A group cannot conduct a meaningful audit just meeting two to three times a week.

CONCLUSION

Collaborating on a communication audit is rewarding, but not simple. Conducting an audit with a team means that one is not only auditing the company's communication, one is also managing the audit team's communication. As the audit team works together, its members learn about the challenges of communicating with each other as much as they learn about communication in the client company. This chapter highlights the kind of detailed planning an audit team should undertake to facilitate that collaboration.

David Cook, PhD, Center for Telemedicine and Telehealth, University of Kansas, Kansas City, Kansas.

James Patterson, PhD, Department of Communication, Miami University of Ohio, Oxford, Ohio.

4

Choosing Focal Areas to Assess

In Chapter 1 we urged auditors to take a process perspective on communication. That means that auditors should view communication as a key organizing process. As such, it must be related to other organizational processes. Taking this perspective affects the focal areas one chooses to study in the audit. As they choose focal points, auditors are in essence setting the boundaries for the audit and determining the kinds of data that they will collect. The best assessments (1) cover a broad range of communication processes and (2) relate at least some of those communication processes to other organizational variables in some depth. For instance, auditors should collect data on the most important organizational elements: the people and their positions, the task processes, the structures underlying task processes, networks, communication of organizational strategies, communication technologies, and the types of information exchanged. The client may also be interested in how these communication variables relate to other organizational variables such as productivity, commitment, and job embeddedness.

In this chapter, we provide guidelines for choosing the investigation's focal areas. Though the content of each communication assessment varies according to the specific client's needs, we designed these guidelines to be useful in multiples settings.

1. Examine how the task processes impact communication.
2. Determine the adequacy of information exchange.
3. Check the directionality of information flow.
4. Assess how well employees use the communication media/technologies.
5. Be sensitive to differences in communication functions.
6. Check the quality of communication relationships.
7. Plot communication networks.
8. Review the organization as a communication system.
9. Relate communication to organizational outcomes.
10. Link internal communication to organizational strategies.

11. Assess the impact of new technologies on communication.
12. Be open to the unexpected.

All these steps are discussed in detail in the following sections. We strive to provide both a theoretical and a practical rationale for each step.

STEPS IN CHOOSING FOCAL AREAS

Examine How the Task Processes Impact Communication

Communication specialists, like organizational psychologists, generally see the importance of motives, attitudes, expectations, human relations, leadership styles, and related variables. Fewer communication experts, though, have been trained to examine the structure of work: for many, it is treated as a given. We believe, however, that no communication assessment can be completed without understanding the task processes necessary for directing, controlling, and coordinating work assignments. Since employees perform many tasks, auditors need to determine how these tasks are coordinated. We construct an *organizational logic,* a listing of the task processes and a description of how the organization functions. By analyzing tasks and how they fit together, we begin to understand the demands made on the communication system.

For example, in an audit of a manufacturing plant, we were asked to focus on the employees' apparent lack of teamwork. Lack of teamwork is generally considered to be a bad thing. But before we could begin to work on the communication steps that might improve teamwork, we had to determine exactly how these employees were expected to coordinate their tasks. What did they do that required teamwork? As it turned out, the employees were unclear about their own task processes, and this uncertainty inevitably led to numerous interpersonal problems.

Auditors can gain a useful sense of how tasks and people are related to each other by actually charting out tasks and who does them. Auditors should also identify whether these people direct, coordinate, or control the tasks. Table 4.1 highlights sample tasks in an organization and identifies employees who are involved in them.

For large organizations, the auditor's task of putting together the organizational logic may seem overwhelming. In those instances, it may be sufficient to diagram out the

TABLE 4.1. Sample Tasks in an Organization

Task	Employees			
	Theresa	John	Joe	Lorrie
Creates strategic report	Directs	Coordinates	Coordinates	Coordinates
Communicates report to superiors	—	Directs	—	—
Communicates report to employees	—	—	Coordinates	Directs
Runs budget numbers	Directs	—	—	—

major tasks by department (rather than by individual) or to look solely at key individual roles in the organization. The auditor should use the logic to gain insight into how work is done, as that affects the communication that needs to occur. The logic reveals to the auditor where integration across tasks is necessary—in other words, where people/departments are interdependent. It also often brings out the formal/informal hierarchy in terms of who has power regarding what decisions. Sometimes the auditor identifies patterns of hierarchy that bear little resemblance to the organizational chart and anticipate that communication issues will arise around these "virtual positions" (Mackenzie, 1986).

Determine the Adequacy of Information Exchange

One ultimate aim of communication is to circulate information. Three issues are related to how adequately this is accomplished: (1) *type of information,* (2) *timing,* and (3) *load.*

Every audit ought to explore whether people get the information that they need to perform their jobs. The need for information relates directly to each task process. The auditor can gauge adequacy in two ways. First, most employees are sensitive to the fact that they do not get certain information, and they generally are willing to share their views with the auditor. Second, employees are sometimes unaware of the existence of information that could be useful; the auditors may become aware of this gap through their own observations. Auditors need to search out what information is, and should be, made available to employees and not be tied to employees' perceptions only. They should ask, "Does the information that the employees desire actually exist, or does it exist in the time frame that they desire?"

Furthermore, because communication is one of the principal ways of integrating people into an organization, they often want information not related to their own task processes. For example, during the economic downturn of 2001, one client fired a key executive. The employees were upset that they had not been informed about this decision in advance. However, there was no way that this information could be distributed companywide in advance without inviting legal liabilities. Indeed, increasingly legal considerations play a role in information dissemination.

Since information is only useful if it is received on time, the auditor can look for ways of developing a timely distribution system. This sounds easier to do than it often is. For example, many companies are plagued by the problem of how to inform their own employees about a story before it is published in the press. Many employees feel cheated or betrayed if they initially get their organizational information through the public newspapers. In working with a public utility, we tried several different formats to solve this problem, but none of them was completely successful. Sometimes the seemingly "simple" communication dilemmas prove to be intractable.

Communication load can be an important variable in assessing the degree of adequacy of information exchange. *Load* refers to the frequency and amount of communication that takes place. An *optimal load* is dictated by the receiver's ability to process some amount of information. Unfortunately, no one has come up with a good definition of optimal load; instead, we are more likely to define it by what it is not. *Underload* occurs when people think they need or could use more information. *Overload* occurs when people have more information than they can possibly process. In such instances, more communication is certainly not better communication.

Although the most common complaint in organizations is that employees do not get enough communication, tension usually develops when moving from underload to overload. For example, a public service company had the following experience. After an assessment, the consultant proposed a new suggestion system. The employees were assured that their suggestions would be reviewed and responded to in writing. As the coordinator received employee suggestions, he placed them in red folders and sent them to the appropriate person for review. The impetus for this program was to draw out the employees—that is, to remedy an underload of suggestions. However, the program was sold so well that one could walk by certain offices and see stacks of those "damn suggestions" on their desks. Replying to employee suggestions took far more time for supervisors than anyone had predicted. In essence, the suggestions created an "information overload" for the people responsible for responding to the employees. As a result, the new suggestion system not only interfered with their other work but also caused a great deal of resentment. Perhaps most significantly, the problems created by the information overload probably made employees wary of future innovations. Many thought, "They say that they will listen to us, but it is a farce. The managers do not respond to us. They probably don't even read our suggestions. Why should we offer new ideas when the company doesn't really believe in them?"

Load may also be related to technology. Computers and new software make it possible to process a greater load of communication. But technology is a mixed blessing. During the audit of a university, we interviewed an employee who identified the photocopier as the organization's greatest communication problem. Too many people copied things profusely and sent them out indiscriminately. The recipients had to at least partially read some of the messages to discover that they did not want them. Therefore, the recipients felt overloaded because reading irrelevant information was taking up too much of their time.

The rise of computers has aggravated this problem. People are constantly searching for ways to differentiate between emails they want and those they do not want. Lotus Notes has amazing capacities to generate elaborate networks for sharing information. Lawson and Downs (1999) audited an organization that had recently introduced Lotus Notes and wanted to assess its effectiveness. The company gave them access to all the messages throughout the organization. One night Downs opened a single file and discovered 10,000 new messages. There was no way he could process all of that. Fortunately, most employees did not have to do so either. In a real sense, the best most assessments can do is to measure whether people feel underloaded or overloaded, but this is important information because it reveals how people are responding to message exchanges.

Check the Directionality of Communication Flow

Because hierarchy is an inherent part of every organization, it is common to analyze communication in terms of the direction in which it flows. The most common types are (1) downward, (2) upward, and (3) horizontal. Knowing the direction is not enough, however, because the importance of any direction depends on the criteria with which the auditors will critique the communication.

Downward Flow

Downward communication refers to those message systems that proceed vertically down the chain of command from managers to subordinates. It takes the forms of orders, company publications, performance judgments, job instructions, company orientations, and training for the job. Employees receive a great deal of information from many different sources but how much of this communication is effective has always been disputed. Investigators have found that "managers are more likely than . . . workers to think that downward communication is taking place" (Farace, Monge, & Russell, 1977, p. 149). Furthermore, there has long been a difference between management's perception of what employees *need* to know and what the employees say they need and *want* to know. This difference calls attention to two functions of downward communication.

First, of course, employees need to have the information necessary to do their jobs. In many organizations such information is late in coming or totally lacking. Second, good downward communication is not limited to immediate work assignments; it integrates people into their environments. This is the aspect that many organizations neglect. In our assessments we have encountered whole units that wanted some downward recognition of their efforts, some sense of how they fit into the total organization, or an idea of how the company planned to meet some general economic problems. When employees do not get such information, they feel left out. Furthermore, they wonder why such information is being filtered out or distorted (Davis, 1968). These feelings arise particularly during the ambiguities brought about by change. According to Smith (1996), "Today's most urgent performance challenges demand that you learn how to manage people through a period of change" (p. 15).

Downward communication may be informal as well as formal; it goes beyond task information; it focuses on the employee, the unit, and the company; it often does not meet the expectations of employees; and it must be constantly adapted to changing circumstances. An audit provides an important means of testing how efficiently and effectively the organization is meeting the comprehensive need for information. Clampitt (2001) addresses the importance of downward communication with this statement: "Managing information effectively is a truly monumental task. Yet, effective information management lies in supervising the knowledge base as well as the processing mechanism" (p. 83).

Upward Flow

Communication also flows from employees up the chain of command, either formally or informally. Whereas many people initially think of downward communication when they think of effective communication in organizations, some of the most important information processing goes from employees at one level to their superiors. Task-oriented reports, for example, are commonly sent upward to provide feedback about performance. Without an effective system of reporting upward, no organization could possibly function for long. Other forms of upward communication include suggestion systems, teams, quality circles, goal setting, and techniques of participative management. Even a job performance review can have an upward dimension as an employee communicates impressions regarding his or her own performance levels and the goals that are relevant to the job.

Upward communication also sets the tone for the communication climate. Whether employees have the freedom to initiate communication with superiors characterizes how employees perceive the communication climate. Employees often deliberately filter upward communication. There is an old observation that no one wants to be the bearer of bad news. Indeed, Downs and Conrad (1982) found that subordinates were often reluctant to bring their bosses bad news. People fear being negatively associated with the bad news. In this sense, upward communication is important not only to the organization but to its individual members. Being able to communicate upward gives one a stake in the organization and promotes a sense of dignity or importance. In terms of organizational outcomes, upward communication affects individuals' satisfaction levels.

It is understandable that employees filter their upward communication out of a need for self-preservation related to their mobility aspirations and their desire to gain their managers' trust (Read, 1962; O'Reilly & Roberts, 1974). However, filtering upward communication can be dysfunctional for overall organizational health. Upward communication also affects productivity. Thus auditors need to assess it closely.

Horizontal Flow

The managers to whom auditors report often consider vertical communication to be most important. However, much of the communication at work takes place horizontally with peers, colleagues, or fellow workers with whom one does not have a hierarchical relationship. Many of these horizontal interactions take place informally for social reasons. We have found that those interactions often stimulate organizational commitment. Many people remain with a particular organization because they enjoy interactions with the people who work there (Downs, Adrian, & Ticehurst, 2002).

Nevertheless, horizontal communication remains absolutely necessary for coordinating task processes. Recently we conducted two audits for managers who specifically requested that horizontal communication be our major focus. The first audit targeted a manufacturing plant where designers had cut down on communication because they thought the engineers "looked down" on them. In the second organization, six units were combined into one department, but one unit considered itself more professional than the others and resisted being identified with the new department. Knowledge can give power, and some people are reluctant to share their power.

Horizontal communication is sometimes neglected not out of intent but out of carelessness. For example, in a university, the people responsible for a change in the school calendar "forgot" to notify the people who ran university student housing. Examples like these demonstrate that some of the richest data in any audit may be found by investigating teamwork and horizontal coordinating patterns.

Assess How Well Employees Use the Communication Media/Technologies

Messages have to be transmitted through some channel or media. These ought to be examined comprehensively since media choice is becoming increasingly complex. Trevino, Lengel, and Daft (1987) note that media choice is not always a simple, intuitive process. Instead, it is often the key to whether or not any communication is effective. In some cases, the wrong choice can impede successful communication and produce disastrous consequences. This description makes choosing a communication channel sound intimidating, but people have to transmit messages through some channel or media. Those choices probably most often reflect what is convenient for the sender, but the choices also reflect certain values employees have about the appropriateness of using certain media for tasks or about the symbolic importance of using those media.

Today, people have more communication channels to choose from than ever before. In many circles, there continues to be a bias in favor of face-to-face communication. Hargie and Tourish (2000) report the work of Kotter, who concluded that the most successful executives exert their influence primarily in face-to-face interactions. Though Kotter's work precedes the widespread use of email, the finding may still be pertinent. Adrian talked with one high-level executive at CitiBank who summed up his view as follows: "Email is not communication."

These examples highlight people's general perceptions of "effectiveness." But as an auditor it is important to think in more sophisticated terms about the interrelationships among channel choice, task, and the people involved in the task. Clampitt (2001) proposes five useful questions to ask:

1. Are the sender's objectives compatible with the attributes of the intended message?
2. Are the messages sent compatible with the channels utilized?
3. Are the sender's objectives compatible with the type of channels utilized?
4. Are the messages compatible with the receivers' characteristics?
5. Are the channels utilized compatible with the receivers' characteristics? (pp. 104–106)

Clampitt's list illustrates that there is more to evaluating the appropriateness of media choice than simply saying, "Is this the most efficient means of communicating this message?" In terms of efficiency, mail may always win the day; one can send a message to everyone in the company without having to interact with (or interrupt) any of them. Gopnik (2003) made the following comment about email:

> The reason this medium has blossomed is not that it gives you *more* immediacy; blessedly, it gives you *less*. The new appeal of E-mail is the old appeal of print. It isn't instant; it isn't immediate; it isn't in your face. Written language gives you a hat and Groucho nose and glasses; it's you there, but not quite you. E-mail has succeeded brilliantly for the same reason that the videophone failed miserably: what we actually want from our exchanges is the minimum human contact commensurate with the need to connect with people. "Only connect." Yes, but *only* connect. (p. 181)

Considerable research has compared computer-mediated communication (CMC) and face-to-face communication (for review of experimental literature, see Bordia, 1997). Much of Bordia's (1997) review explores text-based computer-mediated communication. However, with advances in telecommunications technology and digital compression algorithms, visual media are becoming more prevalent. Researchers have explored how different media connections affect specific communication tasks. Two general research approaches help to define important concerns that influence communicator's perceptions of specific media: *media richness theory* and *social information-processing theory*. Media richness theory focuses on the requirements of the communication task, while social information-processing theory focuses on the communicative participants and their context.

Media richness theory categorizes communication media according to a continuum of interactivity and cues available (Daft & Lengel, 1986). Media offering more interactivity and communication cues (visual and auditory) are on the "rich end" of the continuum. These media typically include face-to-face interactions. As media lose their interactivity and communication cues, they are situated on the "lean end" of the continuum (e.g., reports, data sets). Daft and Lengel (1986) suggest that efficient and effective managers match the ambiguity of the message with the richness of the media. Messages higher in ambiguity would require richer communication media, whereas messages lower in ambiguity require leaner communication media. That is, confirming a meeting with someone (low ambiguity) requires a much less rich medium than persuading someone that it is necessary to restructure the organization (high ambiguity). The communication task is paramount in evaluating the effectiveness of a particular media for successful interaction. However, researchers have discovered that situational constraints also influence media choice (Trevino, Lengel, & Daft, 1987). For example, managers found that time and geographical distance more than task requirements sometimes governed media use. These findings broadened the focus from the specifics of the task to the communicative context itself.

Social information-processing theory expands the focus from the specifics of the task to the participants involved (Fulk, Schmitz, & Steinfield, 1990). Researchers have found that the meaning and use of specific media are constructed by the participants involved. Therefore, a medium that may seem somewhat lean, from a media richness perspective, may be considered rich in certain work environments based on the norms and rules for interaction within that workplace. Drawing on this perspective, we assert that it is critical to explore the characteristics of the communication media in the context of the organization's norms and its formal and informal communication relationships. We suggest the following three steps.

First, auditors should assess their client organization's media comprehensively. Make a thorough list of all the channels used in the organization. Be sure to include institutionalized oral interactions as well as written media. A representative list might include email, intranets, face-to-face meetings, videoconferences, teleconferences, computer conferences, telephone, voice mail, fax, interviews, memoranda, closed circuit television, in-house publications (e.g., newsletters, annual reports, etc.), bulletin boards, and training programs. It is important to tailor the list to the specific organization to get a sense of what the possibilities are. For instance, Adrian assessed one organization in which the most relied-upon interdepartmental channel was their internal email system—"the Pony"—one that she would not have listed on a generic list.

Second, gauge employee reactions to these media. Over time, people develop a general belief that some media provide important information and others do not. Identifying these reactions is integral to identifying whether the message matches the media. We once assessed a large organization in which several people told us, "If it is really important, they [management] send out a memo." In that particular case, management had not sent out a paper memo, but rather had sent an email detailing upcoming organization-wide changes. Ironically, many employees felt that management was not communicating with them about those changes. In reality, management simply was not communicating via the channel that many employees expected for information of that magnitude.

Auditors should also be aware that their own observations can be an important resource. For instance, we have found it quite instructive to attend some meetings to observe communicative patterns. Our observation data provide a rich supplement to the perceptual accounts received from employees. On one occasion, we needed to examine the job performance review system. Obviously, we could not sit in on all the actual interviews, so we did the next best thing: we read the evaluations of every employee for the past 2 years in order to get a sense of how well the review system channel was being used.

Third, evaluate the appropriateness of channel use given the interrelationships among messages, media characteristics, and organizational communicators. One issue that generally arises is a need to determine when oral channels should be used (face-to-face or otherwise) and when written channels should be used. Auditors should be aware that, increasingly, lawyers are having their say about whether messages can/should be put in writing or stated orally. In general, though, everyone tends to have an opinion about which channel is "best." Auditors will find that managers have their own preferences for certain channels. Manager preferences, unfortunately, do not always match the preferences of their colleagues. Sometimes, too, new media are not fully appreciated. We recently conducted an audit in which the two newest media were also the least appreciated. It takes a while for people to grasp their usefulness.

At any rate, because employees have different channel preferences for receiving messages, one guideline is to use multiple channels to send any message. Channel redundancy helps messages reach a wider audience. Here are some other guidelines to help auditors make recommendations:

Does the communication require knowledge sharing? If so, face-to-face channels are generally more effective. Research shows that richer knowledge exchange occurs in face-to-face interactions than in videoconferencing or written media (Clampitt, 2001). There is something about coming together and having primary and secondary conversations that stimulates information exchange in unique ways. The immediacy of feedback may be key.

Do people want to emphasize the message or the source? Some media emphasize the source of the message more than the message. For instance, visual forms of communication place emphasis on who is speaking. With videoconferencing or closed-circuit television, the speaker receives all the attention. Sometimes the most important part of the message is *who* is saying it. For instance, during times of intense change or crisis, some messages have more credibility if employees can see that they come out of the CEO's mouth. On the other hand, sometimes it is desirable to downplay the source in order to emphasize the message. For instance, who originates an idea may cause people to react negatively to that idea, not because the idea is bad, but because of the face they associate with it. In that case, less personal (visual) media such as fax, email, or memos are more effective.

How complicated is the message? Sometimes people convey messages in a more complex way than is necessary. Writing a message down forces communicators to clarify and streamline what they want to say. If the message is truly complicated, having it in writing helps the receiver who may need to go back and read it several times for clarification.

Is immediate feedback desirable? Written messages do not necessarily encourage timely feedback. If rapid feedback is critical, then auditors may wish to recommend face-to-face communication.

Is it necessary for the sender and the receiver to communicate simultaneously? If one needs to confirm a meeting time with task force members, it is not necessary to communicate simultaneously with everyone. In fact, it may be more effective to send out an email request that allows each person to respond and copy the others.

Is the message persuasive in nature or is it more informative? If the message is persuasive, communicating face-to-face permits communicators to adapt to the visual and oral cues of the listeners. It helps to anticipate how the audience will react to the message. If the listeners already agree with the message, then it may be possible to convey the message in written form. If the message requires a demonstration of some kind, use a video presentation.

Naturally, auditors should adapt these recommendations to the specific context of the client organization. We have found that there are organizations that communicate downturns in organizational performance by calling organization-wide meetings that update and reassure people via face-to-face contact; other organizations simply send out an email that explains what has happened. Those decisions reflect, perhaps, organization size and resources, but they also reflect attitudes toward communication. Either communication method, though, would represent organizations with healthier communication policies than the company that decides to say nothing and let employees hear the information from the grapevine, the newspaper, or the evening news on TV.

In addition to thinking about specific media channels, auditors should remember that employees distinguish between formal and informal channels. We find that the informal channels are some of the most important channels to evaluate. Although the distinction between formal and informal channels is not always clear-cut, "informal channel" generally refers to the grapevine (or rumor mill) or to social interactions outside the formal organizational structure. Many employees find these horizontal links to be the lifeblood of their organizations. Informal horizontal linkages help employees accomplish work and establish powerful communication networks. It should not be forgotten, though, that employees also obtain much of their basic information about the organization and its activities through informal channels.

Through our audits, we have determined that informal channels are exceptionally fast, but that members generally prefer hearing information about the organization through formal channels. Employees explain that they prefer these channels because of the potential unreliability of information that circulates informally. Perhaps, too, employees perceive an element of respect when management uses formal channels to communicate important information internally.

It is easy to set up the formal and informal channels analytically as if they were competitors; unfortunately, they sometimes are. Informal channels, however, can also reinforce the formal channels and help to build strong organizational ties. Is it possible to imagine an organization without informal channels? Surely one would question the health of those organizational relationships. When assessing informal channels, auditors should avoid pitting them against the formal system in a good–bad dichotomy; rather, auditors should evaluate how informal channels are being used and whether or not there is an unhealthy reliance on them or a healthy, thriving balance.

Be Sensitive to Differences in Communication Functions

Communication has different functions within the organization, some of which have a higher priority than others. The following five functions are not discrete or mutually exclusive. However, they do provide a general way of thinking about differences in communication function.

Task/Work Function

Organizations succeed by getting work done. An important aspect of communication is its ability to inform, to instruct, to command, to solve problems, to identify goals, and to announce controls. Supervisory instructions, problem-solving meetings, and policy announcements illustrate the ways communication fits the task function. Most of these ways represent some form of downward communication, but many of them will also require important feedback to be reported upward.

Social/Maintenance Function

Modern organizations are where people spend much of their lives, interacting with fellow human beings. For many people, work is their principle means of self-identification. Therefore, the immediate goals of maintenance communication are to enhance the individual's feeling of self-worth, to place high value on cooperative interpersonal and group interactions, and to keep personnel functioning well together. Interpersonal relationships often suffer as people clash trying to accomplish a task; as a result, work may grind to a halt. When this happens, maintenance leadership is necessary to smooth over the disrupted interpersonal relations. Staff socials, some meetings, personnel news in newspapers, and teamwork seminars are oriented toward the maintenance functions.

Motivation Function

Compliance with a management goal cannot always be ordered or commanded. Therefore, persuasive communication is designed to influence, to win approval, and to motivate. Good managers motivate their employees in daily conversations. Colleagues try to motivate each other to cooperate on tasks. Other examples of communication that serve to motivate include performance appraisals, speeches given by managers in organization-wide meetings to motivate people to be more productive, and even something as simple as a poster emphasizing safety on the plant floor.

Integration Function

Communication can build links so that members know what is going on, identify with the organization, articulate its values, participate willingly in its processes, and feel pride in working there. Managers design many Monday-morning meetings to let people know what is happening and to give them a sense of belonging. Other forms of integrative communication include orientation programs, training seminars, state-of-the-organization presentations, and participation in some decisions. Many companies also use social functions such as happy hours to deliver important—usually good—news and to foster relationships. Whenever the integrative function suffers, employees begin to think less of their jobs and their organizations (Adrian & Ticehurst, 2001a). The lack of full integration can lead to a host of work-related problems.

Integrative communication also plays a role in developing external relationships. Sometimes auditors perform an external audit for companies trying to build franchisee and customer loyalty. Downs, Hydeman, and Adrian (2000) found that the leadership at a national beverage company was surprised to learn how much its distributors valued the annual business meeting. Distributors reported that they found enormous value in sharing ideas with their colleagues. They also reported that the focus on interaction and sharing of detailed information left many—especially the smaller distributors—feeling much more "in the know." As a result of the external audit, leadership of this beverage company developed a new appreciation for the concerns of distributors and changed the national business meeting format to include more informal interaction between executives and distributors, the sharing of more detailed information, and efforts to minimize the class distinctions that had arisen between large and small distributors. The external audit gave the distributors a voice. As a result, future business meetings emphasized communication over "putting on a show." Both internal and external audiences appreciate communication that genuinely integrates them.

Innovation Function

Modern organizations continuously change to improve or to adapt to the environment. Increasingly, organizations are turning to their employees as important resources for suggestions. Sometimes organizations institute formal suggestion systems, but more often they look for more subtle ways of programming new ideas. In addition to suggestion systems, problem-solving meetings, quality circles, and goal setting are all means of being innovative.

Managers must also manage change as it is implemented. This is one significant aspect of the innovation function auditors should not overlook. How managers communicate information about the change and when they communicate it affects how employees perceive the change (Ford & Ford, 1995). Smart managers think about what employees' initial reactions to the change are likely to be—that is, will they accept, reject, or be neutral to the change (Shelby, 1991)? It is too simplistic to assume that "people hate change." In our audits, employees are always able to identify changes they would like to occur. Rather than starting from a "people resist change because it is change" position, good communicators think through what a change asks of people—for example, they have to learn something entirely new, they have to do something that they are already good at but learn to do it differently, and so on. Once managers have a sense of why employees might respond as they do, managers can think about ways of talking about the change. Conversations play an important role in managing the change (Ford & Ford, 1995).

Taken in combination these five communication functions characterize a healthy organization. Although auditors differentiate among them for analytic purposes, none of them really stands alone. The functions are not mutually exclusive—performance reviews, for example, could be categorized in all five areas. Likewise, the maintenance and integration functions have some obvious similarities.

The interdependence among the functions is key. Sometimes management may value the task-oriented function most, but a weakness in any of the other areas can affect task communication. Even when management requests an audit targeting a single function, auditors will find that they need to examine the others as well. For example, we audited a manufacturing plant that was producing 50% more than it had the previous year, so the task function seemed to be working well. Management wanted to devise better ways of securing and implementing employee ideas, so they requested a communication audit that would identify problems in the innovative function and suggest ways of improving it. In the actual analysis, however, it became important to look also at the integrative linkages with the organization because integration often seems to be a precondition to innovation. The audit revealed that the production increases had created a rushed, high-pressure climate, and this had led employees to feel apprehensive about their jobs and less informed. Integration and motivation suffered because of a new policy in hiring managers stating that most promotions would no longer come from within. The belief that promotions were blocked caused resentments, and this had to be overcome before employees would be willing to share their activities and their innovative thoughts. The task, integrative, and innovative communication functions were highly interdependent.

Sometimes, auditors find that the functions are working against each other. In one organization, we found that the social functions actually impeded work. In 1995, we audited a British company where the work rules were so stringent that people often worked in their offices so much that they did not feel they knew anything else about the organization. They had few relationships with other workers. Their loyalty to the company was high, but their understanding of it was very limited.

Check the Quality of Communication Relationships

Every message exchange takes place among people in some kind of relationship context. Each new interaction affects the relationship by strengthening, maintaining, or weakening it. Furthermore, the status of a relationship can affect the response to any message. For example, there is a notable difference between the way organization members respond to orders from people they like and the way they respond to orders from people they don't like. In general, dysfunctional, negative relationships inhibit communication. For these reasons, relationships are among the most important communication phenomena to be audited. We next consider the superior–subordinate relationship, the team relationship among coworkers, and the relationship among managers.

Superior–Subordinate Relationships

For most employees, their supervisors are structurally the most important communication links in the organization. Therefore, auditing the relationships between supervisors and subordinates is a crucial focal point of any audit. Such relationships can be analyzed in terms of three elements. First, interpersonal trust "influences the quality, level, content, and directionality of communication" (Klauss & Bass, 1982, p. 23). Trust determines how much credibility one person has with another. Moreover, levels of trust have been found to be significant indicators of communication effectiveness. By asking employees to describe the levels of trust in the organization, auditors can get them to identify many communication strengths and weaknesses of the organization. Lack of trust is invariably rooted in some difficulties with communication.

Second, superior–subordinate relationships largely determine message exchange, especially for upward communication. For example, when employees do not perceive supervisors as being open, employees limit the number of messages they send upward.

Third, the communication style of the supervisor affects his or her relationship with employees. By "communication style," we mean that each individual has a preferred way of communicating information. Some people focus solely on the big picture and omit all the details; others value the details and rarely make connections between those details and larger issues. Some people place an emphasis on presenting information in a logical manner with all the supporting evidence and proofs for each point; others are particularly sensitive to the human issues that arise from any communication and resent a cold presentation of "the facts." The relevance of these styles comes in the interaction of people at work with different styles. For that reason, in addition to describing a style, the audit should measure the response to it. Downs has used his Communication Style Inventory (2000) to demonstrate that people with different style orientations have significantly different expectations concerning their organizations and their bosses. Both Laird (1982) and Clampitt (1983) found that a "productive style" was idiosyncratic to organizational cultures. This simply means that what is effective with one group of subordinates may not be effective with a different group. Therefore, auditors must interpret the appropriateness of a given style on the basis of the people's response to it.

Coworker Relationships

Relationships among coworkers affect both job productivity and job satisfaction (Clampitt & Downs, 1993). It is interesting to note how often people voice displeasure over a lack of teamwork. Recently, in an audit of a manufacturing plant, we encountered one unit in which people would laugh if they observed another employee having problems with a machine; no one would offer to help. Obviously, these relationships were strained and unhealthy. We had to look for the root causes of this behavior because it was not characteristic of the rest of the organization.

Manager Relationships

The relationships among managers profoundly affect the organization's communicative health. These relationships often set the tone for the rest of the organization. Therefore, if one is going to improve organizational communication, one may need to assess the relationships among top managers. On one occasion, Downs was asked to consult with an organization because "those people down there need to learn to communicate." At the same time, some of the top managers were so competitive that they were not even speaking to one another. There was not much that could be done "below" until the problem at the "top" was addressed.

Unit Relationships

Organizations succeed on the basis of coordination. Managers and employees alike increasingly appreciate the importance of interdepartmental communication. Adrian just happened to be on-site at Sony in San Diego the week the first flat screen digital TVs were coming "off the assembly line." The excitement was palpable. Several visiting engineers asked about Sony's big challenges in the future, thoroughly expecting (apparently) a technological response. Adrian was surprised (and pleased) when the manager responded that one of Sony's highest priorities was *to improve interdepartmental communication for the sake of remaining competitive.* He went on to explain that it was absolutely essential that the departments have knowledge of what others were doing or were capable of doing in order to create new products and improve technologies.

The Rules Governing Relationships

Good auditors should be sensitive to the rules that dictate how, when, and about what people communicate. In one sense, all communication is rule-governed because people do not communicate in totally random or erratic ways. Rules may not be explicit; indeed, people may have difficulty articulating them. Nevertheless, the rules are there, and one of the most interesting ways to assess communication is to discover what rules people follow.

Auditors should think about their own behavior. It is likely that they can identify rules about formality, open-door policies, privacy of interactions, what to say to supervisors, when to say it, what "proper" language usage is, and how to control certain situations. If, for example, people use profanity with some people and not with others, what rule are they following? As these examples indicate, rules may involve procedures or content, but in both instances they regulate relationships.

Communication problems result from the different rule expectations that are inevitable in organizations. Stetler (1972) found significant problems between local health nurses and their supervisors because the two groups had different expectations about frequency of contact. After receiving the results of the study, the nurses and the supervisors were able to reconcile some of their differences. Laird (1982) discovered that some employees interpreted a manager's act of stopping by a subordinate's desk as a friendly gesture, while other employees interpreted it as close supervision. We have also encountered many situations in which managers thought they had open-door policies, but either no one came in to see them or the subordinates had learned not to send bad news upward.

Potential rule conflicts can be found in every aspect of the choices people make about communicating. The Coordinated Management of Meaning approach (Pearce & Cronin, 1980) offers some interesting perspectives on communication rules. It assumes that an adequate analysis of communication interactions must include an examination of the meanings that individuals attribute to their interactions. Thus the Coordinated Management of Meaning approach investigates what people mean by what they do and how that may agree or disagree with the impressions that others have of their communication behavior.

Some communication rules vary with individuals, or with specific relationships, and some are organization-specific. Clarke and Clegg (1998) point out vividly that the rules followed inside an organization also may be part of an overall shift in paradigms by the national culture. Suddenly it may be acceptable to speak directly to the boss via email, or to evaluate the boss using 360-degree feedback. Regardless of the level at which the rules operate, communication rules do shift over time. Understanding how people in an organization perceive their communication rules provides auditors with a valuable window into the communicative life of that organization.

Plot Communication Networks

As interaction patterns stabilize in an organization, they develop into structures called *communication networks*. Some networks are *formal* because they follow the organizational structures. For example, if it is accurate, the organizational chart is a description of a communication network because it prescribes who has contact with whom. Other networks are *informal* in the sense that interactions are based on friendships and social ties rather than on position or work processes. By investigating these networks auditors gain insight into the way organization members process information.

Indeed, the very complexity of real-life networks challenges auditors to attain deeper understanding of the organization. There is no one monolithic network structure in any given organization; rather, many different networks operate simultaneously. Different types of information most likely pass through vastly different networks, some of which may be linked to specific communication channels—for example, face-to-face meetings over lunch, email, and so on.

Networks are fascinating because they enable the auditor to see so many aspects of communication at work. Network analysis allows auditors to identify information pathways, to determine real or potential bottlenecks, to determine how communication linkages match the needs of the task processes, and to analyze the roles that specific people occupy. Auditors can plot small networks of 10 to 20 people by hand; modern computer software, though, makes it feasible to plot networks even if the organization contains 1,300 employees.

Many auditors approach network analysis by emphasizing roles (Farace et al., 1977). Basically, communication roles are characterized by how they link together to form the structure. *Isolates* are members who get little information and have few contacts. *Group members* are those who have a majority of interactions with each other. *Bridges* are members of groups who also connect with other groups. *Liaisons* are people who interact with several groups but who are not actual members of any group. Liaison roles are particularly fascinating, since those who hold them have been found to be more gregarious, more influential, and more likely to hold higher official positions, and are also those perceived by others to have a greater number of contacts in the system (Goldhaber, 1979a). In task-related communication networks, Mackenzie (1986) also identified *virtual positions* that float among task processes and that management may or may not recognize and regulate. Auditors should place no value judgments on all these roles; merely identifying who plays which kind of role provides a picture of how the organization operates.

One last consideration for auditors is the way that new technologies are constantly affecting how communication networks form and operate. Email, for example, has given people contacts in their organizations that they never had before. Business software programs such as Lotus Notes have amazing capacities to generate elaborate networks for sharing information within an organization so that the old idea of communication through a chain of command has been severely disrupted. We worked with one company that updated information every 15 minutes so that any designated employee anywhere in the world could have access to the latest information immediately. New hardware and software technologies will have major implications for networks.

In summary, plotting networks can give the auditors some of the most illuminating insights into how the organization really works. There are many different ways of plotting networks, each with a different set of assumptions. Susskind, Schwartz, Richards, and Johnson (2002) outlined some of those methods as they traced the history of network development at Michigan State University, where much of the leadership on network analysis has been developed. We discuss network analysis in greater depth in Chapter 11.

Review the Organization as a Communication System

Researchers developing a branch of organizational theory called *systems theory* have contributed to auditors' ability to conduct meaningful communication assessments. Pioneer writers about systems theory include Ruben (1972), Katz and Kahn (1978), and Weick (1969).

Systems theorists look holistically at the unit being audited. The *system* is the total unit or organization being examined, but it is made up of many *subsystems* that one can define according to one's purpose. For example, in a general audit one may examine a total system, but also break the system down into its component parts or subsystems—for example, the performance review subsystem, the quality circle subsystem, the suggestion subsystem, and the in-house publications subsystem. The systems perspective calls attention to the way things are related, and it underscores the fact that the isolation of any one variable often distorts one's perceptions.

Every system operates in at least one *environment* or *suprasystem*. Sometimes there may be a number of ways to characterize the environment. Society in the United States, for example, can be broken down into the economic environment, the social environment, the legal environment, and so on. Communication experts know that these environments dictate communication choices. For example, the legal system shapes the way that management bargains with employees. Also, the economic system often affects whether management communicates with employees through extensive training programs.

An important way to distinguish how systems operate within their environments is to label them as *closed* or *open*. The closed system is insulated and has apparently impermeable boundaries so that it does not react to and is not influenced by what goes on around it. There are not many totally closed environments—though there are many systems that respond slowly to environmental changes. For example, U.S. automobile manufacturers in the 1980s were accused of being oblivious to the public's changing preferences in size and quality of cars. Faced with serious competition from Japanese automobile manufacturers, U.S. car makers finally began to adapt, but their slow reaction time created economic problems for them. An open system is one in which communication enables the organization to sense its environment and to adapt to the changes taking place. Similarly, the open system may interact freely with the environment in terms of trying to change or modify it.

The system perspective calls attention to several different communication subsystems. Figure 4.1 presents six subsystems, each of which may be important: (1) individ-

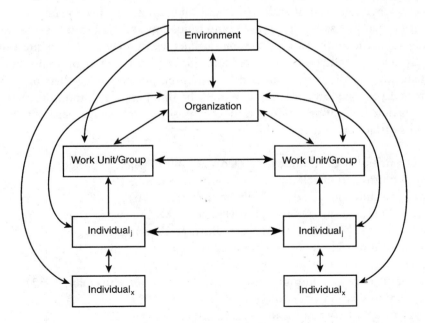

FIGURE 4.1. Visual representation of communication subsystems.

ual to individual within the same work unit, (2) individual to individual across work units, (3) unit to unit, (4) individual to organization, (5) work unit to organization, and (6) environment to each of the other components. Although an audit may focus on one subsystem more than others, auditors should check the different subsystems during an assessment because they are all interrelated. Participation in work group meetings, for example, is one of the most common forms of communication in all organizations. Yet the commitment to one's own work unit may have some bearing on communication patterns with other units. Identifying with one's own unit is normally considered to be a good thing, but there are instances in which such identification is so great that it isolates the unit or blocks coordination with other units when cliques form or competition arises.

Relate Communication to Organizational Outcomes

Organizations exist to accomplish definite outcomes, and communication enables the organization to achieve its purposes: satisfaction, profitability, productivity, and positive labor–management relations (Likert, 1967). We add organizational commitment to these four outcomes because of its importance. A good assessment cannot overlook the relationship between communication and outcomes; in fact, the degree to which these outcomes are achieved is an important standard for judging the adequacy of the communication system.

Satisfaction

As one of the most important end products of organizations, satisfaction has been thoroughly researched—indeed, literally thousands of studies have been generated. Why is it important to examine satisfaction in a communication audit? In a real sense *most communication assessments are heavily based on satisfaction.* In reviews and on questionnaires, organization members share their perceptions about what they like or do not like. Therefore, satisfaction becomes the standard by which employees judge their organization.

In recent years researchers have explored the link between communication and satisfaction in detail. Auditors should note that positive links have been discovered between job satisfaction and the following:

1. Openness in communication (Downs, unpublished experiences in audits)
2. Communication relationships (Downs & Hazen, 1977)
3. Communication load (O'Reilly & Roberts, 1974)
4. Communication apprehension (Falcione, McCrosky, & Daly, 1977)
5. Nonverbal behavior (Sundstrom, Burt, & Kamp, 1980)
6. Communication style (Richmond, McCrosky, & Davis, 1982)
7. Amount of feedback (Downs & Hazen, 1977)
8. Congruence of communication rules (Hatfield & Huseman, 1982)
9. Communication climate (Downs & Hazen, 1977)
10. Accuracy of communication (O'Reilly & Roberts, 1974)
11. Organization commitment (Downs, 1991)

12. Communication from top management (Downs, 2001)
13. Communication satisfaction (Hilgermann, 1998; Pincus, 1986; Ticehurst & Ross-Smith, 1992)
14. Communication quality (Orpen, 1997).

Management values satisfaction because dissatisfied workers tend to leave, and replacing them can be expensive. Therefore, management desires to maintain a general level of satisfaction, at least among high-performing people. Auditors can proactively discover potential problems by discovering what satisfies people and what does not.

However, auditors need to exercise caution here. Sometimes people become dissatisfied with procedures that enhance productivity. For instance, the prevalent reengineering of the 1990s created stress even as organizations cut and refined themselves for the sake of efficiency and economy. In a more specific instance, a manufacturing plant once changed its hiring policy so that it hired mostly college graduates as supervisors. The current employees issued some strong statements of dissatisfaction with the new policy. The auditor decided that in the long run, however, this change would enhance the organization's health and productivity.

Because satisfaction is so important, some considerations about how to measure it are in order. There are several possibilities. One is to ask people how satisfied they are with their jobs. The responses may not tell auditors much, other than how to classify people as being either satisfied or dissatisfied—yet even this can be useful. We once assessed a plant described by management as "heaven on earth." People responded on a 1–7 scale to the question: "How satisfied are you in your job?" The results showed that fully one-third of the employees, mostly on the third shift, had some level of general dissatisfaction. The scale itself, however, did not reveal reasons behind these results.

Some auditors find it useful to use instruments that measure *facets of job* satisfaction. One of the most frequently used is the Job Description Index, which contains 72 items grouped into five dimensions: work, pay, supervisor, promotions, and coworkers (Smith, Kendall, & Hulin, 1969). The index has a modified adjective checklist format, and it is "especially appropriate for employees with relatively low levels of literacy and requires only ten to fifteen minutes to administer" (Dunham & Smith, 1979, p. 77). A similar instrument is the Minnesota Satisfaction Questionnaire (MSQ), developed by Weiss, Davis, England, and Lofquist (1979). Requiring a moderate level of literacy and 20–40 minutes to administer, it has 100 items that measure satisfaction with each of the following:

Ability utilization	Moral values
Achievement	Recognition
Activity	Responsibility
Advancement	Security
Authority	Social service, social status
Company policies	Supervisor; human relations
Compensation	Supervision
Coworker	Variety
Creativity	Working conditions
Independence	

Still another possibility is to devise an original rating scale of satisfaction. Research by Wanous and Lawler (1972) is particularly useful; they surveyed nine different formulas for developing rating scales to measure facets of job satisfaction.

Profitability and Costs

As important as it is, communication is costly. Sometimes alternatives for communicating may be judged on the costs involved. For example, comparing the costs of a house publication with employee reactions to it is one way to determine whether or not the organization is getting its money's worth. Similarly, meetings are one of the most frequently used communication channels; they are also among the most frequently selected solutions for solving communication problems in the United States. One auditor added up all the salaries of each person attending a meeting and plotted out how expensive that meeting was. The participants in the meeting had never thought about the costs involved. Still, a meeting may be more cost-effective than trying to meet individually with each person.

In another example, a state hospital had to cut costs during an economic downturn. One of its major monthly costs was huge telephone bills. The usage of each telephone was audited, and the type of equipment was then evaluated in view of its usage. The auditors found easy ways of saving several hundred dollars a month by making equipment changes. These illustrations point out that expense considerations are legitimate and necessary aspects of communication assessments.

Productivity

Though the link is sometimes hard to measure, there is considerable evidence that communication can be directly related to productivity. Hansen (1987) pinpointed good communication relationships between supervisors and subordinates as a more powerful predictor of profitability in 40 major companies than market share size or capital intensity. Indeed, Clampitt and Downs (1993) found that employees generally could explain how certain communication factors facilitated or detracted from their productivity. Sometimes the relationship may seem less obvious and more indirect because so many complex variables affect productivity.

Executives have often described ineffective communication as an important reason for lagging productivity. An organizational emphasis on communication has been credited with increasing productivity, increasing worker responsibility, and permitting even a struggling company to survive (Semler, 1993).

Several case studies actually demonstrate *how* effective communication can improve productivity. Glaser (1980) found a dramatic increase in productivity after the company introduced new participative management and upward communication programs. Tubbs and Widgery (1978) measured the impact of a new communication program at General Motors and noted a 0.7% productivity increase and a savings of $7 million in production costs. Tubbs and Hain (1979) conducted several studies that found a positive relationship between communication and organizational effectiveness. In one study, they found that departments with the best ratings on grievances, absenteeism, and efficiency had the highest communication effectiveness scores. And in a comparison of two plants, the more productive one received the higher ratings on communication effectiveness.

More recently, Doucouliagos (1995) conducted a meta-analysis of 43 studies and concluded that profit-sharing, worker ownership, and worker participation in decision making were positively related to increased productivity. Interestingly, the Institute of Directors in Britain produced a report showing that, of the companies that had employee communication policies, 65.1% credited the policies with improving productivity, 68.1% credited the policies with reducing the number of industrial disputes, and 80.3% credited them with improvements in employee loyalty (Dawson-Sheperd & White, 1994).

Auditors, though, *should beware of formulating cause-and-effect relations too rigidly.* Work processes depend on complex interrelations among communication, employee motivation and performance, availability of raw materials, organizational design, and economic climate. Because communication is just one of many variables affecting productivity, one needs to be careful in claiming that a given communication phenomenon always affects productivity in a certain way.

This small sampling of research data suggests that the perceived link between communication and productivity is very strong. However, specifying exactly how communication's particular components influence behavior can be difficult. Researchers have related productivity to people's roles in structural networks (O'Reilly & Roberts, 1974); use of communication vehicles, such as teams or quality circles; group relations (Downs & Pickett, 1977); supervisory communication styles (Bednar, 1982); and sending of feedback messages (Downs, Johnson, & Barge, 1984). Such research merely points out that any aspect of communication may be related to productivity, and the auditor must look for the connection in a particular instance. In doing so, there are several factors to keep in mind.

First, the environment has a significant influence. Factors such as federal regulation, changes in energy costs, amount of capital investment, competitors, and general economic climate certainly affect levels of productivity. An organization may be communicating very well and still have poor productivity because of environmental factors.

Second, the link between communication and productivity may not be direct but may operate in a two-step approach. It is possible for communication to affect motivation, which in turn affects productivity (Hawkins & Penley, 1978). As an example, consider that employee X makes a suggestion about a new work procedure. If the idea is accepted and it works, the communication affects productivity directly. But suppose the idea was not accepted. Communication still took place, but now whether or not it affects productivity has nothing to do with the fact that messages were exchanged. The impact on productivity is directly related to how employee X handles rejection. In this situation, some employees think that "communication" did not take place, even though messages were exchanged. In other words, communication may affect the employees' organizational images, and these images then affect the way the employees behave.

Third, organizations have multiple productivity goals, and it is important to sort out which are most important. Some ways that productivity has been measured include input–output ratios, quantity of work, quality of work, absenteeism, project success, number of errors, number of grievances, and performance ratings. This list suggests that there are problems in defining and measuring real productivity, particularly at the individual level. It is probably best, therefore, to relate communication to unit or organizational productivity. However, auditors have a number of alternative measures of productivity from which to choose. While the term "productivity" conjures up connotations of quantification and specific measurement, there is in fact no clear, standardized definition for it. The productivity of a savings and loan institution may need to be measured differently than that of an automobile manufacturer. Within the automobile manufacturer, the productivity of line units may be measured differently than that of office workers, legal staff, design units, and managers. In audits of a service organization and a chair manufacturer, Clampitt (1983) found that the employees in the two organizations had very different impressions of what constituted productivity in their jobs.

In selecting a measure of productivity, any auditor would do well to be guided by the measures that the organization already uses. Management will have access to some productivity data that can be useful. An alternative is for the auditor to develop a new means of measuring productivity.

Fourth, productivity demands may also become points of dissatisfaction. Productivity demands created the reengineering of the 1990s, which certainly created internal organizational stress. And some employees would claim that new technologies have not saved labor but have actually increased it. Being contactable at any hour anywhere in the world means that some people are never really off the job.

Organizational Commitment

An era of seemingly constant change, restructuring, downsizing, and redesigning by organizations may be resulting in an "erosion of corporate loyalty." Organizations are concerned about this problem. We have used audits to check the relationships among organizational commitment and internal communication processes in Australia, China, Guatemala, Finland, Great Britain, Japan, The Netherlands, Thailand, and the United States. These relationships have become one of our most common focal areas for audits (Downs et al., 2002).

We mentioned earlier that the integrative communication function plays a strong role in whether employees remain at work. Some people might infer that it is the strong, informal connections that foster commitment. Here we should clarify that research shows repeatedly that across organizations and cultures, it is the formal communication that affects employees' organizational commitment (Adrian & Ticehurst, 2001; Downs et al., 2002). Indeed, communication from top management plays the strongest role in determining commitment (Adrian & Ticehurst, 2001b). On one level, that result might seem counterintuitive. After all, communication from top management sounds removed from the daily work lives of most employees. Still, top management communicates the organization's identity and vision; it affects how people visualize the organization and what it stands for. It is not surprising, then, that such communication could affect whether or not people internalize the organization's values and choose to commit to it.

Just as there are multiple measures of productivity, there are also multiple measures of organizational commitment. Most definitions include some sense that employees are involved and loyal to the organization. Barge and Schlueter (1988) evaluate four instruments that researchers have used to measure commitment. Choosing one of these common instruments has the advantage of allowing auditors to make comparisons with findings in other organizations.

Because each instrument defines commitment differently, the survey instrument choice affects auditors' findings. For instance, communication's relationship with the commitment component labeled "internalization" may be different than it is with the component part labeled "normative commitment." Choices should be made carefully as auditors keep in mind the organizational questions they are exploring.

Just as we cautioned against drawing rigid causal relations between productivity and communication, we must also caution auditors against taking rigid positions on the link between communication and commitment. We have no doubt that there is some connection; indeed communication appears to play as strong a role as job satisfaction in determining employees' commitment levels. Still, there are many other factors that influence commitment. New concepts such as job embeddedness (Mitchell, Holtom, Lee, Sablynski, & Erez, 2001) look at individuals' communication links to other people in the organization, but also at their perceived fit within their larger communities, and what would be at stake if they left their jobs. The holistic approach behind the idea of job embeddedness is a healthy one for auditors to embrace.

Link Internal Communication to Organizational Strategies

In the past, organizations have often seen communication as a kind of Band-Aid to apply after there is a problem. Auditors can add value to their clients by introducing a strategic view of communication. Tourish and Hargie (1996) define a communication strategy as "a process which enables managers to evaluate the communication consequences of the decision making process, and which integrates this into the normal business planning cycle and psyche of the organization" (p. 12). Indeed, more and more executives see the need for tying their communication thrusts directly to the strategies they set for the organization. For instance, AES, Inc., a global energy company, strategically emphasizes pushing decision making down to the grassroots level. In order to facilitate that, its formal communication policy is to make all information accessible internally. The result is that the lowest level field employee has access to the same information that the CEO does; there is no need to go through "official channels" to ask a question. In that way, AES, Inc. has successfully developed a communication policy that facilitates its larger business objectives.

The focus on strategy requires a paradigm shift for some auditors if their focus tends to be primarily on organizational operations. Brache (2002) defines strategy as "the framework of choices that determine the nature and direction of an organization"(p. 51). Strategy bridges the organization with its external environment, and it drives all operation variables: forms of leadership, forms of organizing, communication roles, and so on.

Too many managers, however, continue to see communication initiatives as a quick fix to apply defensively. This mind-set separates communication from the daily task of accomplishing work and achieving goals. For these managers, communication is about creating glossy brochures and reports to pass on to employees. What managers need to do, and what auditors can help them to do, is see how strategic communication is an integral part of achieving the organization's objectives rather than a separate function. It is useful for auditors to be aware of these objectives and to determine how the organization's communication actually facilitates or inhibits attaining them.

For instance, we audit one organization regularly—nine times in the last 9 years. There are always areas that the employees recognize as being outstanding and other areas that need improvement. These strong and weak areas vary from year to year because the organization changes. Management began to see the fluctuations as evidence that it needed to communicate strategically in order to be effective.

In our own experiences, it is helpful to ask top management what its strategic objectives are for the company. It may be that the company needs to improve its customer relations in order to remain competitive. Or it may be that product development needs a faster cycle in order to maintain the company's competitive edge. Auditors can help by probing the problems that arise around meeting these strategic objectives as a result of ineffective communication. Do the employees dealing with customers on the front line receive relevant information? If departments need to coordinate work, what does the company do to facilitate interdepartmental communication? What does it do that hinders interdepartmental communication? Asking such questions introduces the idea that strategic communication is integral to accomplishing what companies want and need to do rather than something they do on the side to make people feel good.

Assess the Impact of New Technologies on Communication

New technologies affect how people communicate, but they also affect the network, the task processes, and the chain of command. In 1996, we analyzed a company's introduction of Lotus Notes, and found that issuing computers throughout the organization (1) changed the work of secretaries and managers alike because managers were now typing their own messages, (2) changed the chain of command because now everyone could have access to anyone else, (3) forced people to work in more standardized patterns, and (4) gave people access to more information than they had ever before. In short, the introduction of the new technology changed the organization in ways that no one had particularly planned.

Be Open to the Unexpected

Finally, assessments should be open enough to permit observations about the unexpected. If they are arranged too tightly that tightness limits the potential for discovery. Not everyone asks auditors to come in and fix a specific communication problem. For instance, the leadership at a national beverage company simply had a vague sense that they could communicate better with their external audiences (Downs et al., 2000). That audit was designed simply to find out as much about the communication practices as possible and to gain insight into the distributors' perspectives. Going in with preconceived notions about what was probably wrong would have kept the auditors from asking basic questions such as "Why do you come to the annual business meeting?" or "What do you think is the company's purpose in holding an annual meeting for distributors?" When asking such basic questions one often hears surprising answers and thus gains greater insight into the communication relationships being studied.

CONCLUSION

Diagnosis begins with a focus. Communication has many roles and functions, and its different characteristics—for example, frequency, quality, and so on—can be measured. We advocate conducting a thorough analysis of communication in general. Covering all areas referred to in this chapter gives a comprehensive impression of the organization; such a general overview is described in terms of a communication climate or an organizational culture. These concepts reflect an attempt to discover those stable communicative characteristics of the environment, whether or not created purposefully by the organization. To the extent that such climates or cultures "provide a common frame of reference for participants, they would be expected to exert potent influences on individual performance and satisfaction" (Joyce & Slocum, 1984, p. 736).

Our 12 guidelines can help auditors think about general areas for investigation. On the other hand, every assessment can be somewhat different. The examples discussed here were picked to show how one must often choose what is important to examine. If the organization has had previous communication audits, we find it useful to examine that information as we make choices about what to examine currently. Make the choices in collaboration with the management, and keep the areas manageable. Then use instruments that provide the best information possible in those areas. The next few chapters examine these instruments.

5

The Interview

The Most Basic Assessment Technology

Interviews and questionnaires are the two most basic audit methodologies. They can be combined in the same audit quite compatibly. We review interviews in this chapter, and discuss the different alternatives for questionnaires in Chapters 6–8.

For many analysts, the interview plays a supplementary role; however, it is our favorite method. If we are confined to using just one means for learning about small organizations, we choose the interview because it gives high-quality information that can be probed in detail in a face-to-face relationship with the employee. If several means of collecting data are to be used in the assessment, our advice is to *start with the interview.*

The skillful interviewing of employees is one of the richest means of diagnosing an organization's communication dynamics. In addition to learning about people's perceptions, auditors are able to gauge the people giving the information, which lets auditors assess the value of that information. The data are not as easily packaged as with quantitative methods but some insights could never be obtained any other way. Therefore, a round of interviews should be the first diagnostic tool used in any communication audit. Even if the auditor plans to rely primarily on a survey, interview data can sensitize one to the way to frame questions for a particular organization.

ADVANTAGES OF INTERVIEWS

In-depth interviews have five qualities that make them a unique audit instrument.

Familiarity

In conducting interviews, the auditor develops a firsthand familiarity with the people and their work processes. One gets to know the organization in ways not possible through any written media. Furthermore, the interview often permits the auditor to observe the organization at work. For example, in a paper-converting plant, a section manager once took us on a tour of his work area as we talked; this tour enabled us to refine our appreciation of what he did and how he did it.

Fuller Discussion

The face-to-face interview allows a much more detailed discussion of topic areas. People naturally say more in an interview than they will write on a survey. Good interviewers probe interviewees until they obtain complete descriptions and understand the interviewee's thinking. In a short amount of time, auditors can probe a large amount of material and gain in-depth knowledge about the organization.

Serendipity

Every auditor should follow a basic interview guide. Nevertheless, we have found that good open questions often secure answers that we could never have anticipated in designing a questionnaire. It is wise to conclude an interview by asking, "Is there anything that we should have talked about that I have not asked?" We get some of our best information about unanticipated idiosyncrasies of the organization that way.

Interviewee Reward

People like to talk about their jobs and the things that are important to them. Unfortunately, often an organization does not provide a regular opportunity for such interactions. Generally, face-to-face interactions are rated as being more pleasing than written questionnaires, so the interview contains an intrinsic motivator. Recently, a manager told us about a very significant problem in his unit. When asked for more details, he said that he had never discussed the problem with anyone at the company. Yet he felt comfortable in our presence as he thought through the problem aloud.

Organic Nature

One major advantage of interviews over surveys is the fact that during the audit they can grow, be refined, and change in light of new information. This is not to suggest that the same questions or topic areas should not be asked of everyone; initially, they should. However, we often get information from one source that needs to be checked out with other people. Interviews give less of a snapshot view of an organization, because they can be scheduled over a longer period of time. Accordingly, some of the new information learned over time needs to be integrated into the interview guide.

LIMITATIONS OF INTERVIEWS

No data-gathering instrument is perfect, and interviews are only as good as the interviewers. Furthermore, interviews have three inherent disadvantages.

Time

Interviews are time-consuming, which makes them expensive. One must take into account the cost of the interviewer's time and also the cost of taking employees away from their jobs to be interviewed. In fact, in an audit of a university, cost considerations precluded the interviewing of most employees in food services. They were paid on an hourly basis, and the administration was unwilling to pay them to come in early or stay late just to be interviewed. Scheduling interviews in a manufacturing plant has also proven challenging because each employee's work has to be coordinated with that of others, and often the company will not pay them for overtime.

Analysis

Information from interviews is more difficult to code, analyze, and interpret. U.S. society so values numerical data that it sometimes doubts the validity of anything that cannot be put into a numerical scale. How many people have to mention the same problem or strength for it to be considered significant? The interpretive skills of the auditor are tested here. Sometimes a person in an important position may present a good overview of a problem that others have not even mentioned, and it would be foolhardy to disregard it simply on the basis of numbers.

Perceptual Data

Interview data basically comprise perceptual reports of how interviewees see the organization, and these perceptions often need to be verified. As we pointed out in Chapter 1, Odiorne's research (discussed in Filley, 1978, p. 74) demonstrated that when a manager and a subordinate were each asked to describe the subordinate's job, they disagreed on an average of 25% of the things they mentioned. Is it any wonder that there are many different reactions to, and impressions of, the communication in an organization? Also, people's perceptions are sometimes inaccurate. For example, a number of employees for an airline complained that they had not had an appraisal within the last year. We checked this complaint and found signed statements by several of the employees that indicated that they had indeed had appraisals. We did not know what had happened in those appraisals, but there was evidence that the complainers were apparently incorrect with respect to the time frame.

SCHEDULING TWO ROUNDS OF INTERVIEWS

Auditors can maximize the organic nature of interviews by scheduling two different rounds of interviews. These rounds are separate entities that may occur days or even weeks apart in order to tap developments in the organization. This schedule provides the auditor with a perspective over time. The auditor may even learn of some newly developed programs introduced after the first data were collected. It must be remembered that the assessment itself is an intervention that focuses attention on and perhaps motivates changes in the organization. Since changes often occur rapidly during an assessment, it is useful to avoid a one-time snapshot based on a single series of interviews or a single collection of questionnaires. In addition, having two rounds of interviews is particularly useful if multiple data collection methods are used in the audit. Though one should never share data results with interviewees, it is possible to examine the data from the other instruments and build clarifying questions into the second round.

The preparation for each round culminates in an *interview guide,* that is, a list of general questions to be asked of all respondents. The guide allows auditors to achieve consistency across interviews. Interview guides should allow for some flexibility as well, since people in different positions will have access to and insights about different aspects of the organization. We illustrate interview guides that could be used in interview rounds one and two in Tables 5.1, 5.2, and 5.3. In the following discussion, we analyze each round of interviews and the accompanying interview guide in terms of purpose, agenda, questions, and structure.

Interview Purpose

The first round of interviews familiarizes the auditors with the organization, its people, and its communication as a task process. Exploratory in nature, these interviews help accomplish two basic things. First, they provide a general orientation to the organization that lays a foundation for everything else done in the audit. From this beginning, the auditors begin to sense what the organization's communication problems might be. Second, they identify areas that need to be probed further, either with a questionnaire or in a second round of interviews. In other words, the results of the first round give an impression of the organization, but they also stimulate the desire for more information. In general, each successive level of findings helps the auditor create a more accurate picture of the organization.

Whereas the first round of interviews is exploratory, the second round needs to be more issue-oriented. For that reason, several weeks should elapse before the second round is scheduled. In fact, the explanatory potential of the second round of interviews is so great that we recommend waiting until all other information collected from questionnaires and networks or other techniques has been processed. New discoveries prompt new questions, and the interview guide need not be static: let it grow with the understanding of the organization. For example, answers given on questionnaires often tell *how* people react but not *why* they react that way. One may be able to conclude from questionnaire data that 44% of the respondents think their meetings are unproductive. A second round of interviews can help enrich one's understanding by probing why people are dissatisfied with meetings. In one assessment we asked the following question during the second round of interviews:

> "In our survey we found some very positive reactions to some questions and identified some areas that need improving. The general ratings of the organization's overall communication efforts were not as high as they might have been. Why do you think this occurred?"

TABLE 5.1. Exploratory Interview Guide

1. [Auditor: Introduce yourself and explain the purpose of the interview.]
2. Identify name and position of the interviewee.
3. Describe your position in the organization.
   a. What are your chief responsibilities and duties?
   b. With whom or with what positions do you regularly communicate?
   c. What factors tend to facilitate your effectiveness on the job? Please give me an example.
   d. What, if anything, inhibits your effectiveness?
4. Describe the way decisions are made in your organization.
   a. What decisions do you normally make?
   b. What information do you need to make these decisions?
   c. Are these formal or informal policies that determine how you get information?
5. Describe the organization's/unit's primary objectives for this year.
   a. How does the organization know when it has done a good or a bad job? What are the criteria for success?
   b. What are your own personal objectives?
   c. What communication strategies does one use to achieve them?
6. What kinds of communication are necessary for you to have with other work units? How well does this interunit communication work?
7. Describe the formal channels through which you typically receive information. What kinds of information do you tend to receive? How often?
8. Describe the informal channels through which you typically receive information.
   a. What kind of information do you hear?
   b. How active are informal channels?
9. What are the major communication strengths of the organization? Be specific.
10. What are the major communication weaknesses of the organization? Be specific.
11. What do you see as the greatest *unresolved* problem of this organization?
12. What would one like to see done to improve communication here?
    a. Why hasn't it been done already?
    b. What are the major obstacles?
    c. If you had a suggestion to improve communication, how would you make it?
13. When conflict occurs, how is it resolved? What normally causes conflict here? Give examples.
14. Describe the communication relationship you have with:
    a. Your immediate supervisor
    b. Top management
    c. Coworkers
    d. Subordinates, if applicable
15. How do most people react to their managers?
16. How would you evaluate your manager in terms of:
    a. Openness to new ideas?
    b. Willingness to share information?
    c. Ability to clarify expectations?
    d. Ability to coordinate the work in the unit?
17. How do you get ideas about how your superiors feel about your work?
18. How would you evaluate the communication from top management?
19. How would you describe the general communication climate here?
20. How often do you receive information of little value? Give an example.
    a. How often are you overloaded with information?
    b. How often do you feel you get too little information?

(continued)

TABLE 5.1. *(continued)*

21. How does your physical work setting here affect your communication?

22. How does communication here affect your job satisfaction? Is this typical for others?

23. How does communication here affect your productivity? Is this typical for others?

24. If you were to advise me as to what to look for to get the greatest insight into this organization, what would that be?

25. Describe the chain of command in this organization and how it operates.

26. What criteria for effective communication are used in this organization? How do these compare with the way people talk about communication?

27. Is there anything that I have left out that I should have included?

TABLE 5.2. Management-Level Follow-Up Interview Guide

1. Generally when we do an analysis of an organization, we find that people can identify some strengths and some weaknesses for the organization.
   a. What do you see as the strengths of ACME?
   b. What do you see as the weaknesses of communication here?
   c. What strengths do you think the employees will mention?
   d. What weaknesses will they mention?
   e. How accurate do you think their assessment is? Why?

2. A number of our questions deal with perceptions of upper management. What perceptions do you think the employees have of upper management? Why?

3. What is the communication role of the supervisors? How are they trained? Evaluated? What particular communication problems do they have? How do you think employees perceive them?

4. In other organizations, we have found that employees desire increased opportunities to communicate upward on such matters as suggestions for improvement. Do you think that we will find this here? Why? How do you feel about this?

5. How timely is the information exchanged between units and departments within? What, if anything, could be done to alleviate any particular problems in this regard?

6. Generally, how do employees get information that affects them personally? For example, how do they find out about new policies? New management thrusts?

7. Many employees often indicate a desire for more evaluative and informative feedback through face-to-face communication. What keeps this from being given? How does this affect productivity? Job satisfaction?

8. One suggestion we have encountered is that new policies should be programmed into the computers immediately. Is there any reason why this cannot be done?

9. The ratings for communication in ACME vary greatly among employees. The average rating, however, is not as high as it might be. Why do you think this is?

10. Have there been any significant changes in the communication patterns recently?

11. If you could make any changes you wanted in ACME's communication, what would you change? Give us your wish list.

12. How are communication concerns reflected in your organizational strategies?

13. Are there additional areas that we ought to cover?

14. What do you think will happen as a result of this assessment?

TABLE 5.3. Follow-Up Interview Guide

I. *For the write-ups, please group your answers not only according to the question (1, 2, 3, etc.), but also according to the following classifications: Administration, Supervisory Classified, and Nonsupervisory Classified.*

II. *The introduction is very important because many people want to know how they were selected for the interview. We recommend that you take care of this in the introduction by explaining the following:*

  A. **Purpose**: Follow-up to check earlier perceptions and ask more pointed questions, to explore more about strengths and weaknesses. Selection of interviewees was determined by a desire to interview some of the same people in order to check earlier information and to interview others that would give a broader base than was had before—that is, to make certain all areas of the organization are represented.

  B. **How information will be used**: Guarantee anonymity but state that interview data will help to explain some of the results.

III. *The following questions are designed as a broad guide. In some cases, the respondents' answers will make you want to use them in a different sequence. You can also make whatever adaptations in the guide that you believe are needed after the initial interviews.*

  A. Have there been any significant changes in communication patterns recently?

  B. What motivates people in the organization now? What are their principal concerns? How is the communication here relating to and perhaps satisfying these concerns and needs?

  C. Let's look at you as the receiver of information. We'd like to ask you questions about five areas of information that you might receive.
   1. Questions:
      a. What information in these areas would you like to receive?
      b. How would you get it? From whom?
      c. Why aren't you getting it now?
   2. Areas:
      a. Progress in job and how you are being judged.
      b. Organizational policies.
      c. How organization's decisions are made that affect you.
      d. Promotion and advancement opportunities.
      e. Important new service or program development.

IV. *Now let's discuss you as the sender of information.*

  D. How do you know what you need to send to others? How do you make the decision to initiate communication? Do you receive many requests for information?
   1. Do you find yourself requesting information to do your job? What kind? Why is this not sent routinely?
   2. Is there any way in which you do not get to participate in an evaluation of superiors or supervisors? Would you find such participation useful? How high up would you like to evaluate? What would happen if you could do that?

  E. In terms of upward/downward communication, what kinds of filtering are planned in the system?

(continued)

TABLE 5.3. *(continued)*

   F. What happens when you send upward communication to your:
     1. Immediate supervisor?
     2. Middle management?
     3. Top management?
     4. Where is the greatest lag or block? Why?

   G. When there are blocks to communication, what kinds of formal techniques do you use to get around them? What kinds of informal techniques get the best results for you?

   H. How much do you use the informal channels? How are they structured? How do people tap them if they want to?

V. *Let's turn to your evaluation of other communication sources. What should top management be communicating that they are not?*

   I. How would you evaluate your immediate supervisor as a communicator?

   J. How would you evaluate your departmental meetings in terms of:
     1. Information?
     2. Decisions?
     3. Frequency?

   K. Are there important differences for you between communicating with employees in Unit X and communicating with employees from Unit Y?

   L. How do you get the information needed to do your job? What kinds of information do you need to know is available but do not necessarily need to receive all the time? How should it be made available?

   M. What channels are best at keeping you abreast of the day-to-day operations of the organization?

   N. How does the organization reward excellence in:
     1. Productivity?
     2. Service?
     3. Research?

   O. What affects your own commitment to this organization?

   P. Some people have said that there is a need for greater coordination within the organization. How do you feel about this? Are there some examples that you can share?

   Q. What do you think we are going to find as a result of conducting the assessment? What is going to happen as a result of our report?

   R. Are there questions that we have not asked that you expected to be asked?

Note that the initial statement was complimentary enough to allay any defensive reactions. It also gave a rather general expression of findings without really breaking any news to the interviewee. But it did set the stage for probing the rationale behind a fact discovered among the answers to the questionnaire.

Such revelations must be done carefully. *At all costs, one should avoid revealing any information whose source could be identified.* In an audit of a public utility, we used an example to get a basic understanding of the operation. The manager responded, "Oh, yes, and I know exactly who told one that." He happened to be right, but there would have been no justification for acknowledging that he was correct.

One audit team we directed typified the interview development process perfectly. When it finished the first round of interviews in a chemical plant, the members wrote a summary of their findings, which suggested new areas to probe. They concluded:

In the next round of interviews we want to probe: (1) how jobs really are advertised here, (2) whether the rates of suggestions have actually increased or decreased, and (3) the communication impact of putting in a new plant. Another point of interest concerns vocabulary. In several interviews the phrases "efficient" and "mature operation" occurred with an unusual frequency. We should explore their origins.

Interview Agenda

An *agenda* for an interview is simply a list of topics to be covered in the interview. In other words, once the purposes are stated, then the next task is to identify what topics can be explored to accomplish those purposes. Once the topics are developed, then it becomes necessary to frame questions about each of those topics. So the agenda is the bridge between the purposes and the development of questions.

The auditor's goal is to understand organizational performance in all its complexity. With that in mind, Brache (2002, p. 6) offers four general questions that might serve as a general agenda under which auditors could group interview questions:

1. What are the external variables that influence organizational performance?
2. What are the structural variables that influence performance?
3. What are the human variables that affect performance?
4. What are the variables that are both structural and human (e.g., conflict resolution)?

One can then look at each of these general headings and determine what specific topics should be explored for the particular focal organization.

Each round of interviews may have a different agenda—after all, the topics to be explored depend on the issues uncovered. In the first round, target the most useful information for a general orientation. In doing this, the guidelines for focusing an assessment we discussed in Chapter 4 are particularly useful. Preparing the agenda for a first round of interviews is relatively easy, for initially auditors need to explore the colleagues with whom employees communicate, the ways workers get the information they need to do their jobs, communication relationships, reactions to various informal and formal channels, perceived strengths and weaknesses of the unit, the relationship of communication to organizational goals, decision processes, resolution of conflict, and employee suggestions for improvement.

Questions for an Interview Guide

Just as the interview's agenda reflects the purpose, the interview questions should reflect the agenda. Look at the topics, and frame questions for each. When all the questions are determined, one has developed a good interview guide. Developing an interview guide is not difficult, but it is very important. Auditors should carefully craft and choose questions *that will give the kind of information they need.* Just as in questionnaires, the questions in the interview need to be refined to assure that they are asking for useful information. Also like questionnaires, the guide helps auditors consistently ask the same questions of each interviewee. That is especially important when there are multiple auditors. Unlike the questionnaire, however, the order in which the questions are asked can vary from person to person. Many interviews turn into enjoyable conversations; as long as auditors ask all the relevant questions, they should feel free to let the discussion flow organically.

As auditors familiarize themselves with the organization, their needs to vary the agenda may become apparent. Therefore, there may be some important differences between the exploratory and follow-up interviews. The topics may vary somewhat, but Table 5.1 presents the topical questions that were used in an analysis of an airline and a university. The number of possible questions is too great for one interview guide, but auditors can tailor these suggestions to any given organization. Notice that the questions are largely open-ended, explore all levels and aspects of the organization, are oriented to both the past and the future, ask for behavioral examples as well as general perceptions, and ask the respondent to propose solutions for some of the problems.

In the second round, target specific areas that will fill voids in understanding the organization. For illustrative topics, look at the follow-up interview guides in Tables 5.2 and 5.3. In the audit reported in Table 5.3, a different guide was prepared for all employees. The one reported here is for the managers.

Note the references in the guides to such topics as perceptions of upper management, evaluative feedback, and organizational rewards. These were areas that had already been pinpointed as problematic in the first round of interviews and on a questionnaire. It was therefore important to get additional information to help interpret the results already obtained.

Another especially important question in Table 5.2 was Question 14, "What do you think will happen as a result of this assessment?" Conducting this audit caused employees to talk about the whole process, and it was instructive to discover how the managers viewed it. It was also useful to discover what obstacles managers perceived to be hindering the auditors. In other words, this question probed an actual case study: the communication associated with an audit.

While we offer some guidelines for developing an interview guide, auditors should follow the guidelines without feeling tightly restricted. We want to emphasize again that a good interviewer always stays attuned to the possibility of unsought relevant information. Furthermore, some real differences in the questions for managers and nonmanagers are likely. Although the basic guide lets auditors obtain comparative information, it is also possible to adapt the guides: new information is *supplementary as well as comparative*. Table 5.4 contains part of a guide that was particularly adapted to different types of managers. The questions are grouped under certain headings to direct the interviewer's attention.

Ask Primarily Open Questions

Open questions put few restrictions on how the interviewee answers. They are designed to get people to talk at length so that they give in-depth information concerning what they think about the organization. Two examples are "Tell me about your job" and

TABLE 5.4. Partial Guide for Second-Round Interviews

Preliminary Information to Double-Check (Instructions to Interviewers)

1. Some subordinates mentioned a supervisor–employer committee that originated ideas and presented them to a top manager. This is very ambiguous. Check it.
2. Someone was fired, so several people expressed concern over their jobs. How general is this concern?
3. The information about an upcoming move seems to change hourly. How is this circulated?
4. There seem to be wide differences in the company usage of performance appraisals.

Interview Guide to Two Specific Top Managers: X and Y

1. When you have to make strategic decisions, what managers do you typically bring in?
2. For what type of decisions do you need information from _____ in order to decide?
3. What type of information do you need from X in order to make these decisions?
4. How much weight or value do you attach to their input?
5. What is the role of the marketing committee? How do you think the rest of the committee perceives it?
6. Who is on the marketing committee?

Questions for All Managers

1. How much input do you have in decisions made by upper management?
2. In what type of situation(s) is your input necessary or important?
3. What information is needed from you in order to make organizational decisions?
4. How much weight does your input carry?
5. How important are managerial meetings? Why?
6. How important should they be?
7. How many managerial meetings are there now?
8. How many should there be? Is that enough?

Questions for All Managers about Feedback and Performance

9. What do you say or do when you're not satisfied with your subordinates' day-to-day performances? Can you give me an example? How often do you do this?
10. What do you say or do when you're satisfied with your subordinates' day-to-day performance?
11. Do you use definite criteria in judging their levels of performance?
12. Are your employees aware of these criteria? How are they aware (e.g., feedback, job descriptions, "work" contracts)?
13. Do you conduct an annual performance review with your subordinates? What criteria are used? Describe them. (Probe for an example.)
14. Does the criteria used in the annual performance review match the criteria that you use on a day-to-day basis?

"What are the communication strengths of the organization?" Neither question restricts the range of response. By contrast, *closed questions* restrict the respondents in terms of length of response and the topics covered. Typically, any question that calls for a yes–no or agree–disagree response is closed. So are all multiple-choice questions. Although closed questions are analytically useful for classifying people's answers on questionnaires, they are less useful in interviews, where the objective is to get as much information as possible and to identify the range of responses in the organization.

In a sense, the first round of interviews is like a fishing expedition, as the auditor casts about for whatever preliminary information can be "caught." Open questions are well suited to this purpose because they help the auditor discover the employees' priorities, frames of reference, depth of knowledge, and unstructured perceptions of the situation. Furthermore, they give respondents a degree of freedom in structuring an answer and even permit some catharsis as the employees share. Of particular importance here is the fact that open questions permit respondents to identify the areas most important to them. For example, an auditor interviewing workers about how organizational communication affects productivity might want to pinpoint five or six specific areas. Rather than beginning with specific questions about each area, the auditor could first ask the general question "How does communication affect your productivity?" The answers might highlight important areas not on the auditor's list and give him or her better insight into the respondents' thinking; specific questions would limit the auditor to a preconceived list of areas.

Closed questions, on the other hand, do have a place in interviews. When asking for very specific answers in prescribed formats, they save time, are easy to tabulate, and secure answers that can be classified without necessitating explanation. One effective technique is to get the interviewee to commit to an opinion and then to ask open questions as follow-up so that he or she will have to explain the answer. For example, in a recent audit we asked, "Would you say that the communication climate in this organization is better, the same, or worse compared to the climate in your previous work organizations?" Once the respondent had answered, we asked, "Why?" The short answer to the closed question led to a general discussion of the criteria used to make the comparison. In a similar fashion, auditors could ask the respondents to indicate on a 1–10 scale how good the quality of work life is in the organization (closed question) and then ask them what factors determined how they felt about the quality of work life (open question).

Draw the Interviewee Out; Probe Skillfully

A *probe* is a means of asking a respondent to explain the answer in more depth. For example, when someone says that his supervisor is too judgmental, the auditor might probe by asking, "What do you mean by 'judgmental'?" or "Give me some examples of how judgmental he is." Sometimes auditors can anticipate probes as they design the interview guide. Knowing how exhaustive the answers should be is a problem, for one could spend much longer on one question than one has for the entire interview. Therefore, the degree of probing is a matter of judgment. It is important to remember, however, that this interview is a new experience for most people. They have never dissected their jobs in the way the auditor asks them to do. Auditors should not assume that they know what respondents mean by "general statements." It takes time and prompting to secure a good overview.

Avoid Focusing on the Negative

Many auditors fall into the trap of wanting to hear only about the organization's problems—after all, the reason for an audit may be to improve the organization in some way. It is vitally important, though, to develop the positive points as well. The organization's strengths should be probed in as much detail as its weaknesses because the auditors need to understand in detail how the communication system works.

Adapt Questions to Specific Levels or Even to Specific People

We often modify the interview guides for managers versus nonmanagers because managers have access to different kinds and levels of information. We may even create a special guide adapted for a key source in the organization; the questions can be tailored to that person's unique perspective on the organization. We are most likely to create a special interview guide during the follow-up interviews, at which point it becomes clear that specific people can clarify and confirm certain information.

Do Not Reveal What You Find Out about the Organization

Many times interviewees unintentionally (or even intentionally) try to make the auditor violate the basic rules of professional conduct. Specifically, interviewees may try to induce the auditor to tell them what others have said in previous interviews. Some do this quite directly. For example, a manager might say, "Tell me, before I begin, what sorts of things the employees have been telling you." Others are more indirect: "I bet you have found the boys quite helpful, heh, Doc? They tell you everything?" In both cases, the auditor may respond, "The people are most cooperative, and I am learning quite a bit; however, as I promised you, I cannot discuss what others have said any more than I will tell others what you say." When one woman said, "I bet a lot of people have been complaining about wages," the auditor merely answered, "People have certainly been cooperative in expressing their feelings." In this way, the auditor avoids being induced to quote other people (Argyris, 1970, p. 301).

Let the Guide Grow; Do Not Let It Become Static

An assessment is not a scientific study in which everything must be standardized. Although auditors should follow the basic guide, they should also explore any new information they uncover. Moreover, they might decide to add new questions or to modify those that are not yielding much information.

Interview Structure

Arranging the questions on an interview guide develops a structure for the interview. Sometimes, the placement or order of questions makes a difference in how respondents answer them. The following guidelines are useful for thinking about that structure.

Begin Each Interview with an Orientation

Respondents' reactions to being interviewed vary considerably, with some welcoming the opportunity and others being suspicious of the whole endeavor. Nevertheless, everyone appreciates an overview explaining what the auditors are trying to accomplish. A good orientation can be a strong motivator for participation. Basically, the interview orientation should include each of the following.

First, make personal introductions. The auditor is a stranger asking people to divulge information that affects their livelihoods. Auditors should do their best to establish credibility from the outset. Without overwhelming people with details, auditors should allude to their expertise and perhaps indicate who contracted them to conduct the assessment. Auditors should talk about the process even if the audit has been well publicized; one cannot assume that all employees have received the information or paid attention to the publicity.

Second, describe the general purpose of the audit. Employees are often suspicious or fearful of why auditors are collecting information. Auditors should model effective organizational communication by letting people know the rationale behind the audit. Auditors also have the opportunity to let interviewees know how important their participation is in terms of the effect it has on the audits' findings.

Third, assure interviewees of confidentiality. Be sensitive to any nervousness on the respondents' part—remember that some people require more assurance than others. An interviewee's reluctance to say much or, in particular, to offer criticism is often a sign of nervousness, fear, or a lack of trust. Auditors should reassure interviewees that in no way will the audit report information in a way that identifies the sources. For instance, we tell interviewees, "If everyone we interview tells us the same thing, we cannot report that our findings are unanimous as that would reveal what you said." Interviewees appreciate it when auditors indicate that they have carefully thought about protecting their identities.

Fourth, state briefly how the interviewees were selected. Sometimes employees are nervous about how they were selected for the interview. This is often the case when they do not fully understand the audit's purpose. It helps, however, to let them know that many people are being interviewed in order to gain a full picture of the organization's communication. One need not go into great detail; a general comment is usually sufficient to let them know that they were not singled out for any negative reason.

Fifth, explain briefly how one would like to conduct the interview. Setting time constraints lets interviewees know what the auditor's expectations are for their time together. Perhaps more importantly, auditors should emphasize that they wish to focus on communication as that helps people frame their own expectations regarding the conversation.

Sixth, suggest ways in which the information may ultimately be used. Many employees hate exercises that are fruitless and waste their time; many employees complain that they never hear survey results or see anything occur as a result of them (Downs, Smeyak, & Martin, 1980). It is helpful if one can promise them some kind of report that will be distributed to all employees. But auditors should not make such a promise unless they have negotiated it in advance with management as part of the audit contract.

Here is a sample illustrative orientation that follows the six guidelines described previously:

> "Hello, I'm Cal Downs. I'm president of Communication Management, Inc., and you may have already heard that we are here to conduct a communication audit of ACME. Have you already filled out a questionnaire or heard about others being interviewed? From the beginning, we have planned two rounds of interviews. The purpose of this second round of interviews is to clarify and to probe some of the information already obtained in the first group of interviews and the questionnaire. We like to double-check our information to make sure that we learn as much as possible about ACME.
>
> "In order to do this, we don't need to talk to everyone. We select people to interview who represent the diverse units and activities in the organizations. We chose to interview you because we felt that you were in a good position to give us some additional insight into organizational communication, and, although we have questions about several areas, we hope that you'll volunteer as much information as possible to give us the best picture possible of the organization.
>
> "As was the case with the other interviewees, anything that we discuss now will be strictly confidential. We'll give a final report to management, but we never identify individuals. Now, before I ask my questions, do you have any questions about our general process?"

Start with the Job

People find it easy and enjoyable to talk about their jobs, so opening the interview with a discussion of the job motivates conversation. This is also the most logical place to begin for the auditor who needs to know how a particular employee fits into the total system. Finding this out at the beginning of the interview permits the auditor to judge how much information is needed from this individual and how to interpret the answers. One key element to understand at this point is how this person's tasks are interdependent with those of other people.

Probe General Areas before Getting to Specific Ones

A good interview should begin with broad questions and become increasingly specific. We like to use the analogy of a funnel. Such a funnel system allows the auditor to get a better idea of the respondent's frame of reference. For example, it is useful to say, "Tell me about communication on your job" before asking specific questions about interdepartmental linkages or performance appraisals. A more general, somewhat ambiguous question such as this does not structure the respondents' thought processes, and it may give the auditor relevant information that would not be obtained through more specific questions.

Do Not Permit the Guide to Restrict the Interview

The purpose of the guide is to ensure consistent coverage of topic areas. Sometimes there are strategies behind the order in which the questions are asked. For example, we believe that asking questions about strengths first makes talking about weaknesses later seem less threatening. If an interviewee starts talking about weaknesses first, however, it may be useful to pursue this topic. Or if a respondent starts the interview by talking about a topic covered in Question 8, there is nothing wrong in varying the order of the questions.

INTERVIEWEE SELECTION

Every employee is a potentially good source of information about the organization. Unless the organization is very small, however, auditors will not need to interview everyone to get an accurate picture. Since interviews are costly in terms of time and money, selecting interviewees is an important step in the assessment. There is an "art" to making these decisions, for there are no formulas that tell one exactly how many people or exactly who should be interviewed. The general guideline is to interview enough people from sufficient areas of the organization to give a comprehensive view of the communication. Nevertheless, the following considerations may be helpful in making these decisions.

In small organizations, it is both possible and desirable to interview everyone. This prevents anyone from feeling left out. Furthermore, members of small organizations may occupy one-of-a-kind roles, making their individual contributions unique. Examples of organizations in which we have interviewed everyone include a car dealership (24 people), an alumni association's administration office (45 people), a university department (25 people), a savings and loan institution (67 people), and a government office (24 people). The sizes of these organizations made interviewing everyone easier.

When organizations have more than 50 employees, auditors may elect to interview an employee sample. *Sampling* is a scientific method of selecting people to participate in the audit. To make generalizations about the total organization on the basis of a sample, it helps to make the sample (1) representative, (2) random, and (3) stratified.

Make the Sample Representative

A *representative sample* is one in which the auditors have selected the interviewees so carefully that whatever the auditors would have found out by interviewing everyone can be discovered from the sample—in other words, auditors would learn nothing of significance by interviewing additional employees. To be representative, auditors must interview a sufficient number of people; the size of the necessary sample varies with the size of the organization. It is common practice to select 10–20% of an organization that employs 150–200 people. If there *are* 1,000 employees, one might be content with 100 or less (10%). Table 2.2 offers specific guidelines for determining the number of workers to be included. Choosing a sample size is affected in part by whether auditors are relying solely on interview data or using additional means of data collection. If auditors are using interview data to supplement survey data, they may not need as many interviewees as they would if the interview were the only data-collecting tool.

Randomize the Sample

Auditors should desire some randomization of the sample. *Complete randomness* means that every employee has an equal chance of being included in the sample. Randomizing the sample eliminates potential bias that might occur if auditors select people on any other basis. Randomization can be achieved by putting all the names in a hat and drawing out the desired number or by picking from a list of employees using a table of random numbers, found at the back of any statistics book. We say that "some" randomization is desirable rather than complete randomization because auditors want to ensure that they look at the entire organization. For instance, auditors might need to randomly select employees within each of several divisions, rather than risk some units not being represented. The same approach can be taken to make sure that the sample represents people at all levels of the organization.

Sometimes managers in the organization can be helpful in selecting a sample, but be careful that they do not focus solely on one group or one type of individual. A vice-president once tried to pick our interviewees by saying, "Interview Hatfield, Penley, and Smith, but don't interview Cook or Barge because they won't tell you the truth anyway." The vice-president probably thought he was being helpful, but had we taken his advice the results would have been skewed toward his point of view.

Stratify the Sample

As we suggested above, there are limits to the wisdom of choosing only random samples. For example, a graduate student was auditing an organization that had four divisions. He took the names of all employees and tried to create a random sample. But when he finished, he noticed that one of the divisions had been badly slighted, and that three of the four managers were not included. Somehow these oversights had to be corrected. An assessment is a time for all sides and all segments to be represented. One way of doing this is to choose a *stratified* sample. The stratified sample ensures that every segment of the organization is included; this inclusion should be the guiding principle for auditors. The number from any segment is less significant; it may or may not be proportional to its size in the organization. Consider the following examples:

1. *College campus audit.* The interviewers selected 50 freshmen, 50 sophomores, 50 juniors, and 50 seniors. The numbers were not chosen based on gaining a certain percentage from each class, but rather on giving equal weight to each classification. The sample, however, was made proportional on the basis of sex. Since the enrollment was 40% female, 40% of the sample was female.

2. *Airline audit.* There were three main divisions of unequal size in this unit. The total unit included 125 people, consisting of divisions of 60, 42, and 18 people. A total of 40 employees were interviewed. Some auditors might have tried to choose them proportionally to the size of the unit, but in this case interviewees were selected randomly from each division, but the numbers were not proportional. The unit of 18 people probably was overrepresented because the manager of that unit wanted to make certain that enough of his people were included.

3. *Equipment plant audit.* All the interviewees belonged to the same unit, but the job classification fell into four categories: engineers, designers, technicians, staff. We found initial evidence of some communication difficulty across these jobs, so we selected people from each job category; 26 of the 67 people were interviewed. We tried to interview one-third of each category, but the fact that we also accepted volunteers skewed the relative percentages a bit.

4. *Food processing plant audit.* Employees were divided into three shifts. While most workers worked on the first shift, it was still important to interview people on the other two shifts. In this case, it was discovered that the organization's style, its problems, and its communication changed from shift to shift. Which shift gave the most accurate information about "the organization"? In actual fact, they were all accurate because the organization changed with each shift.

Auditors may need to share the rationale for stratification with the interviewees— that is, how they are selecting people and why. Stratification is an important way of gathering a sample that represents the whole organization, but it is not necessary to balance all the characteristics of a population, as pollsters do. There are many characteristics, and auditors have to choose among them. The most obvious characteristic for stratification is the units in which employees work. However, if we had a sense that male–female communication was a problem, we would stratify according to gender; or if we believed engineers and designers were having a problem, we would stratify according to job description. Ultimately, there is no substitute for one's own sensitivity in choosing the sample.

Interview Key People

Generally, managers have more communicative contacts by the very nature of their organizational roles. Therefore, auditors should strive to interview all its people in key positions. In fact, interviewing top management is a good place to begin to get a good overview; these managers have a lot to tell and can often pinpoint problem areas.

Another reason for interviewing key people is that they normally want to participate and feel slighted if they are not included. We learned this quickly in an assessment of a public utility. Since the president had hired us to conduct the analysis, we thought of him as the person to whom we were to give the report, rather than as a person who wanted to contribute to the report. This perception was wrong, as a subordinate manager wisely counseled us.

Do not overlook any key people. Interview as many people as you can, and do not worry whether this part of the sample is random.

Invite Volunteers

Many employees will jump at the chance to "make a contribution," tell the auditor "the way it really is," or get "something off their chests." Obviously, volunteers think that they have valuable information to share, and frequently they are pleased that someone will take the time to listen to them. In some rare cases, volunteers have an ax to grind.

At any rate, special consideration should be given to determine how widespread volunteer concerns are. Auditors always need to be aware that there are some individuals in the organization whose perceptions are not shared by others. In an audit of a university, for example, we discovered that several volunteers came from a special clique in the faculty and that their views did not reflect the opinions of most of the other faculty members.

Even so, volunteers are useful, so how does one get them? There are a number of ways. In the audit of an engineering plant, the manager of each unit sent around a sign-up sheet explaining the reason for the interviews and asking interested people to sign up. A secretary then made out a schedule. In another instance, employees were given a phone number to call if they wanted to volunteer. In an audit of an airline, respondents were given a space on the questionnaire to check if they wished to be interviewed. (This system requires the auditor to know the identity of the survey respondent, so we use the technique sparingly.) Finally, we have asked interviewees to name other workers who might want to be interviewed. It is not the most direct method, but it sometimes results in beneficial contacts. As a practical concern, we generally advocate interviewing volunteers after the selected sample has been interviewed just to make certain those get done.

Allow for Contingencies

Accessibility is a key factor in selecting interviewees. Not everyone is equally available due to vacations, shifts, special work assignments, or crises. Some problems can be overcome if auditors will make themselves accessible at 1:00 A.M. for the third shift, or after work, or on a day during another week. Do what you can.

On the other hand, it may not always be possible to include some of the people that one would like to interview. Some people refuse to be interviewed for personal reasons. Others can't be interviewed because of a work schedule. In one audit the people who worked in the dining room could not be interviewed during mealtimes, and the organization would not pay them to stay for an additional hour for an interview. Therefore, they simply were not included in the analysis.

SCHEDULING TIME AND PLACE

Whenever possible, it is wise to have a liaison in the organization set up schedules and contact people. Whoever takes this assignment should develop a complete timetable well in advance so that interviewees will know exactly when they are scheduled and how much time the interviews will take. This scheduling allows workers to incorporate the interview into their work schedules.

The length of the interview can vary widely, depending on the individual. Thirty minutes to an hour is appropriate for nonmanagers, and 2 hours is not too long for managers. Furthermore, it is wise to schedule breaks between interviews; this time gives the auditor some elasticity. As one cannot forecast the length of each interview, it is better to allow too much time than to cut an interview short because another interview ran long or simply to play "catchup" in the scheduling. Sometimes, for people who have flexible schedules, it is possible to have the liaison let employees know that they are going to be interviewed on a certain day without setting up formal appointments.

Work flow is another consideration in scheduling. Arrange times when people are most receptive to interviews. For example, Monday morning appointments are not good for many managers because they typically have planning meetings on Monday mornings. Similarly, shift workers are often tired and eager to get home at the end of a shift. They might try to shorten the interview if it were scheduled near the end of a shift. Once we audited a manufacturer when management insisted that all interviews be conducted only after employees had completed a certain rush order; that constraint delayed the interviews by 2 weeks.

Where the interview takes place is negotiable. In general, the location should be selected to assure privacy, to stimulate free communication, and to be convenient for the interviewee. Rather than dictating the location, it is wise to give the employee an option. For example, ask a manager, "Where would you like to have the interview?" Most employees prefer their own offices, but we have interviewed some managers at prearranged off-site locations to avoid interruptions—at the suggestion of the interviewees themselves.

Another option is to set up a permanent office and have the interviewees come there. This arrangement saves the auditors some travel time and takes the employees out of their immediate work environments to a place where they can relax and talk. When this option is used, it is particularly crucial to stay on schedule. People are reluctant to sit around and wait when they could be working.

CONDUCTING THE INTERVIEWS

Good planning is necessary for collecting accurate, useful information about the organization. The best planning, however, will not help if the interviewers are not skillful or cannot be trusted. In the following section, we discuss some of the important considerations both for and about interviewers.

Select Competent Interviewers Who Can Be Trusted

Interview time is a precious commodity. The interviewers need to use it wisely. If there is an audit team, one needs to be able to trust that the interviewers actually conduct the prescribed interviews. This is not often a problem, but we know an auditor who did have trouble when an interviewer reported interviews that never actually took place. Thus it is useful to validate that the interviews did indeed occur.

Train Interviewers to Use the Interview Guide

Win acceptance for the interview questions by explaining to interviewers the relevance of each one. It is also important that interviewers are so familiar with the guide that they can ensure all questions will be asked even if the order is not followed. Again, we encourage interviewers to let the interaction flow like a conversation without requiring a definite order to be followed. This maximizes flexibility and prevents the interview from becoming too stilted.

Set a Nonthreatening Climate

There is healthy tension between keeping the interview business-like and on target and allowing it to be an enjoyable experience. Set the tone by explaining the purpose behind the interview but raising questions in a conversational way.

Probe Thoroughly

Since one of the inherent advantages of the interview is the opportunity to probe for in-depth information, skill in probing is the interviewer's ultimate art. Although the interview must not become an interrogation, most answers do need some time to be developed. Therefore, interviewers should be trained to ask both directive and nondirective probes.

Directive probes are pointed questions. They can take many forms. For instance, elaboration is needed when the answer is incomplete—for example, "Tell me more about why you say that." Clarification is useful when terms or concepts are unclear—for example, "I'm not familiar with that organizational term. What does it mean?" Repetition of the question is needed when interviewees give a verbal response that does not really address the question. Confrontation in a nonaggressive way may be necessary when people seem to contradict themselves. Sometimes when the inconsistency is pointed out, they can clarify their positions quite well.

Nondirective probes, on the other hand, are merely designed to keep the employee talking. They include a number of nonverbal behaviors such as maintaining eye contact, nodding one's head, or leaning forward with a look of interest. They also include verbal expression such as "I see" and "uh-huh." One of our favorites, however, is the internal summary, in which the interviewer summarizes for the person what the interviewer thinks has been said and the conclusions that have been drawn. This technique gives the interviewee the opportunity to agree or disagree, thus providing valuable reactions to the interviewer's summary.

Motivate the Interviewees

A motivating introduction to the interview is absolutely necessary. Interviewers must establish their credibility from the start. Normally, this can be accomplished through personal introductions and an explanation of the interviewer's objectives and how the auditor will use the information. Assuring the respondent of confidentiality is usually necessary. We have had a few people walk in and announce "I came in here not to communicate" or "I asked not to be here." Whereas such people present a challenge, this kind of reaction should whet the interviewer's appetite because these people usually have a reason for being defensive that might be important. Getting their unique information will enrich the auditor's picture of the organization.

Anticipate Problems

Interviewers can also be prepared to encounter occasional problems. One common issue is the decision whether or not to explain a question or word. An explanation can sometimes "lead" interviewees into certain areas; but at other times it may be perfectly safe to give examples or explanations. For example, respondents were asked how "involved" they were in their jobs. This was an abstract question, and several people asked what we meant by "involved." In this particular company, we politely explained that we did not want to influence their answers by defining the term and noted that they could define it as they wished. They would be telling a lot about the plant if they discussed their definitions. As this example demonstrates, it is sometimes wise to turn the question back to the person who asked it; however, one should make certain that this does not become a game.

Another problem is coping with the silent or overly talkative employee. In some ways the latter presents the greatest problem. Although most employees are delighted to talk about their jobs, one overly talkative interviewee can ruin the entire interview schedule. Interviewers should be polite, but never lose control of the process.

A third problem is the difficulty of remaining objective. Interviewers, being human, often find it easy to take sides and may express an evaluative reaction to what an interviewee says. In general, interviewers need to remember that the interview is an information-gathering process. Neutrality and objectivity should guide their responses.

Finally, interviewers face the problem of their own boredom. By following an interview guide, even loosely, interviewers will hear the same information over and over. It is a challenge to keep responding with interest, but it is also a necessity. The employee ought to leave the interview feeling appreciated.

RECORDING INFORMATION QUICKLY AND SYSTEMATICALLY

Because interviews are spread over several days or weeks, it is imperative that interviewers register the information they have obtained as quickly as possible. No interviewer's memory is trustworthy when faced with keeping straight the results of many interviews.

There are guidelines prescribing how one should take notes. Some people write notes during the interview itself. Others leave a time for writing general reactions after the interview. Both procedures are useful. A technique that we find has merit is to ask an assistant to take notes while a primary interviewer asks the questions. Having a note taker frees the primary interviewer to concentrate on the interaction. Having the assistant "process" the interview after it is finished provides a different point of view about the answers, which can be provocative and can lead to better write-ups of the interviews. After each interview, a written summary should be formalized. It should include at a minimum the following:

1. Name of interviewee
2. Date
3. Position of interviewee
4. Answer to each individual question
5. Interviewer's subjective reactions or observations
6. Questions or areas that should be explored further in subsequent interviews.

An example of such a summary is presented in Table 5.5.

SYNTHESIZING THE RESPONSE DATA

After conducting many interviews and listening to many answers, the auditor has to determine what all this information means. While it is fun to talk to people about the organization, ultimately it can be quite frustrating to try to make sense out of the various perceptions so that the conclusions really describe the organization. Some of the following procedures might be helpful in synthesizing the data.

Set Aside Time for the Interviewers to Discuss What They Are Discovering about the Organization

Such group sessions need not be delayed until the end of the round; they can take place at the end of each interview day. In an audit of a university, six auditors debriefed each other this way for a week. There is something quite exciting and invigorating about interviewers sharing information that leads to new discoveries about the organization. Furthermore, such processing is a useful tool for checking and refining perceptions.

Develop a Summary Sheet for Each Question

It is not necessary to code each response separately, but the auditors should begin to analyze the answers' content in categories. Then they should look at the range of responses in each category. At the end of this process, the interviewing team should try to write generalizations that can be made from these answers.

Keep the First Analysis Descriptive

Do not go beyond the data. For example, watch out for the tendency to make inferences about why things happen as they do or to provide a rationale for a given behavior. Ultimately one will want to develop explanations and theories; however, at this

TABLE 5.5. Individual Interview Write-Up for Second Round Interview

Name: Jane Doe
Position: Supervisor; Sales Support
Interviewer: Carl Smith
Date: March 15, 2004

1. Communication Role of Supervisors

To communicate changes that take place and the whys behind them—"the people have a right to know"; to make yourself available to the employees on a personal level as well as the job level.

HOW WELL DO THEY FUNCTION? Supervisors communicate "only as good as the people that work with them do"; there must be an equal exchange between supervisor and employee. She expresses that there should be an equal give-and-take in communication with employees and supervisors for the sake of getting the job done and providing a good interpersonal atmosphere. ANY PROBLEMS WITH SUPERVISORS IN THEIR COMMUNICATION? MAKING THEMSELVES AVAILABLE TO THE AGENTS FOR THIS NEEDED AMOUNT OF GIVE-AND-TAKE COMMUNICATION.

Note: She took an overall defensive attitude to the first two questions by saying she felt as if they're "hounding" her to tell how she personally has been performing as supervisor.

2. How Much Information Do Employees Receive about Being Judged?

DAILY: not much individual judgment or recognition, but a comment on the overall unit's daily work is made. She doesn't like to evaluate agents that much verbally or informally because she says she doesn't want to seem to be "hounding" the agents about their work. No comment was made on possible informal positive evaluations though.

PERSONAL FEELINGS AND SUGGESTIONS FOR IMPROVEMENT: Personally, she says it's hard to evaluate people, that is, in terms of effort or in comparison to others. She didn't like the written evaluation in use. The previous form had "no middle ground," that is, an employee was rated either excellent or fair to unacceptable. The old form also judged an employee on areas not related to CDP and left important areas such as punctuality and attendance out. The new form is more tailored to the organization.

3. Perceptions We'll Find about Upper Management

Dissatisfaction; that they're stupid, *but* she interjects by saying that upper management is not always responsible for the mix-ups and neither are supervisors because corporate headquarters interferes too much and upper management must answer to them.

4. Perceptions We'll Find about Supervisors

She says most complaints occur because many supervisors will further mess up mix-ups by not properly following through with communication about them (e.g., communication and feedback they get from management about mix-ups). Also, perceptions will include that supervisors don't respond enough to personal needs, which she feels greatly affects job performance. "Employees want attention." SUPERVISOR SELECTION AND TRAINING: Big problem with training—it's on-the-job training. She feels training programs would help.

5. Favoritism

She avoids it by having certain rules for herself to follow. She says most of what is labeled favoritism is just grumbling by employees who "sit on their butts all day and talk instead of work." She says the promotions that have been called favoritism she sees from a supervisory position as valid promotions based on job performance and not favoritism.

(continued)

TABLE 5.5. *(continued)*

6. Job Satisfaction

Obtained through merit increases, through cross-utilization of employees. This is letting employees learn what they want and can learn in other departments as well as within the division, so they can be used elsewhere (therefore beneficial to the company) and so they can always have hopes of promotion (thus giving them individual incentive and motivation and keeping them happy). JOB DISSATISFACTION: People create their own dissatisfaction. People can do what they want in their jobs if they have the incentive. Those that are dissatisfied are the ones who don't do anything to improve their situation. They think something is going to be handed to them.

7. Grapevine

Detrimental to her because sometimes overrides or arrives before supervision does, then subordinates ignore supervision and make supervisor look dumb because they already know.

8. Suggestion System

Good because chance for employees to tell management directly. Management really is concerned and she expresses that she doesn't think agents know or feel this. Management can't always do anything about the problem (here she again points out corporate headquarters) but they really want to know and help.

point, limit oneself to what can be described from the direct statements from the interviews.

Analyze the Data from Each Round of Interviews Separately

It is important that some tentative descriptive conclusions be drawn after the first round of interviews. These conclusions provide targets to be checked by the collection of additional data. Since they are the first data on the organization, the conclusions must be tentative, and the auditors should look for evidence in the follow-up interviews that would allow the auditors to question or reject them.

Look for Qualitative Interpretations

We are only somewhat interested in numerical data gathered from the interviews, so it is not necessarily appropriate to report frequency counts of how many people gave what response. Nevertheless, one cannot hide the fact that the frequency of related comments may indicate how widespread or intense a problem is. For example, in response to a survey within a small academic unit, every graduate student gave the same answer to the question "What is the chief weakness of the organization?" This frequency was significant. On the other hand, none of the undergraduates or the faculty members mentioned it as a problem. In the total scheme the particular weakness might not have shown up as significant, but in communicating with graduate students it was the most important communication phenomenon. The challenge for us was to integrate that information into our overall picture of the unit in an appropriate way: representing the perspective of a certain group. (And, as we mentioned earlier, we could not report the response as being unanimous as that would have betrayed the identities and answers of the graduate students.)

Draw Conclusions across Questions

Communication operates in the organization as a system with many subsystems. The goal is to obtain a good view of the entire system. This view cannot be achieved by looking at answers to individual questions. Therefore, one must examine data intuitively across all dimensions to see how things are related. Table 5.6 demonstrates how this was done in an industrial plant.

EXAMPLES OF AUDIT CONCLUSIONS

The following conclusions were drawn from several audits to suggest the kinds of observations that are obtainable. Please note that in each case these were preliminary conclusions for the auditors themselves to discuss, and were not necessarily communicated back to the organization as they appear here. These observations would have to be coordinated with data from the questionnaires that were used.

Manufacturing Plant

"People here think that this is a good place to work. In fact, this is the most pervasive perception encountered in the interviews. When anyone compares this company with a previous job, this one was always rated as the best. Motivation has been affected by a perceived change in hiring only college-educated managers. Workers resent the fact that internal promotions are now blocked. This is a communication problem, because actually 50% of the promotions are still from within."

Manufacturing Plant

"The communication climate has changed dramatically in the last 2 years. Specifically, work pressures have increased and teamwork is lacking across the board, that is, among shifts, among departments, and among management levels. Productivity is up 50%, but the pressure leads people to believe they are uninformed. Major decision making seems to be mostly downward, even though management talks of looking for ways to increase participation to improve the climate. Meetings are not seen as being the best avenue for securing participation."

Airline

"Ratings of supervisors differ remarkably and run the gamut from excellent to poor. When there is a negative rating, the reason is usually noted as lack of experience or technical expertise. Interestingly, there seems to be a high degree of empathy for a supervisor's job demands.

TABLE 5.6. Sample Summary of Interviews, Industrial Plant

OVERALL:

CDP appears to be a fairly pleasant place to work whether you are management, supervisory staff, or production worker. The attitude coming through in interviews was generally positive with a few exceptions. Upper management was most positive, and satisfaction seemed to diminish as the management hierarchy was descended. The most negative interviews were of workers who had no subordinates and handled production, maintenance, or production support work. Even though some negative attitudes showed through, no one complained of not having someone to complain to or offer suggestions. At the same time, some workers mentioned that the flow of complaints and suggestions upward was often blocked somewhere so that many received no response. This was mentioned at the third tier, as well as at the bottom.

The chain-of-command hierarchy was viewed as certain and for the most part rigid. Lower-level employees suggested that they could communicate with upper management and that to do so they would send the message through proper channels. Communication among department heads, general management staff, and the resident manager seemed more informal; yet the hierarchy remained clear in everyone's understanding. Note that communication funnels neatly through the system. That communication which does not funnel well comes from outside the local plant. The division office of CDP communicates directly to plant personnel at various levels of the hierarchy. The information is technical or directly related to raw materials shipment production plans and changes, research and development of products, and manufacturing techniques, as well as marketing and shipping. Such messages come from across the hierarchical strata within the division office.

Formal channels at CDP include monthly department reports, a monthly plant report (derived from department reports), an in-house local newspaper, a corporation magazine and newsletter, the bulletin board on which all information for employees is posted, safety meetings, and department meetings. In addition, the resident manager holds a weekly staff meeting attended by his immediate subordinate and the general superintendent holds a weekly staff meeting of his subordinates, the department heads. Brief written reports of operations every 24 hours are prepared and sent to the general superintendent as well as other interested managers and superintendents. Work plans are sent from shift to shift via log books, which indicate the production plan, progress toward it, and other vital operations information.

Evaluating these channels, interviewees were generally positive toward each one. The monthly reports were criticized lightly as excessive but only insofar as the government required the reporting of things that seem to be unimportant to production. The paper received split reviews, with most negative comments coming from line workers and some supervisors. Those who criticized it thought of it as a waste of paper, a gossip sheet, or both.

The bulletin board was also seen as being both positive and negative. The majority of comments about it stated that all employees read it regularly and that important information was put on it such as job notices and employee benefit information. Most of the negative comments came from line workers and some supervisors. They complained about the job listings (referring to openings within the plant and in the plant being built) being incomplete or late.

Department or communications meetings were seen as positive by some and negative by others. The negative comments were more evenly spread across the authority strata. Often the meetings were criticized for being a waste of time and unimportant. The meetings are intended in part to air employee questions and grievances, but those that are sent in seem to seldom make the agenda. Safety meetings, which in many cases precede the department meetings, are generally seen as important and useful.

The resident manager's weekly staff meeting is not loudly applauded. It was seen as too long and as a gathering where each staff member was expected to contribute something no matter how trivial. The "result" then was supposedly an informed staff knowledgeable of the goings on in each unit. One critic felt that the result came from informal contacts and seldom from the meeting. Other channels are perceived as positive.

(continued)

TABLE 5.6. *(continued)*

One strikingly positive aspect of the CDP operation is decision making in general. Although a few negative comments about insufficient subordinate input or involvement are noted, on the whole those who wanted to contribute knew of a channel through which to express their views. Others considered to have necessary information were accessible and were contacted. The bulk of the decisions have to do with production. Others deal with employee issues.

All or most seem to follow the same format. Decisions are made very close to where they will have an effect. Line workers make decisions. They are trusted to do their job and to be reasonably autonomous in that effort. The same is generally true on up the hierarchy. At each level, the job holder has a range of decisions for which he or she is responsible and information necessary to make the decisions is easily accessible by talking with whoever should know, face-to-face or on the phone.

Another feature of decision making that was fairly clear was that an individual usually has final responsibility for any particular decision. He or she may solicit any and all the information he or she feels is necessary and consider all the points that seem significant, yet one person makes or takes responsibility for the decision.

Workers in the lower strata did *complain* of not being heard on up the line. This decision-making system may stifle or weed out some of their remarks. Some claim that for all the emphasis on safety, employees in fact do unsafe things at management's request, and an injury or two has been glossed over to maintain a good record. Suggestions about safety and production efficiency seem to get lost sometimes. The industrial relations unit has a reward system for such suggestions. Workers are selected to go out to dinner, to a ball game, or to an amusement park at company expense in exchange for the best suggestions of the month. Evidently the system is lax, not serving rewards on time, and it is charged with pulling unimportant and repeated suggestions. On balance, though, the safety emphasis was seen as a sign of management interest in employee welfare and safety meetings were viewed positively.

Upper-level managers complained of a lack of interdepartmental coordination. The meetings being held by the general superintendent may correct this. Another issue at this level is the use of MBO. The system is seen as ineffective. Departments get their objectives in order and send them up for approval. The approval comes usually after management has revised and sent back the objectives to be resubmitted in the revised form. It was suggested that a meeting time be established to hash out an agreement on objectives. This could eliminate some frustration, at least, if not the contradiction of the intent of the system.

Workers at the lower levels wanted two things in particular. They want a cleaning crew for the plant. They want this so that operators don't have to clean their own areas. Second, they want a more responsive and effective maintenance operation. Complaints about maintenance were only general and directed at slowness and unsatisfactory work.

In the *next round of interviews,* we want to probe the areas of advertising jobs, the impact of putting in a new plant (some hints of an issue, although a necessarily short-term one, come through in this round), and whether the rate of suggestions has increased or decreased. Another point of interest is one of vocabulary. In several of the interviews the word "efficient" came up often, as did the phrase "mature operation." The occurrence of these seemed unusually frequent and we're curious about where they came from.

"All supervisors mention overload and the fact that everyone in unit ABC is spread very thin. Some supervisors think that ABC is over committed and that people are often trying to handle more than they can be responsible for.

"There seems to be a uniform desire for information to be communicated through multiple channels. Many supervisors expressed the desire for written notification of all information that affects overall operations, rather than so much reliance on oral messages. Twilight shift supervisors specifically mentioned the need to put more information in writing.

"Most managers contend that communication among them is very good and that they keep each other informed. Supervisors and agents share this perception of the managers. One notable exception seems to be the communication to and from _____ [specific person]. [Note: while a specific person is named here, we do not mention who made the comments. It is crucial to the observation, however, to note that particular people or positions may be at the chief focal point of a general conclusion.]"

Public Utility

"The informal channels are rated the least effective means of communication. In Unit A, it is almost nonexistent. Unit B has an active grapevine, but most people seemed to doubt its reliability. Of all the communication areas considered, the greatest dissatisfaction was expressed over an apparent lack of information about job vacancies and advancement. Some workers were not even certain that a system existed. They seem to rely on word-of-mouth almost as much as published information. Those employees who desire mobility want an updated, more effective system.

"Group managers saw very little conflict either within their units or between units. Isolated incidents were not thought to be important. Nevertheless, there is a kind of competitiveness communicated between the officers at Unit B and Unit C.

"Training generally gets high marks as a communication vehicle, new policies are developed, employees are advised by their managers, meetings, by booklets, and through special quizzes. The employees generally thought these procedures were both adequate and satisfactory."

Corporate Headquarters

"Top management has designed three major thrusts to improve productivity in the workplace; however, only one-third of the respondents were supportive of any of the three. The degree of openness is perceived as limited."

Police Department

"Personal feedback is perceived as being inadequate. People say there is a not only a lack of recognition for their performance but there is a lack of clarity as to where the department is going.

"Upper management feels that rumors are a major problem. It is difficult to get the facts out due to the nature of shift work and the fact that the officers are not located in the same place. One particular problem is that dissidents can feed rumors to the press."

Public Relations Firm

"Job insecurity has surfaced as the overwhelming concern in the organization. Technically, it is not a communication problem since employees are aware of the 2001 downtown in the general economy, but they still blame top management for not steering them through the crisis. This has led to a desire for more complete communication from top management about the business and the future strategic directions of the company. Upper-level managers feel there is little they can do to change the economic outlook."

CONCLUSION

Face-to-face interviews offer a perfect opportunity to establish and sustain auditor–client relationships. Although auditors are strangers at first, they soon become fixtures for a while in the organization. People grow accustomed to their presence at work, and the informal channels often discuss them. A new relationship develops, and the wise auditor nurtures it. Alderfer (1968, pp. 260–265) reports several ways of doing this. First, "be as visible and as approachable as possible." Look for special opportunities to interact with employees informally while eating or visiting their workstations. Next, "preserve the confidentiality of the data without damaging the self-esteem of the people who seek information." Finally, "be accessible to key members of the organization, even if it means altering a research design." These points suggest that collecting useful information is not limited to formal interviews or other data-generating methods.

Finally, interviews familiarize auditors with an organization and its people in ways that no other data collection technique can. There are no limits to the depth with which topics can be explored. In fact, one never quits learning about the organization. We often treat the final report as an interview by asking managers to respond to what they are hearing. In our last audit, we were having dinner with the chief executive officer after having given the final report. During the dinner, he made two comments that really reshaped the conclusions of one of the auditors. Since it involved his own personal standing in the organization, we were able to discuss that in a constructive manner with him. The report continued.

6

Diagnosis through Questionnaires

Despite our emphasis on triangulation of methods in Chapter 1, the mainstay of most comprehensive audits of larger organizations is some type of questionnaire because questionnaires have advantages over other methods of data collection. Although their advantages vary according to the methods with which they are being compared, the primary advantages are efficiency, large sample size, cheap costs, assured confidentiality, sampling of many topics, and having a permanent original copy of the responses.

Whereas an auditor can interview only a limited number of employees in sizable organizations, he or she can distribute a questionnaire to all employees, if that is desired. Furthermore, it can be given to all in the same time frame, so it is a faster means of getting information. The questionnaire is also one of the cheapest audit procedures. Not only is it inexpensive to reproduce and circulate, but it avoids the expenses incurred from paying interviewers or taking people away from their jobs. Generally, a questionnaire can be filled out during slack periods when it does not compete with work time. A major advantage to a questionnaire is that a certain amount of anonymity can be assured, so sensitive information can be obtained from people who might not risk disclosing it in another way. A questionnaire provides a permanent written record, so it can be restudied during the analysis phase of the audit, and it can be designed so that tabulating standardized answers is easy. Finally, a questionnaire has the advantage of comprising more topics than is normally covered in other methods of data collection.

These advantages are suggested under the assumption that one has a *good* questionnaire to administer. Basically, two options are available: (1) designing an original questionnaire or (2) using a standardized one developed by others. Each option will be explored in depth. The rest of this chapter describes the process of designing a new questionnaire. Chapters 7 and 8 examine two frequently used standardized questionnaires.

DESIGNING A QUESTIONNAIRE

Designing a good questionnaire sounds easier than it actually is, but it is profitable when done well. Therefore, considerable time ought to be spent planning the questions and the format of the questionnaire. Some of us can easily think of questions to ask, but it is important to design them so that the auditors always know *in advance* how to make the best use of the information obtained in the answers. Some of the following considerations may facilitate a well-developed design.

Develop a Focus

Decide what information is most crucial to the audit. Chapter 4 described the variety of communication information that it is possible to collect, but because so much is available one must decide whether to sample numerous topics with a few questions each or to probe a few topics in depth with many questions each. Auditors often face pressure to cover as many of the communication processes and systems as possible. Remember that the preliminary interviews may be very helpful in identifying areas to be investigated. As we described in Chapter 4, the most important potential topic areas include:

1. Kinds of information needed to be received and to be sent
2. Reactions to sources of information
3. Adequacy of channels used
4. Relationships among people
5. How communication network or structure affects the work processes
6. Directions of communication: upward, downward, and horizontal
7. Communication outcomes such as satisfaction and productivity
8. Feedback mechanisms and performance
9. Communication problem areas
10. Interdepartmental communication
11. External variables that affect internal communication

Choose Questions for Each Topic Area

Generally, it is useful to start off with more questions than you need and later to evaluate which ones are most important for your purposes. Ask whether a question is necessary and how an answer to it can be used. There is a kind of science about question development. Some of the major considerations are identified in the following sections.

Scope

The wider the scope of any question, the more difficult it may be to obtain comparable answers across respondents and to properly interpret each respondent's responses. Sometimes several questions are needed to tap the multidimensionality of the topic area. A good example is the superior–subordinate relationship. There are too many aspects to this relationship to be covered in one question. An auditor can explore the superior's receptivity to upward communication, the adequacy of downward communication, the communication climate between the two, and so on. Therefore, this relationship may need to be explored through several questions, each of which identifies a different aspect of the relationship. The choice seems to be whether to ask general, open questions or to explore specific issues.

Specificity

Here the auditor is in a bind. On the one hand, the more specific the question, the more questions that are necessary to probe an area. On the other hand, the more abstract or general the terms in the question, the less certain you can be about understanding what the answers really mean. For example, in one audit we asked employees to react to "how organizational decisions are made that affect your position." The employees indicated that they wanted a great deal more information than they were receiving on this topic. Although this was one of our most significant findings, we did not know from the question exactly what decisions interested the respondents. Furthermore, it would be rather tedious to list on a questionnaire all the major kinds of decisions that could be subsumed under that question. This case demonstrates how follow-up interviews can be helpful.

Wording

It is important to anticipate how the respondents may interpret the questions. If a question *can* be misunderstood, it *will* be misunderstood. That is why it is better to consider the question "How can this be misunderstood?" rather than the question "Can it be understood?" The frame of reference is never exactly the same for everyone, but a sensitive designer can reduce the likelihood of some problems occurring by considering several points. Is the wording biased toward an expected answer? Couching a question in terms of a "problem" may be biasing, because some people try to avoid problems. Are there unstated assumptions in the questions? For example, asking "How does your job satisfaction affect your productivity?" may imply a connection between satisfaction and productivity that has not been supported by research. Finally, avoid evaluative words like "bad," "good," or "fair" because the criteria used by different respondents for these evaluative words will not be known unless they are probed specifically.

Relevance

Questions should be relevant to the goals of the audit, but they should also be relevant to the individual respondent's experience. Novice auditors often become enamored of asking as many questions as they can, and the answers to many of these questions are never used. In other words, questions need to be focused on meaningful areas with an intended use in mind. For example, there is a tendency to ask for too much demographic data, most of which are never used in the analysis. Similarly, we have found it useful to make sure that certain questions are posed only to those individuals who have the experience necessary to answer them.

Choose an Appropriate Response Format

Open versus Closed Questions

Choosing whether a question should be open or closed is one of the most important decisions to be made. Each type has particular strengths, as we initially mentioned in Chapter 5. We recommend that most questionnaires have a mixture of both.

An *open question* does not restrict the answer in any way. A good example is "What improvements would you like to see in communication in your job?" The respondent can answer any number of ways. The advantages of this type of question are many. Since this question does not structure the respondent's thinking by asking for comment on any specific element, it may uncover both the individual's priorities and his or her frame of reference. Also, the responses are likely to be longer and more detailed, providing richer information. Open questions are particularly useful when the subject is complex or when the list of alternatives is either too long or unknown. For example, asking the question about improvements mentioned previously often generates a list of things that the auditor could not have anticipated, and therefore that could not have been framed in a closed question.

It is also important to be aware of open questions' limitations. Because answers to them are not standardized, tabulation may be more difficult. Some answers will include irrelevant information, and others will be too sketchy to be of real value. Another problem we have encountered is that a majority of respondents will not take the time or make the effort to fill them out—although we have found that posting questionnaires online seems to motivate people to give longer answers.

By contrast, *closed questions* typically restrict the answers in specific ways. They take the forms of rating scales, ranking, dichotomous alternatives, inventories, checklists, or grids. This makes them easier and faster to answer, to code, to compare, and to sample many different topics quickly. Multiple-choice test questions are good examples of closed questions.

On the other hand, closed questions are limited in some ways too. Some respondents are frustrated when they cannot elaborate on, clarify, or qualify their responses. Furthermore, variations among responses are artificially removed through forced choice, and differences in interpretation go undetected. The auditor cannot be certain whether the respondent is guessing or taking the responses seriously. Finally, closed questions provide less in-depth information than well-answered open questions provide.

Table 6.1 offers examples of the closed and open questions about one general area. One can readily see that the answer to an open question could reveal a great deal. But if the respondents do not talk about the same issues, tabulation and thus generalization may be difficult. A closed question may require respondents to pick a number on a scale—thus, for example, the coder can readily see how many people do not trust their supervisors. However, the only aspect of the relationship that is investigated is "trust." In the absence of the respondents' comments and elaborations, the auditor may not even know what they meant by the term. Therefore, it is best to use closed and open questions in supplemental fashion. In the case of the trust question, one could use the scale to get people to commit themselves, and then follow with an open question such as "Why?" or "What could be done to make this relationship better?"

TABLE 6.1. Contrast between Open and Closed Questions

Example:

1. (Open) Describe your relationship with your supervisor.

    versus

2. (Closed) To what extent do you trust your supervisor?

    Little   1   2   3   4   5   Great

Because there are so many aspects of communication to cover in an audit, well-designed closed questions are very helpful. An important part of their design is the choice of a rating scale. Contemporary research would urge a degree of consistency throughout the questionnaire because changing rating scales from section to section may throw respondents off. Since there is no particular pattern that ought to be followed, we will discuss several possibilities.

Agree–Disagree Statements

A statement is made, and the person is asked to indicate how strongly he or she agrees or disagrees with it, as is depicted in Table 6.2.

This scale forces the respondent to make a choice and also assesses the intensity of the respondent's feelings. Make every effort to avoid framing of questions around a confusing double negative. Suppose the statement had said that "the supervisor does not give you personal feedback." Some people would be confused about how to respond. The respondent would need to mark "disagree" in order to make a positive statement about the supervisor. In other words, the respondent has to select a negative to counter the negative phrasing of the question.

U.S. society seems to be fascinated with numbers. Thus the rating scales used most often are numerical. Generally, an item is mentioned and the respondent indicates the strength of the response by a number. It is common practice to use odd numbers so that there is a middle ground. Also, the longer the continuum, the more sensitive it is; for example, scales of 1 to 5 give more variation than scales of 1 to 3. However, there is a point of diminishing returns such that extensions from 1 to 11 may render the difference be-

---

TABLE 6.2. Example of Forced-Choice Question

Your supervisor gives you personal feedback about
the progress in your job.

_____ 1. Strong agreement

_____ 2. Agreement

_____ 3. Disagreement

_____ 4. Strong disagreement

TABLE 6.3. Example of Question with Likert Scale

How satisfied are you with the amount of personal feedback
you get from your supervisors?

Little   1   2   3   4   5   6   7   Great

tween a 7 and an 8 relatively meaningless. The most common scales are either five or
seven choices long. Table 6.3 offers an example. Nevertheless, Clampitt now uses 0–100
scales, thinking they achieve greater reliability. Similarly, Downs et al. (2002) found the
0–100 scales useful in investigating how much impact a number of aspects of internal
communication have on organizational commitment.

Finally, whatever scale is chosen, one must be careful that potential respondents
find the scale simple to use. *Simplicity is an overwhelming consideration in motivating respondents to participate.*

Semantic Differential

This popular scale has been around a long time. It is popular because it provides a very
large amount of information quickly. Basically, the respondent is given a concept followed by a series of bipolar adjectives that describe the concept (Osgood, Suci, &
Tannenbaum, 1967). The respondent is asked to check one of the spaces between each
adjective pair. Gribas and Downs (2002), for example, used a semantic differential scale
to measure how organizational members regarded the concept of "teams." Table 6.4
presents one example.

When you employ a semantic differential scale, choose the adjectives carefully and
vary the list so that not all of the positive attributes are listed on the same side. This variation may help to prevent a response bias resulting from individuals' tendency to answer
everything on the same side. This variation technique can test whether or not people are
filling out the questionnaires carefully. Again, in analyzing the responses, each blank is
coded with a number. In the example here, the range would be 1 to 7.

TABLE 6.4. Example of Semantic Differential Scale

Communication with supervisor

Adequate	_____	_____	_____	_____	_____	_____	_____	Inadequate
Cold	_____	_____	_____	_____	_____	_____	_____	Hot
Trusting	_____	_____	_____	_____	_____	_____	_____	Distrusting
Late	_____	_____	_____	_____	_____	_____	_____	Timely

Rank Order

If you ask a respondent to use a rank order scale, you must not allow the original order of listing to influence the response. Some auditors vary the listing on various questionnaires to randomize any error that comes from the order itself.

Whatever the rating scale employed, a good question allows for a complete range of responses. Sometimes forcing a choice can be useful, but it still is forced. That is why the agree–disagree scale may contain an undecided component or an indication of the degree of strength, and the satisfied–dissatisfied continuum will let a respondent choose among a range of responses so that different degrees of satisfaction are evident. An answer's degree of strength may be very important. For example, if the questionnaire asks the respondent merely to indicate whether he or she agrees or disagrees with a series of statements about communication, he or she could agree with them all; but the response format would not allow discovery of either his or her highest priorities or the things about which he or she feels most strongly. Therefore, some way of measuring the degree of agreement is often helpful.

Use Companion Responses

Ask for similar information in more than one question. For example, one questionnaire asked both "Do you like the kind of work you do?" and "Are you satisfied with your job?" Although both questions contain the element of satisfaction, there are some subtle differences in what they are asking. Furthermore, companion responses may allow you to check the reliability of the answers.

Prepare Simple Instructions and a Cover Letter

The purpose of this instruction is similar to the introduction in an interview: to motivate people to take the time to fill out the questionnaire and to explain to them how to complete it. Motivation is extremely important, because many employees have filled out other questionnaires without ever having received any follow-up. Therefore, motivate them by explaining why it is useful for them to complete the questionnaire and, if possible, suggest how the information is going to be used. Assuring them of confidentiality also has a motivational quality. In addition, we like to have a top manager send a cover letter with the questionnaire to lend credibility to the project as well as to encourage employees to complete it.

Order the Questions

Experience has taught us that the following suggestions about order have merit.
  Ask easy-to-answer questions first. This "hooks" the respondent.
  Ask interest-arousing questions early.
  Intersperse some open questions among the closed ones. Doing so taps the respondents' frames of reference before they are completely structured by the closed questions.

Look for natural ways of grouping questions by topics. In some cases they may be grouped under headings, such as channels or outcomes. There are circumstances, however, when one may also wish to mix up the topic areas. For example, in an audit designed to explore reactions to the communication climate and supervisor–subordinate relations, questions were distributed throughout the questionnaire to investigate either topic. The idea was to circumvent the possibility that the answer to one question might influence the answer to another or that grouping all questions about a certain topic together might condition respondents to answer them all in the same way.

Vary the order in which the questions appear, which also reduces such an effect. Watch for possibilities that answers are conditioned undesirably by answers to preceding questions. This is not often done with standardized questionnaires, but it can be useful in the development of original questionnaires. Furthermore, one can do this easily without affecting coding. Note, however, that coders need to be carefully programmed to make certain the questions are coded appropriately.

Balance positive and negative questions. If organizational weaknesses are probed, also ask about organizational strengths so that it does not appear that the audit is merely interested in the negative side of the organization.

Leave demographics questions until last. Some respondents worry that auditors or managers may try to identify them; therefore, asking for personal information at the beginning of the questionnaire deters them from answering. Ask only for the demographic data that is definitely going to be used. In this way, a consulting audit differs from academic research that often asks for as much demographic data as possible in order to generate as many analyses as possible. The difference is that respondents do not expect the results of research necessarily to be fed back into their organizations.

Pretest the Questions

Pretesting requires that a number of people similar to those in the organization answer each question so that the auditors can determine whether or not respondents are interpreting questions as the authors had intended. Also, we often show a pretest questionnaire to representatives of the organization to get their reactions to its suitability for that organization. Such pretests are valuable in detecting variations in interpretation and range of response. Auditors simply cannot anticipate all the ways that people might interpret a question. *What seems obvious to auditors as they labor over the questionnaire may be lost to the respondent who is viewing it for the first time.* Finally, the pretest is also valuable in determining whether or not the answers can be analyzed in ways that fit the auditor's objectives.

Be Realistic about Response Time

Lengthy questionnaires are not only intimidating at the outset, but they also generate fatigue. If respondents become discouraged, they may skip questions or choose not to complete the questionnaire. Although circumstances may vary, 15–45 minutes is a good time range for completing questionnaires. The expected time to complete the questionnaire should be forecast in the introduction. Keep in mind that filling out a questionnaire is an unusual (and undesirable) activity for many employees.

Somewhat related to this issue is the format for the questionnaire. It is possible to design it so that many questions are put on the same page using a common scale. However, sometimes people put the scale after each question, and this process will take many more pages. We have found that presenting a questionnaire with many pages is disheartening even though respondents are told that they can fill it out quickly. The image of the questionnaire and the promise of quickness appear contradictory.

Present an Attractive Product

Remember that the design affects people's impressions. Therefore, provide wide margins and sufficient space between items. Distinguish carefully between instructions and questions, and use good-quality paper. The more professional the questionnaire looks, the more incentive people have to respond to it.

ADMINISTERING THE QUESTIONNAIRE

Administering a questionnaire involves the distribution and collection of the completed questionnaires. These two processes are quite separate in terms of the mechanics involved, and each is important to the success of the audit.

Distribution

Two things need to be accomplished during distribution. First, the questionnaires should reach all employees at about the same time. Second, the process should *motivate* the employees to respond. Some of the following procedures have been found to be useful.

1. *Publicize the process.* As a part of the publicity, an officer of the company should write a memo backing the audit. This memo is frequently attached to the questionnaire.

2. *Include a cover letter with the questionnaire.* A sample letter is included in Table 6.5. The letter should explain the purpose of the audit, assure confidentiality, forecast how long it might take to answer the questionnaire, and attempt to motivate employees to make their contribution.

3. *Give each individual a personal copy of the questionnaire.* Whenever possible, an auditor should actually hand them out individually and let the employees fill them out according to their own schedules. The advantages of this system are that (a) employees can complete the questionnaire when they want to, (b) anonymity is assured, and (c) costs are minimized since it does not interfere with work. The disadvantages are that (a) some people forget to return the questionnaires and anonymity prevents one from knowing who did not return them; (b) several respondents may discuss the questions, so the answers are not completely uncontaminated; and (c) there is no opportunity for the

TABLE 6.5. Example of Cover Letter

Dear ACME Employee:

For the next 2 weeks, representatives of Communication Management will be conducting a Communication Survey of ACME. The enclosed questionnaire is one part of that survey. The results of the survey will be analyzed and a complete report will be given to ACME. This is an important survey that gives you an opportunity to provide information that might improve the operation of ACME. Therefore, we hope that you will fill it out.

There are several things that we want to emphasize.

1. YOUR COMPLETE ANONYMITY IS GUARANTEED. NO PERSON FROM ACME WILL SEE THE COMPLETED QUESTIONNAIRES.
2. ONCE ALL THE QUESTIONNAIRES ARE COLLECTED, A GENERAL REPORT WILL BE GIVEN TO ACME, AND A SUMMARY REPORT WILL BE GIVEN TO YOU.
3. PLEASE MARK YOUR ANSWERS DIRECTLY ON THE QUESTIONNAIRE, AND PLEASE ANSWER EACH QUESTION, AS EACH HAS SOME SPECIAL MEANING.
4. For the purpose of this survey, certain terms require the use of common definitions.
   - *Immediate supervisor:* The most direct management person of the unit to which you are assigned.
   - *Middle management:* This category represents the managers to whom your supervisor reports.
   - *Top management:* This term refers to the Manager of ACME, Manager of Passenger Systems Development, and Director of Reservation Services.

5. When you have completed the questionnaire–which should take you 15–20 minutes—PLACE IT IN THE BROWN DISPATCH ENVELOPE, AND PUT IT IN THE BOX LOCATED NEXT TO THE EXTRA LIFT CLERK NO LATER THAN 12:00 P.M. WEDNESDAY, (DATE).

PLEASE COMPLETE THEM BY:

Thank you for your cooperation,

David Smith, Director

---

auditor to answer questions about the questionnaire. Although individual distribution by an auditor is the ideal, circumstances sometimes require an adaptation. We have used three alternatives.

First, members of the organization have distributed the questionnaires. For example, in one audit the questionnaires were given to the managers of each unit, who in turn passed them out individually. In this case, a 90% return rate indicated that the process worked well, and it seemed to demonstrate management's backing of the survey.

Second, the questionnaires have been mailed to employees or put in their work mailboxes. This system is much less personal, and the response rates tend to drop. Nevertheless, this may be the only viable alternative. In the audit of a public seminar organization, since the speakers traveled constantly, the only way to obtain their responses was to mail them a questionnaire.

Third, people can assemble in groups to fill out the questionnaire. Such groupings suffer from the fact that time away from work is expensive and that people do not work at the same rate, thus wasting some employees' time. Nevertheless, this group method has three big advantages: (a) The rate of return is high. When we have an opportunity to explain the purpose of a questionnaire or to answer questions, we have rarely had someone refuse to answer the questionnaire. (b) It is fast because the answers are collected immediately. (c) The interaction between the auditor and respondents allows for instructions, questions, and the development of trust. We have used the group process in many settings. One of our manufacturing clients insists on this method as a means of ensuring that everyone fills them out.

Finally, auditors are increasingly putting questionnaires online for respondents to fill out. This works only if everyone has access to the Internet. Security, of course, is a potential problem associated with electronic distribution.

4. *Set a reasonable response time for the questionnaires to be returned.* Three days is generally adequate. If you permit respondents to take longer, they may put the questionnaire on the "back burner." filling out the questionnaire loses its urgency. The time frame should rarely exceed a week.

Collection

Privacy and anonymity must be ensured; these requirements often eliminate the option of individually picking up the completed questionnaires. However, we have found two other systems to be effective. The first is to put a box clearly labeled "audit" in an area of the organization easily accessible to most—that is, a coffee room or receptionist area—and to let respondents seal their questionnaires in envelopes and drop them in the box. In this case, provisions should be made to pick up the envelopes at the end of each day. The second method came at the insistence of an organization who wanted to avoid any possibility of invasion of privacy. Each employee mailed his or her responses directly to our office, using the U.S. Postal Service.

ANALYZING THE QUESTIONNAIRE DATA

Which questionnaires have all the advantages mentioned earlier, you should never lose sight of their limitations. Basically, they report what people think or feel at a particular time. *These self-reports may not represent actual behaviors; the auditor simply infers behavior from the reports.* Auditors should always be mindful of the possibilities for lying, distortion, and misinformed responses caused by a reader misunderstanding a question. The questionnaires can be analyzed in the following ways.

Frequency Distribution

The first task is to prepare a frequency distribution for every question. If we look at the data in Table 6.6, we note immediately how varied the responses are. There is little consensus on many questions. This range of responses is noteworthy. Even though a review of all responses may indicate that there is a problem in a particular area, there may still be people who feel very good about this same area.

Means and Ranks

Once calculated, means can be rank-ordered in descending order to determine what kinds of information people are receiving successfully or least successfully. This process is illustrated in Table 6.6. In this example, Question 96 has the most positive mean and thus would rank first among these items. Question 92 has the least positive mean, and thus the lowest rank, of these questions. Note, however, that even though Question 92 had the lowest rank, a slight majority of respondents were still positive about "up-to-date tools." Furthermore, these results might describe the organization very well in that some groups have better tools than others. The quest would be to discover if those pockets needing improvement can be identified.

Once the process of rank ordering is complete for the data in Table 6.6, compare the means for each item on "amount of information received now" with the "amount I want to receive." For example, "How are you being judged" ranked 13th in terms of information the plant employees now receive, but it ranked fifth in terms of what they wanted to receive. This difference between *what they get* and *what they want* indicates that there may be a problem. It is also possible to discover some areas where more information is given than is needed. In this organization, company policies ranked second in amount of information received, but ranked ninth in terms of what information was wanted. Discrepancies in the rank orders of more than four or five points may point out areas to begin looking for problems. At this time it is perhaps useful to look at some artifacts of this particular scale. Notice that very few people indicated that they want little information

TABLE 6.6 Example of a Frequency Chart

Question	SA 1	A 2	MA 3	I 4	MD 5	D 6	SD 7	Mean
92. Employees have up-to-date tools to do their jobs effectively.	5	22	30	9	16	12	21	4.1
93. ABC's overall business strategy responds to competitive markets proactively.	6	35	36	19	6	10	2	3.2
94. ABC works interdependently as a team.	4	40	43	7	12	6	2	3.1
95. ABC makes me feel successful in my work.	16	37	32	11	11	7	2	2.9
96. Working at ABC is more than a paycheck to me.	29	47	20	8	5	4	1	2.4
97. Classes in ABC's training program are relevant to our agency's strategic intent.	8	35	31	27	9	2	0	3.0
98. I feel secure in my position at ABC.	11	35	25	7	18	11	8	3.6
99. ABC rewards employees who identify needed changes and help implement them.	9	20	29	27	13	10	7	3.6

Note. SA, strong agreement; A, agreement; MA, moderate agreement; MD, moderate disagreement; D, disagreement; SD, strong disagreement; 1, most positive; 7, least negative.

on any topic. Furthermore, in every case they said that they want more information than they are getting. Because people generally feel a need for more information, regardless of how much they receive, we may be measuring a "curiosity index" here rather than a true information need.

Differences between Actual Means

Difference scores can be found by subtracting one mean from another. For example, the score for the amount of information received can be subtracted from the score for the amount that people want to receive.

The possible assumption is that the greater the differences, the more likely it is that a problem exists, because the discrepancy represents a dissatisfaction on that item. These differences can then be rank-ordered to determine the greatest problem areas. An example from the manufacturing plant is given in Table 6.7. The greatest difference occurred for "How you are being judged" (3.86 – 2.08 = 1.78), so the auditors concluded that more information needed to be circulated in this regard. Later, the company implemented a positive discipline approach that spelled out exactly what procedures and standards would be used for infractions. One of the managers praised it for eliminating the ambiguities of judgments.

Such differences in means provide a useful way to assess the strengths and weaknesses of each category, but the categories must also be examined in terms of other data. For example, in a different case, we noted that the greatest discrepancy between what employees wanted and what they were receiving was on a certain item. Nevertheless, when we examined the rank orders of the means on the frequency distribution, we found that the item ranked seventh out of nine on what the workers wanted and nine out of nine on what they received. This finding indicates that the difference may not be really important after all. *Not all statistical differences are meaningful to the analysis.*

Correlations

One of the most popular ways of analyzing data is to select one important item on the questionnaire and determine what other items correlate with it. Actually, correlations identify how answers to questions vary together. A high correlation between two questions, for example, simply means that fluctuations in one answer covary with fluctuations in another answer. Therefore, correlations are often used to explain how communication phenomena coexist. Although correlations do identify positive or negative relationships between items, they *do not necessarily explain cause-and-effect relations.* When we find that satisfaction with personal feedback has a high correlation with job satisfaction, we cannot say that one necessarily *causes* the other.

Statistical Comparisons among Demographic Groups

Most of the information presented so far has been at the organizational level, with data from all employees combined to represent the total organization. This is useful as a beginning point. However, to make some data more meaningful, it is often wise to analyze

TABLE 6.7. Example of Double Scale for Each Question

Topic area	Amount of information received							Amount of information wanted						
	Very little	Little	Some	Great	Very great	Mean	Rank	Very little	Little	Some	Great	Very great	Mean	Rank
Progress in your job	17	22	37	16		2.57	8			39	36	16	3.74	8
Your job requirements	5	21	35	23	5	3.02	4	1	1	22	43	21	3.93	2
The company policies	7	6	45	24	9	3.24	2	2	3	32	39	14	3.67	9
Pay and benefits	2	2	31	42	11	3.66	1		1	17	46	24	4.06	1
How technological changes affect your job	16	18	30	17	9	2.83	6	4	4	35	32	14	3.54	12
Mistakes and failures of the company	31	26	25	6	4	2.20	11	6	5	45	25	9	3.29	13
How you are being judged	35	26	17	11	1	2.08	13	2	2	29	31	26	3.86	5
How your job-related problems are being handled	23	22	33	8	4	2.42	9	1	2	25	38	23	3.90	4
How organization decisions are made that affect your position	34	22	21	10	4	2.20	12	3	3	22	39	22	3.83	6
Promotion and advancement opportunities in the company	22	17	30	19	4	2.63	7	2	2	22	39	26	3.93	3
Important new service of program developments in the company	11	8	45	24	4	3.02	3	2	2	34	40	13	3.66	11
How your job relates to the total operation of the company	12	14	35	21	9	3.01	5	1	3	28	41	17	3.78	7
Specific problems management faces in the company	28	23	27	9	5	2.35	10	2	3	37	30	19	3.67	10

the data across certain demographic parameters. Normally, these comparisons involve some analysis of variance (ANOVA) of the data. For an explanation of analysis of variance, consult a standard text on statistical analysis.

Work Units

There are many ways to divide a company into work units, but four examples will illustrate the point. In a telephone company, management wanted us to compare two groups of operators because they thought there was some friction between the groups. Our audit revealed none. In our audit of an equipment engineering group, we compared the answers of engineers versus nonengineers. These people had to work together. We discussed important differences in their reactions to communication in meetings. In an audit of an airline, we compared the units of three different managers in a department. Finally, in auditing a university, we analyzed each school within the university.

In addition to revealing information about the individual work units, these comparisons help develop comparative standards.

Productive or Less Productive Units

If the auditor has access to data concerning different levels of productivity for units, these data can help determine whether the units differ significantly in terms of communication. Discovering the relationship between communication and productivity is one of the chief aims of any audit.

Gender

It is increasingly popular these days to compare the responses of males versus females. However, in the audits that we have conducted, we have never found meaningful impact on internal communication on the basis of gender.

Satisfied versus Dissatisfied Groupings

Many audits have a measure to report job satisfaction. It is important to find out what communication phenomena really differentiates the satisfied employees from the dissatisfied employees. This analysis can be helpful in identifying what communication problems seem to coexist with the dissatisfaction. It is also a very useful way of determining what problems are most significant.

Managers versus Nonmanagers

Because communication patterns often differ widely between managers and nonmanagers, this is an important comparison to make. Managers generally occupy more central roles in communication networks, and their view of communication adequacy is likely to differ from that of nonmanagers.

Tenure

Length of time on the job sometimes can be a factor in surprising ways. We have found both strengths and dissatisfactions when we had not anticipated them. For example, in a manufacturing plant, we used seniority to judge the reaction to the company's overall communication efforts on a 1–5 scale, with 5 representing the greatest satisfaction. The findings were as follows:

Years	Mean
–1	4.01
1–5	3.23
6–10	3.22
11–15	2.77
15+	3.60

All tenure groups were fairly satisfied with communication except for the 11- to 15-year group. Therefore, we began to probe what was operating within this group. The problem seemed to be related to both age and to career stage. Over time in many audits we have noted a common trend for the members who have worked for a company less than a year to be the most satisfied group; this finding can lead to even more interesting explorations.

Additional Demographics

You may wish to make other comparisons suitable to the organization, the audit, or any research questions. Some additional ones include whether the respondent has had communication training; age; work status (full-time vs. part-time); length of time in the job; pay categories such as salary, hourly, exempt or nonexempt from overtime pay; salary earnings; or mobility (number of previous jobs).

Themes from Open-Ended Questions

One of the limits of any objective questionnaire is that the auditor obtains information that is limited by the question. When answers to open-ended questions are included, however, answers often include themes that would not have been tapped by the objective questions. For example, in a recent audit, we measured the level of commitment to the organization. Then we asked, "What affects your commitment?" There was no great coherence among the answers, but we were able to divide them into "positive" and "negative" categories. Within each of these areas, we then detected the most prevalent themes. Listed below are three themes derived from the comments made about each. Just a year prior to 2001 these comments would never have been made, but this audit was taken after the disastrous terrorist destruction of the World Trade Center on September 11, 2001, and the resulting downturn in the economy. Since there are not many comments made about some themes, there is always the question of how many comments should be made before a theme is reported.

Job Insecurity

This was by far the greatest concern, mentioned by the most respondents. In fact, this was a consistent theme that occurred in answering several of the questions.

"Will my job suffer because we do not get enough new business?"
"ACME represents a large chunk of our business. What would happen if we lost that?"
"Job security."
"Job security is my greatest concern. I am fearful that because I have little billable that is not internal my position may be cut. I am also concerned by the lack of projects that are on the horizon."
"With the economy, loss of clients, and no new big business, job security is a concern."
"The industry is very tight right now and several places have laid off employees. I think a lot of employees are anxious about job security."
"With the loss of Total and the economy, will we have a future here?"

Organizational Loyalty to Me

"That the organization is also loyal to me."
"Organizational loyalty to employees who do good work."
"Loyalty to people and the work they have contributed."

Personal Growth

"A distinct lack of concern regarding my personal growth."
"Training for new people seems minimal."
"That I am always exposed to new things and growing professionally."
"Growth within my department."

CONCLUSION

The ability to design a questionnaire is an important skill for auditors to develop. In Chapter 1 we urged auditors to tailor an audit to the organization; designing an organization-specific questionnaire may be the ultimate way of tailoring the audit.

As desirable as it is to develop one's own questionnaire, another possibility is to use a standardized questionnaire that has been refined through research, has been used extensively, and has produced practical information of immediate use to managers. Three such questionnaires that analyze communication will be reviewed in depth in subsequent chapters: (1) the International Communication Association Survey, (2) the

Downs–Hazen Communication Satisfaction Questionnaire, and (3) ECCO Analysis by Keith Davis. Two new books have been published recently that would be good reference points for viewing other questionnaires: Allen Kraut's *Organizational Surveys* (1995) and Rebecca Rubin et al.'s *Communication Research Measures* (1994).

Finally, we often use a blend of the two options above. We may use a standardized questionnaire because it gives us something that has already been worked out by experts. However, in order to adapt completely to the organization, we may also add our own questions that are specifically designed for that organization. In this case, all the points covered in this chapter will maximize the likelihood of having a thorough, practical questionnaire.

7

The International Communication Association Survey

Under the leadership of Dr. Gerald M. Goldhaber, members of the International Communication Association (ICA) worked together from 1971 to 1979 to develop and refine a method to diagnose communication in organizations. The total assessment package included a standardized survey questionnaire, interviews, observations, network analyses, critical incidents, and a communication diary. Although all of these techniques were incorporated into the ICA audit process, the survey was the one truly unique methodology because others had independently derived the other methods. Therefore, this chapter provides an overview of the ICA survey and offers it as an alternative resource that is readily available and very practical. It should be remembered that the survey is generally used in conjunction with other methods, but it can stand alone and still give practical information.

AN OVERVIEW OF THE SURVEY

One of the outstanding advantages of the survey is its comprehensiveness. Its 122 questions are divided into eight major sections, designed to cover the most important aspects of organizational communication. Some sections are divided into discrete subsections, identified as follows:

1. Amount of Information Actively Received about Topics.
   Amount of Information Desired about These Topics.
2. Amount of Information Actually Sent about Topics.
   Amount of Information Desired to Be Sent about These Topics.

3. Amount of Follow-Up by People Now.
   Amount of Follow-Up Needed.
4. Amount of Information Received from Sources.
   Amount of Information Desired from These Sources.
5. Timeliness of Information Received from Key Sources.
6. Organizational Communication Relationships.
7. Satisfaction with Organizational Outcomes.
8. Amount of Information Received from Channels Now.
   Amount of Information Desired from Channels Now.

Because questions under the various sections are grouped together, it is possible to use some sections while not using others and to get a quick overview of what is actually covered in each individual section. Each section is described separately in this chapter.

For each of the items two scales are used. These scales exist horizontally side by side. The reason for this arrangement is to allow one to subtract the "receive now" score from the "need" score in order to come up with a difference score that may describe gaps.

Scale 1	Scale 2
"This is the amount of information I receive now."	"This is the amount of information I need to receive."
Very little	Very little
Little	Little
Some	Some
Great	Great
Very great	Very great

Information Received

In designing the questions presented in Table 7.1, it was important to decide which kinds of information were most crucial to one's job. A quick review indicates that the two general areas are information useful in doing the job (items 1, 3, 5, 9, 13, and 15) and information useful in keeping informed about the organization (items 11, 17, 19, 21, and 25). While the latter may not be necessary to do the job, this type of information possesses a motivational quality that helps workers identify with their organization.

Sending Information to Others

Because most people seem to be concerned with information they do or do not receive, that area was listed in the first section of the survey. However, workers also need to send information. The questions in Table 7.2 concern the amount they send. Question 37, "Evaluating the performance of my immediate supervisor," may be problematic because not every organization permits the sending of this type of information. Note that all of

TABLE 7.1. Receiving Information from Others

	Amount of information I receive now					Amount of information needed to receive				
	Question	Very little / Little / Some / Great / Very great				Question	Very little / Little / Some / Great / Very great			
How well I am doing in my job	1.	1 2 3 4 5				2.	1 2 3 4 5			
My job duties	3.	1 2 3 4 5				4.	1 2 3 4 5			
Organizational policies	5.	1 2 3 4 5				6.	1 2 3 4 5			
Pay and benefits	7.	1 2 3 4 5				8.	1 2 3 4 5			
How technological changes affect my job	9.	1 2 3 4 5				10.	1 2 3 4 5			
Mistakes and failures of my organization	11.	1 2 3 4 5				12.	1 2 3 4 5			
How I am being judged	13.	1 2 3 4 5				14.	1 2 3 4 5			
How my job-related problems are being handled	15.	1 2 3 4 5				16.	1 2 3 4 5			
How organization decisions are made that affect my job	17.	1 2 3 4 5				18.	1 2 3 4 5			
Promotion and advancement opportunities in my organization	19.	1 2 3 4 5				20.	1 2 3 4 5			
Important new product, service, or program developments in my organization	21.	1 2 3 4 5				22.	1 2 3 4 5			
How my job relates to the total operation of my organization	23.	1 2 3 4 5				24.	1 2 3 4 5			
Specific problems faced by management	25.	1 2 3 4 5				26.	1 2 3 4 5			

126

TABLE 7.2. Sending Information to Others

Instructions for Questions 27 through 40: For each topic listed on the following pages, mark responses on the answer sheet that best indicate: (1) the amount of information one is sending on that topic and (2) the amount of information one needs to send on that topic in order to do one's job.

	Amount of information I receive now						Amount of information needed to receive					
	Question	Little	Very little	Some	Great	Very great	Question	Little	Very little	Some	Great	Very great
Reporting what I am doing in my job	27.	1	2	3	4	5	28.	1	2	3	4	5
Reporting what I think my job requires me to do	29.	1	2	3	4	5	30.	1	2	3	4	5
Reporting job-related problems	31.	1	2	3	4	5	32.	1	2	3	4	5
Complaining about my job and/or working conditions	33.	1	2	3	4	5	34.	1	2	3	4	5
Requesting information necessary to do my job	35.	1	2	3	4	5	36.	1	2	3	4	5
Evaluating the performance of my immediate supervisor	37.	1	2	3	4	5	38.	1	2	3	4	5
Asking for clearer work	39.	1	2	3	4	5	40.	1	2	3	4	5

these questions are oriented toward upward communication in the form of reports, complaints, or requests for more information. It would be possible to phrase additional questions about sending information horizontally to colleagues and downward to subordinates. An example may validate such additions. When we conducted a teamwork seminar for a division of an organization, one of the workers' most frequent complaints was that they did not get enough recognition for their efforts. The employees thought that it was management's responsibility to do the recognizing. Of course, this is management's responsibility—but not management's alone. In fact, our audits have often demonstrated that employees enjoy the people with whom they work and value a very supportive mutual climate. Positive feedback exchanged horizontally becomes a kind of glue that holds groups together, and each member of a group has a responsibility to send such information. An audit reminds one of that responsibility.

Follow-Up on Information Sent

The key to understanding this section is the word "follow-up." We send messages to people, we expect them to be open to those messages, and then to acknowledge or use that information in some way. The question in Table 7.3 attempts to get an impression of how well the major groups with whom one works respond to messages.

Sources of Information

One of the earlier sections focused on the types of information received by employees; this section lists the various sources from which that information can come. It gives each employee an opportunity to indicate how much information he or she receives from each source and how much he or she needs to receive from that source. The list presented in Table 7.4 includes normal classifications for organizations and can be easily adapted to fit the unique sources in the organization under study.

TABLE 7.3. Follow-Up on Information Sent

Instructions for Questions 41 through 50: Indicate the amount of action or follow-up that is and needs to be taken on information one sends to the following.

	Amount of follow-up now					Amount of follow-up needed				
	Question	Little	Very little	Some	Great	Very great	Question	Little	Very little	Some	Great	Very great
Subordinates	41.	1	2	3	4	5	42.	1	2	3	4	5
Coworkers	43.	1	2	3	4	5	44.	1	2	3	4	5
Immediate supervisor	45.	1	2	3	4	5	46.	1	2	3	4	5
Middle management	47.	1	2	3	4	5	48.	1	2	3	4	5
Top management	49.	1	2	3	4	5	50.	1	2	3	4	5

TABLE 7.4. Sources of Information

Instructions for Questions 51 through 68: One not only receives various kinds of information, but one can receive such information from various sources within the organization. For each source listed below, mark responses on the answer sheet that indicate: (1) the amount of information one is receiving from that source and (2) the amount of information one needs to receive from that source in order to do one's job.

	Amount of information I receive now						Amount of information needed to receive					
	Question	Little	Very little	Some	Great	Very great	Question	Little	Very little	Some	Great	Very great
Subordinates (if applicable)	51.	1	2	3	4	5	52.	1	2	3	4	5
Coworkers in my own unit or department	53.	1	2	3	4	5	54.	1	2	3	4	5
Individuals in other units, departments in my organization	55.	1	2	3	4	5	56.	1	2	3	4	5
Immediate supervisor	57.	1	2	3	4	5	58.	1	2	3	4	5
Department meetings	59.	1	2	3	4	5	60.	1	2	3	4	5
Middle management	61.	1	2	3	4	5	62.	1	2	3	4	5
Formal management presentations	63.	1	2	3	4	5	64.	1	2	3	4	5
Top management	65.	1	2	3	4	5	66.	1	2	3	4	5
The "grapevine"	67.	1	2	3	4	5	68.	1	2	3	4	5

Four observations should be made about the interpretation of the data generated from this section. First, these questions involve only general reactions to the sources. They do not, for example, tell the auditor specifically what information is needed but is not being passed on.

Second, a relationship with top management is the one thing that everyone in the organization has in common. Therefore, most audits pinpoint problems with the communication from management. Of course, top management has the responsible for setting some basic mechanisms and establishing the climate for communication. "The buck stops there." Nevertheless, one needs to recognize that part of the result is often an artifact of the audit. Top management is the only category on the questionnaire that is the same for everybody. Employees are not responding to the same coworkers, department meetings, or immediate supervisors. In some cases, it might be wise to note on the questionnaire who constitutes top management because we have found that some employees do not know who the top managers really are.

Third, because of the differences just mentioned, the responses must be compared by units or by departments to make this information meaningful. What good is it, for example, to know that 50 out of 250 people rated their immediate supervisors low in communicating information? What makes a difference in the usefulness of the information is to know whether those 50 complaints are spread across all departments or whether they are concentrated in one or two departments. If it is the latter, specific individuals can be counseled or offered training. When they are shown the data, the supervisors themselves often ask for help.

Fourth, all but one question refers to formal sources. The grapevine, on the other hand, refers to the informal channels so pervasive in most organizations. An interesting tendency we have found is that employees often want less information to come to them through informal channels. It is the only case in which "less is better." For some reason, employees tend to think that information necessary to them should come through formal channels.

Timeliness of Information

There can be no doubt about the importance of timing in the processing of communication. People want information exactly when they need it: if it comes too early, they are temporarily overloaded; if it comes before a useful context is provided for them, then they will not know how to interpret it; if it comes too late, then they face an underload. Therefore, timing is a crucial area to investigate in an audit. Table 7.5 presents the questions concerning timeliness. The focus in this section is again on key sources. Although information derived from these questions contributes to an overall impression of the adequacy of the sources, it does not precisely measure the kinds of information not being received on time. To identify specific needs, one could easily formulate additional questions that ask about the kinds of information that need to be communicated more quickly or one could check it out in follow-up interviews. Some information we have found to be communicated late in organizations include availability of jobs (chemical plant), ticket price changes (airline), summer schedules (university), management

TABLE 7.5. Timeliness of Information Received from Key Sources

Instructions for Questions 69 through 74: Indicate the extent to which information from the following sources is usually timely (one gets information when one needs it—not too early, not too late).

	Question	Very untimely	Little	Some	Great	Very untimely
Subordinates (if applicable)	69.	1	2	3	4	5
Coworkers	70.	1	2	3	4	5
Immediate supervisor	71.	1	2	3	4	5
Middle management	72.	1	2	3	4	5
Top management	73.	1	2	3	4	5
"Grapevine"	74.	1	2	3	4	5

changes (manufacturing plant), new business (public relations firm), and benefit changes (public utility). These examples suggest areas where an auditor might develop meaningful categories. Timeliness is an example of an area where a questionnaire can identify problems that need probing in a second round of interviews.

Although they are not part of the ICA survey, it is sometimes useful to tailor questions about timeliness to the specific circumstances of the organization.

Organizational Communication Relationships

Every time two people communicate, they are not only exchanging information but they are also building, maintaining, or destroying a relationship between them. Therefore, communication relationships are among the most important areas to be examined in any communication audit. The questions presented in Table 7.6 are oriented toward relationships with coworkers, the immediate supervisor, and top management. They also consider the employee's general relationship to the organization. There are more questions about the employee's relationship with his or her immediate supervisor than questions about any other relationship because of the employee–immediate supervisor relationship's extreme importance in communication. In a number of audits the supervisors have been identified as the most important communication link between the employees and the organization. Furthermore, Downs et al. (2002) found the relationship with the supervisor to be one of the most important determinants of an employee's commitment to the organization.

Organizational Outcomes

Organizational communication accomplishes specific purposes. At a basic level, one purpose is to exchange information, but the exchange is supposed to result in something that we call "outcomes." Rensis Likert (1967) listed these outcomes as satisfaction, productivity, union–management relationships, and profit. Characteristically, communication scholars have always had difficulties in isolating the actual impact of general communication on organizational outcomes. These difficulties arise not only from the process nature of communication but also from the difficulties of measuring outcomes.

On the ICA audit, the outcome measured is the individual's satisfaction with the organization. In fact, many items in this section are the same ones that other writers use to measure communication climate. It is important to measure the level of an individual's satisfaction with the organization, the job, and the pay associated with it. Thirteen outcome questions are presented in Table 7.7. The questions in this section do not address level of performance or level of productivity. The auditor must not necessarily assume that low satisfaction results in low productivity. Research does not support such a con-

TABLE 7.6. Organizational Communication Relationships

Instructions for Questions 75 through 93: A variety of communication relationships exist in organizations such as one's own. Employees exchange messages regularly with supervisors, subordinates, coworkers, etc. Considering your relationships with others in your organization, please mark your response on the answer sheet that best describes the relationship.

	Question	Little	Very little	Some	Great	Very great
I trust my coworkers	75.	1	2	3	4	5
My coworkers get along with each other	76.	1	2	3	4	5
My relationship with my coworkers is satisfying	77.	1	2	3	4	5
I trust my immediate supervisor	78.	1	2	3	4	5
My immediate supervisor is honest with me	79.	1	2	3	4	5
My immediate supervisor listens to me	80.	1	2	3	4	5
I am free to disagree with my immediate supervisor	81.	1	2	3	4	5
I can tell my immediate supervisor when things are going wrong	82.	1	2	3	4	5
My immediate supervisor praises me for a good job	83.	1	2	3	4	5
My immediate supervisor is friendly with subordinates	84.	1	2	3	4	5
My immediate supervisor understands my job needs	85.	1	2	3	4	5
My relationship with my immediate supervisor is satisfying	86.	1	2	3	4	5
I trust top management	87.	1	2	3	4	5
Top management is sincere in efforts to communicate with employees	88.	1	2	3	4	5
My relationship with top management is satisfying	89.	1	2	3	4	5
My organization encourages differences of opinion	90.	1	2	3	4	5
I have a say in decisions that affect my job	91.	1	2	3	4	5
I influence operations in my unit or department	92.	1	2	3	4	5
I have a part in accomplishing my organization's goals	93.	1	2	3	4	5

TABLE 7.7. Organizational Outcomes

Instructions for Questions 94 through 106: One of the most important outcomes of working in an organization is the satisfaction one gets or fails to receive through working there. Such satisfaction can relate to the job, one's immediate supervisor, or the organization as a whole. Please mark your response on the answer sheet to indicate the extent to which you are satisfied with the following.

	Question	Little	Very little	Some	Great	Very great
My job	94.	1	2	3	4	5
My pay	95.	1	2	3	4	5
My progress in my organization up to this point in time	96.	1	2	3	4	5
My chances for getting ahead in my organization	97.	1	2	3	4	5
My opportunity to "make a difference" and to contribute to the overall success of my organization	98.	1	2	3	4	5
My organization's system for recognizing and rewarding outstanding performance	99.	1	2	3	4	5
My organization's concern for its members' welfare	100.	1	2	3	4	5
My organization's overall communicative efforts	101.	1	2	3	4	5
Working in my organization	102.	1	2	3	4	5
My organization's effectiveness, as compared to other such organizations	103.	1	2	3	4	5
My organization's overall efficiency of operation	104.	1	2	3	4	5
The overall quality of my organization's product or service	105.	1	2	3	4	5
My organization's achievement of its goals and objectives	106.	1	2	3	4	5

clusion. On the other hand, high levels of dissatisfaction do generate problems, and dissatisfied workers often leave the organization. Therefore, do not minimize the importance of knowing something about people's levels of satisfaction. We assume that if people are really dissatisfied, the level of dissatisfaction is indicative of a problem that ought to be addressed.

Channels of Communication

Every organization communicates through channels, and these channels need to be evaluated periodically. To make this section really valuable, each of the organization's individual channels must be listed. Because the channels will differ among organizations and also within the same organization over time as new technologies develop, there is no standard list. Nevertheless, the ICA survey always contains this section, but the items on the list must be adapted to the specific organization. For illustrative purposes, the comprehensive list shown in Table 7.8 was developed for an audit of a manufacturing plant. The items were generated in conferences with management. Rank ordering the discrep-

TABLE 7.8. Channels of Information

Listed below are a variety of channels through which messages are transmitted. Please indicate on the answer sheet (1) the amount of information you now receive through that channel, and (2) the amount you need to receive through that channel.

	Amount of information I receive now						Amount of information needed to receive					
	Question	Little	Very little	Some	Great	Very great	Question	Little	Very little	Some	Great	Very great
Face to face	107.	1	2	3	4	5	108.	1	2	3	4	5
Telephone	109.	1	2	3	4	5	110.	1	2	3	4	5
Written memos, letters, and notices	111.	1	2	3	4	5	112.	1	2	3	4	5
Bulletin boards	113.	1	2	3	4	5	114.	1	2	3	4	5
Corporate newsletter	115.	1	2	3	4	5	116.	1	2	3	4	5
Plant newsletter	117.	1	2	3	4	5	118.	1	2	3	4	5
Procedural manual	119.	1	2	3	4	5	120.	1	2	3	4	5
Home mailings	121.	1	2	3	4	5	122.	1	2	3	4	5
Pay envelope suffers	123.	1	2	3	4	5	124.	1	2	3	4	5
Communication committee minutes	125.	1	2	3	4	5	126.	1	2	3	4	5
Safety steering committee	127.	1	2	3	4	5	128.	1	2	3	4	5
Shift briefings	129.	1	2	3	4	5	130.	1	2	3	4	5
Meeting with supervisor	131.	1	2	3	4	5	132.	1	2	3	4	5
Meeting with divisional management	133.	1	2	3	4	5	134.	1	2	3	4	5
Meeting with plant management	135.	1	2	3	4	5	136.	1	2	3	4	5
Departmental safety meetings	137.	1	2	3	4	5	138.	1	2	3	4	5

ancy scores is a quick way to see the general reactions to each of these channels. One can also evaluate the effectiveness of the media in terms of cost or effort. An organization may choose not to continue a channel if it costs a lot and does not yield useful results. One manager asked us after introducing a whole new technology to his company, "How will we ever know if it was worth it?" We did not have an answer for him (Lawson & Downs, 1999).

ANALYSIS AND INTERPRETATION

Some of the interpretive implications of the survey have already been explored. This section indicates traditional ways that the data from this questionnaire are analyzed.

Frequency Counts and Means

A basic approach to analyzing the data collected about an organization is to plot the frequencies with which each question is answered on each part of the scale and to compute a mean for all of the responses to that question. The frequency count permits an auditor to examine how individual responses vary across the scale for each question. Such spectrum analysis allows one to determine the degree of agreement in the organization about strengths and weaknesses. The mean, or average, on the other hand, allows comparisons among the items. A rank ordering of the means indicates what employees rate as being most and least effective about the organization.

Difference Scores

Questions 1–68 are designed to gather data about the amount of information being received currently versus the amount needed. Subtract the score of the amount received from the score of the amount wanted or needed, and the resulting difference score theoretically gives one a measure of satisfaction on that question:

Satisfaction = Amount Needed/Wanted − Amount Received Currently

The assumption is that the wider the gap between "need" and "current amount received," the more a problem exists. Therefore, a rank ordering of all different scores will indicate where the major problems occur. This is a legitimate way to analyze the ICA Survey in its entirety or by individual sections.

Demographic Comparisons

Like other questionnaire data, the ICA Survey can be analyzed across all demographic data as was reviewed in Chapter 6. The results allow one to identify where groups are significantly different from one another. In turn, calling attention to group differences can help explain what happens in the organization. We nearly always compare departments as well as make comparisons between management and nonmanagement answers.

ADVANTAGES OF THE ICA SURVEY

The comprehensiveness of the survey has already been noted, but there are other positive aspects that should be mentioned. Conceived by scholars and seasoned through years of pilot testing, the ICA Survey has received great academic scrutiny. Although it has been somewhat controversial, many auditors have used it successfully. Furthermore, frequent usage has prompted people to refine it in significant ways, such that the end product is a highly usable instrument. The survey has proved to be adaptable to many kinds of organizations: banks, colleges, military units, governmental organizations, hospitals, unions, manufacturing plants, airlines, utilities, volunteer organizations, and retail operations. Furthermore, the sizes of the organizations have varied widely. The reliability and validity of the survey questions have been thoroughly researched and documented. Goldhaber and others have tested each section of this questionnaire extensively. Their reliability and validity scores are demonstrated in Table 7.9. The reliability coefficients show the extent to which people answer the question the same way across time. Validity determines whether or not auditors are measuring what they think they are measuring. In this case, the coefficients measure the correlations between each scale and the organizational outcomes scale. Finally, the discrimination ability percentages indicate the number of items that significantly discriminated between the top 17% of the respondents and the bottom 17% (Goldhaber & Rogers, 1979, p. 34).

The fact that a data bank is available gives this instrument an enormous advantage. From the beginning, the ICA scholars set out to build a data bank that might generate the compilation of norms for comparative purposes. In 1979, for example, Porter synthesized the results of 17 audits representing responses from 4,600 people. While the expectation of building truly national norms has never been fully realized, the data banks are available for comparative and research purposes. They are currently housed at SUNY–Buffalo, Ohio University, Purdue University, and the University of South Florida. Access to them can be obtained by contacting members of the communication departments at these universities.

TABLE 7.9. Measurement Adequacy of the ICA Survey

	Reliability	Validity	Discrimination ability
Amount of information received	.88	.69	100%
Amount of information desired	.85	.07	100%
Amount of information sent	.83	.56	100%
Amount of information desired to send	.79	.10	100%
Amount of information received from sources	.70	.63	78%
Amount of information desired from sources	.76	.06	89%
Relationships	.90	.70	n.a.
Organizational outcomes	.88	n.a.	100%

Note. n.a., not available.

Although it is exciting to be able to compare one organization with others, extreme caution must be used when comparing data from a local company with data from many different organizations throughout the country. For this reason, some auditors have begun to develop regional data banks. DeWine, James, and Wallence (1985) have done this at Ohio University, and they have found that the regional norms often differ from the national data.

The ultimate testimony to this instrument is that it has performed well as a practical analytic tool. DeWine et al. (1985) surveyed several organizations that had been audited, and they discovered "noticeable improvement" in most communication variables except load. Despite the advantages, the survey is vulnerable in some significant ways, which are discussed in the next section.

VULNERABILITIES OF THE ICA SURVEY

Some of the vulnerabilities of the instrument have been exposed through extensive use. These are pointed out here not to attack the survey but to suggest that any potential user may encounter certain problems.

Many respondents have complained about the length and complexity of the survey. There have been reports that some people do not finish it, and some managers resent the "downtime" at work because it takes so long to fill out. Because this liability is indeed inherent in the instrument, extra care must be taken in administering the survey to motivate respondents.

Originally, a 5-point Likert scale was used; this is what is described in this chapter. As auditors have become more sophisticated, they have looked for more refined scaling techniques. Today, some people have rejected the Likert scale and have replaced it with different kinds of scales. The differences in scaling sometimes make it difficult to compare data from new and old audits.

Ambiguous terms also constitute a problem. The respondents are sometimes uncertain what is being asked or the auditors are not certain how the question was interpreted. For example, in one section employees are asked to contrast the amount of information wanted and the amount currently received. The amount received is then subtracted from the amount wanted to compute a difference score. One question emerged as a significant difference score in two different audits; it was ranked as the number-one difference score in one audit and as number two in the other. The topic area was "how organizational decisions are made that affect your position." Employees in both organizations wanted a great deal more information than they were receiving about this topic. It was one of our most significant findings, and we were at a loss to interpret how employees perceived the question. In which decisions were they interested? The ambiguous item thus stymied the interpretation.

Another significant result that was difficult to interpret was the extent to which "I have a say in decisions that affect my job" (Question 91). Since the question did not ask the respondent to contrast the amount he or she wanted with the amount now received, the finding is problematic. Should we assume that low participation is necessarily a problem? This question may reflect a bias toward participatory decision making, but not all workers want to have more say than they have. *The problem with questions such as these is not that the analysis cannot generate possible interpretations, but rather that these interpretations may not be faithful to the meanings intended by respondents.*

The form of the comparison of the amount of information needed or wanted minus the amount received creates another difficulty in interpreting the questionnaire data. Using the terms "want" or "need" apparently biases the respondent to indicate that high levels of information are desired, implying deficiencies in sharing information in the organization. Perhaps the most telling proof for this conclusion is that in audits, every respondent, on every difference question pair except one (information from the grapevine), always indicated that they needed more information than they received. Thus, the scale may be more of a "curiosity index" than an information needs inventory.

The ICA Survey is basically a self-report, perception-based instrument. Therefore, it is subject to questions about the congruence between the report and actual communication realities. This, of course, is a legitimate objection. It can, however, be answered in two ways. First, discovery of perceptions is important because these perceptions often determine how people behave. Second, the survey instrument is rarely used alone. The complete audit calls for it to be used with other methodologies that may overcome the reliance on mere self-report. In this regard, what the auditor observes about actual communication is important, but it may not be any more important than the members' beliefs about the "truth" of the matter.

Occasionally, auditors discover that this instrument, while comprehensive, still leaves out significant areas. Since the survey does not analyze structure, networks, or the environment context in which the organization is working, it would not meet all of the needs of people interested in those topics. For these kinds of objections, however, one should remember that the ICA Survey is merely one tool available for use in conjunction with other methodologies to build a comprehensive assessment of the organization.

CONCLUSION

The descriptions of the ICA Survey have been brief by necessity. A greater appreciation of its history, development, and significance can be obtained from Goldhaber and Rogers (1979), Goldhaber and Krivonos (1978), and Greenbaum et al. (1983). Since 1979 the pooled effort so instrumental in the survey's development has declined. The emphasis on the ICA Survey diminished because of administrative and legal considerations. At one point, the ICA officers decided that they could not be liable for its use. Therefore, the coordinated effort that had constructed the instrument was diminished and no one individual or no group really had control or influence over its use. To our knowledge, there has been no effort to coordinate all the results from audits using it. Nevertheless, it continues to be a viable tool for individual auditors, and as such it merits attention.

8

Downs–Hazen Communication Satisfaction Questionnaire

PHILLIP G. CLAMPITT
CAL W. DOWNS

The Communication Satisfaction Questionnaire (ComSat) was developed about the same time as the ICA Survey. It grew out of the same discussions with other ICA members. It is less comprehensive than the ICA Survey, but it offers both an efficient and a comprehensive approach to auditing the communication practices of organizations. One significant difference between the two questionnaires is how they were developed. The questions on the ICA Survey are a theoretical compilation of all those areas that the team thought might be significant to measure in an organization. Downs was a member of that team. By contrast, the questions on the ComSat were selected on the basis of factor analysis out of an original pool of many questions. *Factor analysis* is a statistical technique that combines into clusters those questions that seem to be measuring the same phenomena.

Composed of only 60 items, the ComSat has proved to be easy and quick to administer while being remarkably thorough in covering a variety of communication practices that range from personal feedback to corporate-wide communications. In fact, it has been the basis for more than 30 PhD dissertations and MA theses. During the past decade it has been used in several foreign countries as well as the United States; some translations can be obtained from Communication Management, Inc. at *www.commgt.com*. It has also been used in many different kinds of organizations, including manufacturing plants, television stations, school districts, consulting firms, banks, hotels, mental health centers, advertising agencies, airlines, hospitals, and police departments. In short, this instrument has proved to be exceptionally useful in a variety of organizations. This chapter discusses how to utilize it in a communication audit.

HISTORICAL DEVELOPMENT

Traditionally, communication satisfaction was thought to be a unidimensional construct. Thayer (1968) defined *communication satisfaction* as "the personal satisfaction inherent in successfully communicating to someone or in successfully being communicated with . . ." (p. 144). Redding (1972) reviewed some of the literature about communication satisfaction and asked whether communication satisfaction may indeed be a multidimensional concept. Such questions often spur theoretical and empirical research.

Indeed, two research efforts have suggested that communication satisfaction is multidimensional. Osmo Wiio's (1976) work suggested four dimensions of communication satisfaction: job satisfaction, message content, improvements in communication, and channel efficiency. He conducted 22 organizational communication audits in Finland and factor-analyzed the results.

Downs and Hazen (1977) used similar procedures to investigate the communication satisfaction question. They developed a questionnaire and administered it to 225 employees from many kinds of organizations, including a military unit, a hospital, professional organizations, businesses, and universities. The results were factor-analyzed, and a new questionnaire was refined and administered to four different organizations. Factor analysis led to the identification of eight stable dimensions of communication satisfaction, all of which are described below.

1. *Satisfaction with communication climate* reflects communication on both the organizational and the personal level. On the one hand, it includes items relating to the extent to which communication in the organization motivates workers to meet organizational goals. On the other hand, it includes estimates of the degree to which people's attitudes toward communicating are healthy in this organization. Workers often tend to think of climate when they respond to general questions about communication.

2. *Satisfaction with communication with supervisors* includes both upward and downward aspects of communicating with superiors. For example, it measures subordinate's perceptions of how open the managers are to their ideas as well as how adequately manager keep subordinates informed.

3. *Satisfaction with organizational integration* revolves around the degree to which individuals receive information about the immediate work environment such as departmental plans and personnel news. Such information makes them feel a vital part of the organization.

4. *Satisfaction with media quality* obtains reactions to meetings, written directives, and several other important communication channels. It also covers the degree to which the total amount of communication in the organization is seen as adequate.

5. *Satisfaction with horizontal and informal communication* concerns the degree to which the grapevine is active and the degree to which horizontal and informal communication is accurate and free-flowing.

6. *Satisfaction with organizational perspective* concerns the degree to which employees receive the broadest kind of information about the organization as a whole. It includes notification about changes, information about the organization's financial standing, and information about the overall mission of the organization.

7. *Satisfaction with communication with subordinates* focuses on upward and downward communication with subordinates, who are expected to be responsive to downward communication and also to anticipate the supervisor's needs and initiate upward communication that will be helpful.

8. *Satisfaction with personal feedback* is one of the strongest dimensions because workers in general have a need to know how they are being judged and how their performance is being appraised.

Downs and Hazen (1979) concluded that "it is possible that the various dimensions of communication satisfaction can provide a barometer of organizational functioning, and the concept of communication satisfaction can be a useful tool in an audit or organizational communication" (p. 72). Hecht (1978) reviewed various instruments used to assess communication satisfaction. Generally he was quite critical of most approaches used to measure communication satisfaction, but his remarks on the ComSat were positive:

> The thoroughness of the construction of this satisfaction measure is apparent. While one could comment on the fatigue factor in requiring respondents to complete 264 scales (88 items multiplied by three scaling styles), the strategies employed in the original study are exemplary. Input into initial item construction was obtained from a wide variety of sources, and items were tested and factor analyzed for variety of scaling styles. Internal consistency, reliability for each dimension, and validity information as a whole are lacking. (p. 363)

Crino and White (1981) reported a study that answered most of Hecht's concerns. The subjects were 137 first-line supervisors from five textile mills. After their data collection, the researchers sought to determine the dimensional stability and intrascale internal consistency of the measure. Their results show that the eight-factor solution is reasonable. While the intrascale internal consistency is not as strong as it could be, the scales are still useful. They conclude that "although still in a somewhat embryonic stage of development, the construct, communication satisfaction, appears to possess few of the problems which have plagued the construct, organizational climate" (p. 832). Thus, the ComSat provides a uniquely theoretical and empirically sound method of gathering information about organizational communication. And, as was pointed out in the beginning of the chapter, people have continued to investigate the ComSat through dissertations and theses, as well as numerous consulting projects, making it a thoroughly studied instrument with great credibility. Downs has used it productively in 14 different countries, thus illustrating its practical significance.

OVERVIEW OF THE QUESTIONNAIRE

Of particular importance to the auditor is the actual content of the survey. Table 8.1 contains the basic questionnaire used in numerous organizational audits.

Two questions are open-ended and seek to determine what types of communication changes could be made that would increase employee satisfaction and productivity. Analysis of the responses to these open-ended questions provides a useful check on the statistical data generated from the closed questions. Frequently the problems highlighted in the open-ended responses serve to confirm the results of the other parts of the survey; sometimes they fill gaps not tapped by the closed questions. In addition, when reporting the results to a company, a well-turned phrase garnered from the qualitative data can sometimes be more persuasive than statistical data.

Four survey items are reflective of end-product variables. Two of these questions ask employees to indicate their degree of job satisfaction and whether their level of job satisfaction has decreased, increased, or stayed the same during the past 6 months. Similar questions are used to assess employee productivity. As a group these four questions are often the focus of much discussion in feedback sessions with management. Through the use of statistical correlations, the auditor can frequently "explain" the productivity and satisfaction levels by relating these variables to the communication satisfaction factors. In recent years, Downs and his colleagues have added an outcome variable of organizational commitment.

Forty items ask about employee satisfaction with various types of communication that correspond to the eight factors discussed previously. Each factor consists of five items determined through initial factor analyses. Various scaling devices have been used. Originally it contained a 1–7 scale, ranging from "satisfied" to "dissatisfied." Downs and Adrian continue to use this scale, partly because of the large respondent pool, which numbers more than 6,000. However, Clampitt prefers the 0–10 scale because it offers greater choices to respondents. When describing this kind of scale on the survey, it is important to use the language "by placing a 0–1–2–3–4–5–6–7–8–9–10 in the blank provided" instead of "by placing a number from 0–10." Using the latter often results in respondents only utilizing zeros, fives, and 10s on the surveys. Hence, the full value of the scaling device is not realized, which is like using only certain gears on a 10-speed bicycle.

Organizations frequently wish to add other questions to the survey. We encourage these additions for two reasons. First, they allow the company to develop ownership of the survey, which may strengthen commitment to the process and ensure a higher return rate. The aim is to move the discussion from "the auditor's questionnaire" to "our company survey." Second, adding their questions can help ease pressure to change the wording of questions at the heart of the survey. Any changes in the wording of the 40 key items hinder the reliability of the survey. While encouraging additional questions is useful, it is important to avoid an overly enthusiastic response so that too many questions are added. Sometimes we have to deal with a client that wanted to double the size of the instrument. Remember that part of the charm of this instrument is its brevity.

TABLE 8.1. Communication Satisfaction Questionnaire, by Cal W. Downs and Michael D. Hazen

INTRODUCTION: Most of us assume that the quality and amount of communication in our jobs contribute to both our job satisfaction and our productivity. Through this study we hope to find out how satisfactory our communication practices are and what suggestions you have for improving them.

We appreciate you taking the time to complete the questionnaire. Hopefully, you should be able to complete it in 10–15 minutes.

Your answers are completely confidential, so be as frank as you wish. This is not a test—your opinion is the only right answer. Do not sign your name; we do not wish to know who you are.

The answers will be combined into groups for reporting purposes. An initial report will be given to management and a brief report will be distributed to all employees.

1. How satisfied are you with your job? (Check one)
   1. Very dissatisfied
   2. Dissatisfied
   3. Somewhat dissatisfied
   4. Indifferent
   5. Somewhat satisfied
   6. Satisfied
   7. Very satisfied

2. In the past 6 months, what has happened to your level of satisfaction? (Check one)
   1. Stayed the same
   2. Gone up
   3. Gone down

3. If the communication associated with your job could be changed in any way to make you more satisfied, please indicate how. _____

A. Listed below are several kinds of information often associated with a person's job. Please indicate how satisfied you are with the amount and/or quality of each kind of information by circling the appropriate number at the right.

   1 = Very dissatisfied   2 = Dissatisfied   3 = Somewhat dissatisfied   4 = Indifferent
   5 = Somewhat satisfied   6 = Satisfied   7 = Very satisfied

4. Information about my progress in my job.	1	2	3	4	5	6	7
5. Personnel news.	1	2	3	4	5	6	7
6. Information about company policies and goals.	1	2	3	4	5	6	7
7. Information about how my job compares with others.	1	2	3	4	5	6	7
8. Information about how I am being judged.	1	2	3	4	5	6	7
9. Recognition of my efforts.	1	2	3	4	5	6	7
10. Information about departmental policies and goals.	1	2	3	4	5	6	7
11. Information about the requirements of my job.	1	2	3	4	5	6	7
12. Information about government regulatory action affecting ACME.	1	2	3	4	5	6	7
13. Information about changes in ACME.	1	2	3	4	5	6	7
14. Reports on how problems in my job are being handled.	1	2	3	4	5	6	7
15. Information about employee benefits and pay.	1	2	3	4	5	6	7
16. Information about profits and/or financial standing.	1	2	3	4	5	6	7
17. Information about achievements and/or failures of the organization.	1	2	3	4	5	6	7

(continued)

TABLE 8.1. *(continued)*

B. Please indicate how satisfied you are with the following by circling the appropriate number at right.

18. Extent to which my managers/supervisors understand the problems faced by staff.   1 2 3 4 5 6 7

19. Extent to which ACME's communication motivates me to meet its goals.   1 2 3 4 5 6 7

20. Extent to which my supervisor listens and pays attention to me.   1 2 3 4 5 6 7

21. Extent to which the people in ACME have great ability as communicators.   1 2 3 4 5 6 7

22. Extent to which my supervisor offers guidance for solving job-related problems.   1 2 3 4 5 6 7

23. Extent to which communication in ACME makes me identify with it or feel a vital part of it.   1 2 3 4 5 6 7

24. Extent to which ACME communications are interesting and helpful.   1 2 3 4 5 6 7

25. Extent to which my supervisor trusts me.   1 2 3 4 5 6 7

26. Extent to which I receive in time the information needed to do my job.   1 2 3 4 5 6 7

27. Extent to which conflicts are handled appropriately through proper communication channels.   1 2 3 4 5 6 7

28. Extent to which the grapevine is active in ACME.   1 2 3 4 5 6 7

29. Extent to which my supervisor is open to ideas.   1 2 3 4 5 6 7

30. Extent to which communication with other employees at my level is accurate and free-flowing.   1 2 3 4 5 6 7

31. Extent to which communication practices are adaptable to emergencies.   1 2 3 4 5 6 7

32. Extent to which my work group is compatible.   1 2 3 4 5 6 7

33. Extent to which our meetings are well organized.   1 2 3 4 5 6 7

34. Extent to which the amount of supervision given me is about right.   1 2 3 4 5 6 7

35. Extent to which written directives and reports are clear and concise.   1 2 3 4 5 6 7

36. Extent to which the attitudes toward communication in ACME are basically healthy.   1 2 3 4 5 6 7

37. Extent to which informal communication is active and accurate.   1 2 3 4 5 6 7

38. Extent to which the amount of communication in ACME is about right.   1 2 3 4 5 6 7

C. Please indicate your estimates of your productivity.

39. How would one rate your productivity in your job?
    1. Very low
    2. Low
    3. Slightly lower than most
    4. Average
    5. Slightly higher than most
    6. High
    7. Very high

(continued)

TABLE 8.1. *(continued)*

40. In the last 6 months, what has happened to your productivity?
    1. Stayed the same
    2. Gone up
    3. Gone down

41. If the communication associated with your job could be changed in any way to make you more productive, please tell how.

D. Indicate your satisfaction with the following *only if you are responsible for staff* as a manager or supervisor.

42. Extent to which my staff are responsive to downward-directive communication.	1	2	3	4	5	6	7
43. Extent to which my staff anticipate my needs for information.	1	2	3	4	5	6	7
44. Extent to which I *can avoid* having communication overload.	1	2	3	4	5	6	7
45. Extent to which my staff are receptive to evaluations, suggestions, and criticisms.	1	2	3	4	5	6	7
46. Extent to which my staff feel responsible for initiating accurate upward communication.	1	2	3	4	5	6	7

ANALYSIS

Quantitative and qualitative data can be used to arrive at conclusions. The related data analysis techniques that have special significance for the instrument are reviewed next. All of the data used for illustration in this chapter came from actual audits.

Quantitative Data

Few research activities are more routine than entering data in a computer and utilizing statistical packages to calculate means, standard deviations, and frequency counts. Assuming that this step has been completed, there are several approaches that can be used at this juncture: (1) categorize item groups; (2) rank-order items; (3) utilize factor scores; and (4) make data comparisons.

Categorize Items

A thorough examination of the means and standard deviations for each survey item can prove revealing. In a very rough and tentative fashion, those mean scores that fall well below the conceptual midpoint (a 5 on a 0–10 scale or a 4 on a 1–7 scale) can be thought of as weaknesses. Those scores that are well above the conceptual midpoint can be seen as strengths. Scores falling around the mean are areas of average satisfaction. For instance, if a company had percentages of employees giving the following responses to Question 9, the auditor would be safe in tentatively concluding that the feedback area was an area of concern for many employees. More specifically, the auditors would want to explore the issue of praise and how individuals are recognized for good work within the organization.

Question 9: Recognition of my efforts.

Level of satisfaction					
Low				High	Mean
0–2	3–4	5–6	7–8	9–10	
24%	10%	34%	18%	13%	3.94

On the other hand, should the results reveal that the mean for Question 25 is 8.64, it would be reasonable to conclude that supervisory communication is an area of strength. However, that may be a hasty conclusion if other questions about the supervisory relationship are not rated equally high. Remember also that not everyone is responding to the same supervisor, so there is often a need to tease out unit responses. Hence, the auditor must use a great deal of discernment in coming to these conclusions.

Question 25: Extent to which my supervisor trusts me.

Level of satisfaction					
Low				High	Mean
0–2	3–4	5–6	7–8	9–10	
9%	6%	19%	34%	32%	8.64

The difficulty with this approach is that sometimes no items fall in the dissatisfied area. Is it proper to assume that this company has no communication difficulties? Conversely, there are companies that have been audited in which few items fall in the satisfied area. Can the auditor then assume the organization has few communication strengths? Or, more to the point, can the argument be made that all companies have at least some communication strengths and some weaknesses? No doubt that proposition could be debated at some depth. Yet making such an assumption is a sound strategy in actually reporting the results. For ineffective organizations, designating certain strengths can be motivating and encouraging. For effective organizations, designating weaknesses can stimulate even better performance. If this assumption can be made, some other method is needed to arrive at conclusions, which leads us to the next method.

The Rank-Order Method

Each of the 40 communication satisfaction items can be rank-ordered on the basis of the means from 1 to 40. Statistical tests can be used to determine which items are significantly different from one another. Hence, a group of relatively high, moderate, and low means emerge. These groupings can be examined to determine conceptual patterns within each group. Based on the auditor's knowledge of the organization, certain items will appear to cluster together naturally, pointing to certain areas of strength and weakness. For instance, Table 8.2 contains the items clustered at the top of the ranking in one audit.

What kinds of observations can one draw from these data? Clearly, a number of the questions cluster together around supervisory communication and coworker communication, suggesting that these are areas of relative strength in this organization. Formal communication practices such as written directions and information about pay/benefits also seem to be relatively theoretical dimensions of communication satisfaction. In this case the auditors, using other supporting data as well as the survey items, concluded that the area of "formal communication" was a unique strength of this particular company. Hence, an item-by-item ranking of the questions, used in conjunction with other methods, can suggest conclusions other than those designated by the eight communication satisfaction factors. The obvious difficulty with the rank-order method is that communication strengths and weaknesses are always discovered. In the context of the rank-order method, an item of average satisfaction could actually emerge as a strength if the absolute standard method suggested previously is used. In the last example, some of the items may be thought of as strengths but may actually fall in the "average satisfaction" area. Hence, the auditor should always temper this type of conclusion by underscoring the fact that these are *relative* strengths or weaknesses.

Factor Scores

Another method of arriving at conclusions is to calculate the factor scores for each of the eight communication satisfaction dimensions. In fact, one of the most compelling analytic tools is to analyze everything in terms of the factors. The factor key can be obtained from Cal W. Downs, Communication Management, Inc., Box 3242, Lawrence, KS,

TABLE 8.2. Sample Rank Order of Means on a 0–10 Scale

Rank	Mean	Question
1	6.88	Extent to which my work group is compatible.
2	6.87	Extent to which the grapevine is active in our organization.
3	6.68	Extent to which my supervisor trusts me.
4	6.66	Extent to which the amount of supervision given to me is about right.
5	6.35	Extent to which my supervisor is open to ideas.
6	6.31	Extent to which written directives and reports are clear and concise.
7	6.29	Information about employee benefits and pay.
8	6.15	Extent to which my supervisor listens and pays attention to me.
9	6.04	Extent to which horizontal communication with other employees is accurate and free-flowing.
10	5.55	Extent to which my supervisor offers guidance for solving job-related problems.

66046. Permission is readily granted to people wishing to use the questionnaire for academic purposes if they (1) will furnish a copy of their report, (2) will not publish the factor structure, and (3) will limit their use to academic purposes.

The factor scores could be compared to the conceptual midpoint. Clampitt consistently uses a 10-point scale; Downs uses a 7-point scale. With the 0–10 scale this midpoint would be 25 for each factor, because there are five items per dimensions. Rank ordering the factor scores and testing for statistical significance could also prove to be useful.

Theoretically, utilizing the factor scores should prove revealing because each of the five items that make up an individual factor are measuring the "same thing." Yet using only the factor scores may obscure subtle differences unique to a particular company. Hence, auditors should examine individual survey items in addition to the factor scores. Note that, in addition to factor analysis, statistical analyses such as principal component analysis can be used to explore the unique groupings for each organization.

Correlations

A *correlation* is a common statistical technique used to show how two variables vary together. Correlations are often used to determine which factors are most closely connected to levels of satisfaction. For example, it is assumed that there may be a close relationship between job satisfaction and personal feedback if they have a high correlation. These kinds of results can give information useful in interpretation.

One problem with the ComSat is that sometimes several factors correlate highly with each other. From a statistical viewpoint, these relationships blur the distinctions between the factors and create problems if researchers are trying to use certain kinds of statistical tests on them; on the other hand, the high correlations do not create practical problems for analyzing a particular organization in terms of factors. Theoretically, it makes sense for communication factors to be correlated to each other.

Data Bank Comparisons

One of the more exciting alternatives now available is the comparison of one organization's results to those of other companies. Such an opportunity is enthusiastically embraced by most organizations because most want to know "how they stack up." Comparisons often add meaning to the actual numerical scores obtained in the audit. To date, the communication audit data bank at the University of Wisconsin–Green Bay's Communication Research Center has responses from more than 1,400 individuals in 18 companies. The database collected during a 4-year period includes a wide range of organizations, such as banks, TV stations, and manufacturing companies. Furthermore, the response rate from the various organizations surveyed is relatively high at over 84%. Hence, a reasonable cross section of individuals and organizations is represented in the data. One of the problems of the database is that it has been generated in only one section of the country. Yet the firms are representative of the types of organizations found in other locales. In spite of this minor difficulty, the data bank provides a useful research base. There are two formats of output. Table 8.3 indicates the summary rankings of the

TABLE 8.3. Summary Rankings of Communication Satisfaction Factors

Overall rank	Range	Dimension
1	1–4	Subordinate Communication
2	1–4	Supervisor Communication
3	2–6	Organizational Integration
4	1–8	Horizontal Communication
5	3–8	Media Quality
6	2–8	Corporate Perspective
7	4–8	Communication Climate
8	5–7	Personal Feedback

ComSat factors in the Green Bay data bank. Auditors can examine how closely the rankings of factors in the target organization compare with these database rankings.

Table 8.4 lists the actual means and standard deviations for the respondents in the Green Bay data bank. Once the means and standard deviations for the client organization have been determined, standard statistical tests can determine if the differences are significant.

The data bank compiled by Downs not only covers over 6,000 people in different kinds of organizations, it also contains analyses from organizations in many different countries: Mexico, Nigeria, Guatemala, Thailand, Australia, Scotland, England, The Netherlands, Finland, and Taiwan. Therefore, some cultural comparisons can also be made. Table 8.5 contains the results of 10 audits from the Downs Data Bank. Examine the results closely and see what observations or trends you can determine. Is there, for example, any statements you can make about which factors are rated highest and which tend to be rated lowest? If there are organizations that do not follow these trends, what might be happening?

TABLE 8.4. UWGB Data Bank Norms

Rank	Dimension	Mean	SD	N
1	Supervisor Communication	34.18	10.50	1,370
2	Subordinate Communication	33.43	8.62	323
3	Horizontal Communication	31.81	7.84	1,344
4	Organizational Integration	29.62	9.54	1,371
5	Media Quality	29.17	9.14	1,344
6	Communication Climate	26.56	10.23	1,358
7	Corporate Information	26.35	11.12	1,360
8	Personal Feedback	23.99	10.68	1,366

Note. All results are based on a 0–50 scale, with 50 designating the maximum satisfaction. Only complete cases can be used for analysis, so the size of N varies from factor to factor.

TABLE 8.5. Sample Means from Downs Data Bank

Nation	Type and number	Sup.	Sub.	Horiz.	Climate	OP	OI	Media	PF
USA	Hospital (100)	3.5	n.a.	3.7	4.3	4.1	3.6	3.8	4.2
USA	Service (250)	3.0	n.a.	3.4	4.0	3.9	3.3	3.5	3.7
USA	Marketing (200)	2.3	2.7	3.0	3.4	3.1	2.9	3.1	3.1
USA	Manufacturing (400)	3.4	3.2	3.5	4.5	4.0	3.5	4.1	4.4
USA	Government (161)	3.0	3.2	3.7	4.7	4.2	3.6	3.8	4.1
USA	Airline (201)	3.8	2.7	2.7	3.8	3.2	3.3	3.4	3.8
Guatemala	Service (121)	2.6	2.2	3.2	3.0	3.6	2.2	2.9	3.6
Australia	Manufacturing (100)	2.6	2.4	2.9	3.4	3.3	3.2	3.0	3.8
Australia	Government (54)	2.7	2.8	3.2	3.8	3.7	3.0	3.3	3.8
Thailand	Manufacturing (117)	3.1	n.a.	3.2	3.4	3.5	3.3	3.3	3.4
Korea	Manufacturing (131)	3.7	n.a.	3.6	3.8	4.0	3.7	3.7	4.0

1, very satisfied; 7, very dissatisfied; n.a., not available.

Since companies differ in terms of functions, procedures, competitive environment, and goals, it may not always be appropriate to compare some organizations to others in the data bank. However, there is a capability to evaluate the target organization against similar types of organizations. For example, the auditor could compare a savings and loan to other financial institution in the data bank.

A more perplexing problem can occur when this technique is used in conjunction with the other approaches detailed in previous sections. In the first three methods, the basis of comparison is internal. The organization is examined essentially in isolation, which is similar to asking the question "What are the strengths and weaknesses of the Green Bay Packers compared to the other teams in the NFL?" This situation can set up some interesting dilemmas. An item or factor that emerges as a weakness using the rank-order method may turn out to be a strong point when the data bank analysis is conducted. The situation would be like the Packers rating their linebackers as the weakness of their team when they look internally, even though when compared to other NFL teams the Packer linebackers look fairly impressive. Resolution of this dilemma can only occur when the auditor and the client agree on adopting a given perspective in light of the objectives of the audit.

Qualitative Data

One of the most enlightening aspects of the audit is reading through the responses to the open-ended questions. But this step can also be the most misleading. One particularly insightful or impressive comment may become overly persuasive in weighing the actual evidence. To avoid these difficulties, a rigorous system of analysis, known as *content analysis,* is needed. The process has been reviewed in considerable depth elsewhere (Krippendorff, 1980), but typically the following steps are involved.

- *Step 1.* Read through the entire list of responses and try to discern central concerns that are common to many of these respondents. After you make a thorough review of all the responses, you should notice the emergence of a series of nonoverlapping categories for ____ of the open-ended questions. For example, assume that the following comments were made to the question about communication changes needed to prove job satisfaction.

    A. "More listening by managers."
    B. "Would like more responsiveness to upward communication."
    C. "More meetings."
    D. "More coverage of our department in the newsletter."
    E. "There are not enough meetings."
    F. "The newsletter is frivolous."

The categories that emerge could be as follows:

    1. Improvement of upward communication (Responses A and B)
    2. More meetings (Responses C and E)
    3. Changes in newsletter (Responses D and F)

- *Step 2.* Another auditor should read through the same list of responses and, without discussion with the first auditor, should make his or her own list of categories.
- *Step 3.* The two auditors should reconcile the differences between their category lists. A working list of categories should be agreed upon for each open-ended question.
- *Step 4.* Both auditors should separately categorize each response according to their working list.
- *Step 5.* The reliability of the coding procedure should be determined by comparing the number of coding agreements between the judges. The following formula should be used to calculate the reliability (Holsti, 1969, p. 40):

$$\text{Reliability} = \frac{2\,(M)}{N1 - N2}$$

where M is the number of coding decisions on which there was agreement, $N1$ is the total number of coding decisions by person 1, and $N2$ is the total number of coding decisions by person 2. The reliability should be 90% or better. If this level of reliability is not achieved, the category system should be reevaluated.

Content Analysis Exercise

Listed below are some actual statements made to an open-ended question on an audit conducted in 2001. What themes seem to be emerging about the company?

"My relationship with my supervisor and my great friends here are the only things keeping me going."
"We have excellent supervisors."
"Expectations from my boss are communicated well."

"Some people who worked here a long time have been let go and that brings a lot of uncertainty. We keep wondering who is going to be next."

"The amount of trust, commitment, and responsibility that is placed on me by my supervisor makes me committed to him."

"I really enjoy working for my supervisor."

"That my supervisor is a sane, intelligent, and effective person; that there are consequences for those who consistently do not perform well."

"After some lean times, we have a person in place who I honestly believe has a mission and a vision."

"There is a lot of job insecurity here because of the general economy."

"Friends; we work hard but play hard too."

"I have good relationships with clients and coworkers."

"My team gets along very well."

"Being part of a productive and smart team."

"Freedom to do my job. Make decisions and do the right things without unreasonable interference or bureaucracy."

"This place remains fun and free of bureaucracy."

"Compensation is extremely important to me and ACME shares its financial performance with employees. This is good."

"Some people here are time bombs—anger, outbursts."

"People need to treat people how we want to be treated."

"ACME used to be about its people and now it is more about money and getting research published."

"Money."

"People remind me that the way to make money in this business is to move around, and my desire to stay with one company is being taken advantage of."

"Several of my teammates are like family to me."

"Working for ACME is like being with family. I know everyone."

"I am left alone to do my job."

"I like working for ACME because I am trusted to do my job."

"I am empowered to do my best."

"Top management does not value employees."

"I feel it is a quality organization."

"The company goes out of its way to make its employees feel appreciated."

"The way we are perceived by the community is very favorable."

"Commitment of the company to move forward with strategy."

"If we are not seen as being on the cutting edge, who wants to come to work here?"

"Morale is very low."

"We are operating out of a fear mode."

"Lots of political things are going on now."

"Many are worried over hiring freezes and turnover. If the worry is unwarranted, let everyone know."

"No trust between executive committee and the employees."

"Right now we are Obligated Involuntary Employees—we meet under the pretense that our input means something but if it does not address the topics of interest to the Executive Committee, it is directed back to topics that the common employee cannot understand."

"Executive managers without appropriate experience."

"Executive management's desire to be on the cutting edge and forcing speed is costing the company more than what is readily apparent. There is nothing wrong with operating at warp speed if one is built for it, but we are like a toddler on a tricycle trying to go down the side of a mountain (inexperienced driver and inappropriate vehicle). We need to invest time and money into both the driver and the vehicle if we are going to achieve our strategic intent."

INSTRUMENT EVALUATION

All research instruments have strengths and weaknesses. Furthermore, development of instruments is constantly exposed to new challenges as scholars become more sophisticated in analysis. Nevertheless, in a decade of experience with the ComSat instrument, we have encountered relatively few difficulties. A review of ComSat's reliability and validity is reported in Rubin et al. (1994):

> Test–retest (2 weeks interval) reliability of the CSQ was reported at .94 (Downs and Hazen, 1977). Coefficient alpha reliabilities for the 8 dimensions have been consistently high, ranging from .72 to .96 for studies in the United States (Potvin, 1991/1992) and Australia (A. Downs, 1991). (p. 115)

Rubin et al. also comment on the instrument's validity:

> Construct validity of the CSQ has been determined primarily through factor analysis. Evidence of concurrent validity exists. CSQ factors have been found to be highly correlated with job satisfaction (C. W. Downs and Hazen, 1977), strong predictors of organizational commitment (A. Downs, 1991; Potvin, 1991/1992) and related to turnover (Gregson, 1987) and need fulfillment (Kio, 1980). It is unrelated to demographic variables. (p. 116)

However, there are two areas of concern. First, most of the questions have a conceptual bent toward the communication behaviors of others. However, the relatively few items that ask for self-evaluation of communication tend to have an upward bias. For example, the items for the subordinate communication factor all ask supervisors to evaluate their own communication with their subordinates. Even the question about the "extent to which the supervisor trusts me" may be interpreted in terms of the respondent's trustworthiness rather than as an evaluation of the supervisor's behavior. Having a data bank available for comparison can to some extent alleviate this difficulty.

Second, the original survey did not contain any specific items about interdepartmental communication. Analyses of the open-ended questions have revealed this to be a prevalent problem in many organizations. Consequently, Downs and Adrian have added five questions to the instrument for their own investigations. Just as in the qualitative data, interunit communication tends to be one of the lowest rated communication aspects of most organizations. However, since it was not part of the original factor analysis, it is not reported here.

Nevertheless, the instrument has proved useful in a variety of organizational settings and cultures. Table 8.6 reviews some of the theses and dissertations that have used the instrument to date. These studies have yielded a number of insights. Across various audits, the subordinate communication and supervisory communication factors tend to be deemed the most satisfactory areas of communication, while the feedback and climate dimensions are considered to be areas of less satisfaction. The University of Wisconsin–Green Bay (UWGB) data bank, alluded to previously, shows a more precise picture. Table 8.3 presents those findings. Note that the supervisory communication and subordinate communication factors cluster at the top, just as found in previous research (Clampitt & Downs, 1983). The personal feedback dimension, as before, settles at the bottom. Such findings are particularly useful to practitioners seeking to deal with typical organizational difficulties. For the auditor, these findings can provide a yardstick of comparison for the particular organization being investigated and may suggest a context for interpreting the data.

TABLE 8.6. Communication Satisfaction Research

Researcher	Organization	Subjects	Size	Country
Avery (1977)	Government	Agency employees	135	USA
Thiry (1977)	Hospitals/clinics	Nurses	1,069	USA
Kio (1979)	Government and Business	Administrators/line workers	134	Nigeria
Nicholson (1980)	Urban schools	Administrators/teachers	290	USA
Jones (1981)	Rural schools	Administrators/teachers	142	USA
Duke (1981)	Urban schools	Business education teachers	309	USA
Alum (1982)	Social service	All employees	274	Mexico
Wippich (1983)	School district	Teachers	150	USA
Pincus (1984)	Hospital	Nurses	327	USA
Lee (1983)	Church schools	Teachers	224	USA
Downs (1991)	Packing firm	All employees	99	Australia
Potvin (1991)	Retail agency Hospital Electronics	All employees		USA
Downs (1994)	Hospitals	All employees	981	Scotland
Adrian (1997)	Food processing	All employees	769	Australia
	University	All employees	699	Australia
	Service	All employees	578	Australia

RESEARCH TRENDS

Numerous investigators have uncovered a series of trends. Reviewing all of these studies in depth would prove too lengthy an endeavor for the present purpose. Of particular interest to auditors is the relationship of communication to end-product variables. Hence, this section examines the relationship communication has to job satisfaction and the relationship communication has to productivity.

Of particular interest has been the fact that there is some consistency in the way the factors are rated across a number of the studies. Clampitt reviewed nine studies and discovered the overall ranking for the factors as well as the range for the factors. These are included in Table 8.3 and may be compared with the UWGB data bank norms included in Table 8.4.

Communication and Job Satisfaction

Most of the studies that have used the ComSat have sought to relate communication to job satisfaction. Different techniques have been used, but almost every study shows some relationship between job satisfaction and the communication satisfaction variables. Based on a thorough review of the theses and dissertations in Table 8.6, three communication factors seem strongly related to satisfaction: personal feedback, communication climate, and supervisory communication. The results of the UWGB data show similar trends. The correlations between the factors and a simple satisfaction measure are shown in Table 8.7. All the factors show statistically significant relationships ($p < .01$). In short, results from numerous sources show that the communication satisfaction factors are related to job satisfaction.

Communication and Productivity

The relationship between communication and productivity seems evident, yet surprisingly little research has been conducted to verify this assumption. The strong relationship of individual communication satisfaction factors to job satisfaction does raise some

TABLE 8.7. Communication Satisfaction and Job Satisfaction Correlations

Factor	Job satisfaction (r)	N
Personal Feedback	.5316	1,328
Communication Climate	.5207	1,321
Supervisory Communication	.5028	1,332
Organizational Integration	.5023	1,332
Media Quality	.4966	1,307
Corporate Perspective	.3916	1,321
Horizontal Communication	.3888	1,307
Subordinate Communication	.833	311

question about this assumption. Other research has suggested that increasing job satisfaction does not always produce a related increase in productivity—indeed, in some cases productivity can actually decrease. What has the research shown?

One study explored how employees thought each communication satisfaction dimension affected their productivity, with supervisors rating employee productivity. In the study employees were asked to rate the impact of the factors on their productivity and the productivity of their department (Clampitt & Downs, 1983). One-hundred-point scales were used in which 0 represented no impact on productivity, 50 designated an average impact, and 100 represented a maximum impact. Employees from two different companies were interviewed and their opinions solicited on why and how each factor affected productivity.

The results, shown in Table 8.8, detail the effect of the various dimensions on productivity. Employees perceived each of the communication satisfaction factors to have an "above-average" impact on productivity, but certain factors appeared to have greater impact than others. The personal feedback dimension had a significant effect on productivity in both companies, while horizontal communication, media quality, and corporate information had a relatively lower impact on productivity. In sum, the interview data seem to suggest that the perceived relationship between communication and productivity is strong and concrete.

The implication of the research trends is fairly clear. Auditors must realize that the various communication satisfaction dimensions are related to job satisfaction and productivity in different ways. Like manipulating a Rubik's Cube, a strategy designed to increase employee satisfaction may have no impact on perceived productivity. Another twist of the communication variables meant to align productivity may throw out of kilter an array of job satisfaction variables. For instance, the data bank shows a fairly strong relationship between the communication climate dimension and job satisfaction, but not between communication climate and the self-productivity estimates. Hence, when auditors make suggestions to an organization based on the use of the ComSat, they must carefully focus on the end-product variables with which the organization is most concerned.

TABLE 8.8. Communication Satisfaction and Productivity Correlations

Factor	Self-estimate of productivity (r)	N
Subordinate Communication	.1747	322
Organizational Integration	.1635	1,368
Supervisor Communication	.1592	1,368
Personal Feedback	.1116	1,363
Corporate Information	.1075	1,358
Horizontal Communication	.1006	1,343
Media Quality	.0979	1,342
Communication Climate	.0688	1,356

Communication Satisfaction and Organizational Commitment

A major thrust has been made in recent years to determine how the dimensions of the ComSat relate to organizational commitment. A positive relationship has been demonstrated between communication and organizational commitment both through correlations and regression analyses. However, the exact nature of this relationship varies among the (1) communication dimensions, (2) the individual organizations, and (3) the national cultures in which they operate. In a cross-cultural study by Downs, Adrian, and Ticehurst (1996), all dimensions of the ComSat correlated positively with commitment, and six ComSat factors predicted communication in at least some of the organizations. These close ties do suggest that understanding individual differences among organizations is important in making audit assessments.

CONCLUSION

The ComSat has a noteworthy heritage. Grounded in a firm developmental process, possessing a rich theoretical orientation, and utilized in a variety of organizational settings, it has proved to be a useful, flexible, and efficient means to audit organizational communication. Well-established analytical techniques have yielded many research findings that are useful to practitioners and theorists alike. The research trends have underscored the importance of auditors thinking carefully and deeply about how planned changes in communication affect key end-product variables. Indeed, these very ponderings may prove to be the greatest challenge of all for the auditor.

After having used this questionnaire for many years, we still find it necessary to measure aspects of organizational life that it does not cover. Therefore, we offer this questionnaire as one tool among many that might be helpful. And when we add questions to measure other aspects of organizational life, we follow the advice given in Chapter 6.

Phillip G. Clampitt, PhD, Department of Information Sciences, University of Wisconsin–Green Bay, Green Bay, Wisconsin.

9

Critical Communication
Experience Survey

When the Air Force was looking for a better procedure for air crews during World War II, it created the Aviation Psychology Program under the direction of John C. Flanagan. This program developed studies to discover why some pilots were eliminated from flight school, why some bombing missions failed, why some pilots became disoriented in flight, and how cockpit design could be improved. In their studies psychologists developed a systematic method for collecting descriptive behaviors, which later became known as the "critical incident method." The basic objective was to focus on concrete behaviors while eliminating statements of opinion, gross generalizations, imprecise evaluations, and stereotypes.

The critical incident technique was so successful that after the war psychologists continued to use and to perfect it. In 1949, for example, Thomas Gordon determined the critical requirements for airline pilots. Use of the technique spread, and by 1972 Fivars had compiled a list of 600 studies using this technique. Target groups have included public school administrators, teachers, judges, college administrators, extension agents, military police, salespeople, and industrial foremen.

The technique is well respected, and it can be a valuable audit tool. In fact, Downs used this technique in a 2002 study of the relationships among cultures and religion. Respondents answer a standard questionnaire, but as part of the questionnaire they are asked to describe two effective and two ineffective experiences they have had in another culture. However, we have since changed the name from "critical incidents" for political reasons. In 1971 we used the technique on a questionnaire while auditing a public utility. When we showed the president the preliminary draft, he balked at the word "critical" because to him it implied that we were asking the respondents to provide only negative information. Even though the word "critical" is intended to mean "vital" in this instance, we changed the name from "critical incident method" to "critical communication experience survey" in order to get a more positive response. The name is different, but the goal is still the same: to determine the most critical communication behaviors on which success or failure depends.

It is noteworthy that collecting the experiences of people in organizations has become one of the most popular academic means of analyzing organizational cultures.

ADVANTAGES OF THE METHOD

The technique itself is guided by some basic principles but is not governed by rigid rules. This gives it several advantages.

1. *The technique focuses on specific behaviors.* The purpose is to collect representative samples of observed behavior, which Flanagan (1954) asserts is the "only source" of data regarding critical requirements of a job.

> It should be emphasized at this point that observations of the behavior of the individual, or of the effectiveness of this behavior in accomplishing the desired results in a satisfactory manner, constitute not just one source of data but the only source of primary data regarding the critical requirements of the job in terms of behavior. (p. 327)

2. *The technique focuses on behaviors that have been directly observed—but not necessarily observed by the auditors themselves.* The observations are made by those people who actually experience the organization. It is true that they look at the experiences through their own communication filters and that the data they provide are susceptible to all the subjectivity of self-report. However, people behave in objective ways in their organizations. Learning about their subjectivities can enhance the value of an audit. Auditors constantly battle the tension between subjectivity and objectivity, but David Smith (1972) maintained that auditors sometimes need to reject the concept of total objectivity to gain a grasp on reality.

3. *The responses are unstructured by the auditor.* Questionnaires and interview guides are normally planned in detail so that the auditor can gather data about predetermined areas. Since the communication experience technique gives the respondent complete freedom in describing any experience, it stresses those incidents respondents themselves assess to have high priority. Furthermore, such incidents are likely to deal with phenomena that have a strong impact on the success or failure of an operation.

4. *The technique can be adapted to any specific observable situation or context.* Furthermore, it can be left entirely open, or certain areas can be specified. For example, Downs and Conrad (1982) indicated that they wanted to collect critical incidents about supervisor–subordinate relations. Mackintosh (1973) audited an organization of prison guards and specified that he wanted to collect incidents involving communication between guards and inmates, guards and guards, and guards and other prison elements. In still another audit the assessors gathered critical incidents concerning interdepartmental relations.

5. *The technique is both reliable and valid.* Anderson and Nilsson (1964), after auditing store managers in a Swedish grocery company, concluded:

> The material . . . seems to represent very well the behavior units that the method may be expected to provide. After a relatively small number of incidents had been classified, very few new behavior categories needed to be added. . . . It would appear justifiable to conclude that information collected by this method is both reliable and valid. (p. 402)

6. *The rich qualitative data obtained from critical incidents is invaluable in interpreting the data from questionnaires.* For example, one may be able to report accurately from questionnaires how many people are satisfied or dissatisfied with their performance reviews, but the findings are not likely to explain what creates that satisfaction or dissatisfaction. Critical incidents can help fill that void. By focusing on specific behaviors, the technique asks the respondents to evaluate the behaviors as being either effective or ineffective and to explain what makes them so.

THE BASIC FORM

Tables 9.1 and 9.2 depict the basic form for recording the incident. Note that the forms are simple, provide lots of open space for writing, and include very explicit directions. The amount of detail provided by respondents is not likely to be great unless the auditor coaches them to offer details. The Mackintosh (1973) form was the primary means of auditing a prison facility, whereas the form in Table 9.1 was integrated into a longer questionnaire.

TABLE 9.1. Communicative Experience Form

Think of an experience in which communication was particularly effective or ineffective, and describe that experience in as much detail as you can. In doing so, please be certain that the following questions are answered.

1. With whom were you communicating? (position)
2. What happened?
3. Why did it happen?
4. Was it effective or ineffective?
5. Is this experience typical of the communication in this organization?

Describe the communicative experience, the circumstances leading up to it, what the person did that made him or her an effective or an ineffective communicator, and the results (outcome) of what the person did. PLEASE PRINT. THANK YOU.

TABLE 9.2. Mackintosh Form Used in Study of Prisons

BACKGROUND DATA

1. My personnel grade is (write in one's personnel grade) _____
2. I have worked in a correctional facility for: _____ (years) _____ (months)
3. The communication incident below was significantly effective or ineffective (circle one) in providing correctional treatment, care, and custodial supervision to inmates.

SITUATION

Please write a short but complete description of the incident. Tell just what the people said or did. (Who, what, when, where, and with what effect.)

RESULTS

What was there about the communication behavior of the prison guard that made it significantly effective or ineffective?

NOTE: YOUR ANSWERS ARE TO BE ANONYMOUS!!
PLEASE DO NOT RECORD THE NAMES OF THE PERSONS INVOLVED.

ADMINISTERING THE QUESTIONNAIRE

Specify the Need for Both Effective and Ineffective Experiences

Both forms presented in Tables 9.1 and 9.2 allow the respondent to determine whether to report an effective or an ineffective incident. This is a strategic decision, for one would normally expect people to focus on what they do not like. If this were the case, the data from the incidents would be overwhelmingly negative. One variation on the procedure is to give the respondents several forms, with some specifying effective incidents and others specifying ineffective incidents. This method attempts to get a more balanced view. Remember: an audit should look at strengths as well as weaknesses.

Choose the Most Appropriate Means of Collecting Data

There are four ways of gathering information: individual interviews, questionnaires, group administrations, and over the Internet. These may be used alone or in combination.

If the communication experiences are integrated into questionnaires, coverage is increased. However, we have encountered a low response ratio for this method. Moreover, many of the returned questionnaires are likely to have insufficient details to be useful. For example, Page (1973) received a return rate of only 34%. It appears that many employees either do not like to write or to take the time to write. This is a basic problem with the critical incident methodology. On the other hand, both an interview and group administration are two important methods of communication that increase the return rate and utility of reported incidents. First, face-to-face interaction during an interview allows the auditor to be persuasive. Second, the respondents can be coached about how to complete the form, and questions can be asked that probe for more details.

Response rate and depth of details have been improved by the use of computer technologies. For some reason, many people are more likely to provide information when they can type it rather than write it out. Of course, this may also be affected by the kind of person who uses computers because not everyone has access to them or has skill in their use.

ANALYZING THE DATA

Although the ratio of return is not great for communication experiences, they can still add unique insights to the audit report. Flanagan (1954) maintained that 50–100 incidents might be enough to analyze a job (p. 343). Anderson and Nilsson (1964) found that after a small number of incidents had been classified, not much new information appeared. To make the most of the findings derived from incidents, you should follow these guidelines:

Screen the Experiences

Unfortunately, not all communication incidents are usable. Sometimes the descriptions are too vague, are too incomplete, or do not meet some other important criteria. It is important that the auditor decide at the beginning what criteria he or she will employ for accepting the incidents. The most important criteria include:

- *Observer.* Was the reporter the actual observer? If not, the incident is hearsay and may not be used.
- *Time frame.* Did the incident occur within the last 6 months or the last year? If the incident is not recent, the organization or person may have changed.
- *Evaluation.* Was the experience classified as either effective or ineffective? The auditor needs to know how the respondent viewed the behavior. For example, some employees respond to the same supervisory behavior in different ways. Whereas some classify a supervisor's asking questions about a project as "sincere interest" (effective), others view it as "supervising too closely" (ineffective).
- *Behavior.* Are actual behaviors reported in sufficient detail? In his study of trial judges, Page (1972) rejected the following incident because it did not describe actual behaviors and the details were insufficient.

> I watched two attorneys in action. I thought one had the evidence while the other seemed to be more persuasive. The one with the weaker evidence seemed to identify with the jury, and the jury voted in favor of him. If I had been judging, I would have gone for the other person.

- *Focus.* Sometimes the auditor has specified that the incidents should be about a definite area, such as supervisory communication or interdepartmental communication. If the incidents fall outside this defined area, they should be rejected.

Identify Incidents with Specific Person, Position, or Department

To interpret trends, it is useful to know exactly where the incident originated. Such identification permits checking it against other questionnaires or against interview information from the respondent.

Divide the Incidents into Effective and Ineffective Groups

It is relatively easy to put all the effective incidents together in one group and all the ineffective ones together in another group to look for trends. The two groups should be analyzed separately. This is illustrated in Table 9.3, which contains the exact statements made by the respondents.

Classify the Incidents into Themes or Categories

Sometimes categories can be identified in advance. Table 9.4 contains a classification used in the audit of a large university. This system was developed in part because a quick analysis was needed. Respondents read the list and identified the areas about which they were going to write incidents.

On a separate form, they indicated the person to whom the experience related, whether the incident was effective or ineffective, and the number of the item on this list to which the experience primarily related. They were then asked to write up the incident.

Although this system has merit, it does impose a great deal of structure on the respondents' answers. Consequently, we prefer the use of ad hoc categories, that is, classification schemes that come to the auditors while they read them. This makes for more work in the short run, but it does sometimes force the auditor into new ways of thinking. Table 9.5 contains actual summaries of incidents obtained in a public utility.

Sometimes a single incident can be classified in several categories. Mackintosh (1973) recalls such an incident in auditing the communication behavior of prison guards. The incident description recounted how a guard requested assistance in handling a belligerent inmate, and it also related the subsequent communication behavior of another guard answering the call for assistance. Therefore, the incident was classified in both the guard-to-inmate category and the guard-to-guard category.

There is no established format for grouping the incidents. The initial step may be to look for references to basic communication phenomena (described in Chapter 3), such as relations among people, certain types of messages, use of channels, or communication outcomes. These can be as elaborate as the system warrants. Table 9.5 lists some of the actual incidents reported in the analysis of one organization; the numbers on the left side refer to a certain respondent's questionnaire.

TABLE 9.3. Summary by Categories

I. Effective Incidents
   A. Job-related information
      1. Supervisor took the time to familiarize individual with job duties for new job.
      2. Supervisor gave detailed and basic explanations.
      3. Employee received praise, and errors were corrected in helpful way.
      4. Used visual aids in explanation.
      5. Coworker gave information that helped with a work problem.
      6. Supervisor gave critical yet helpful evaluation.
      7. Praise and recognition received from superiors.

   B. Personal situations
      1. Understanding with a personal situation.
      2. Understanding and development of procedures related to a health problem.
      3. Concern about an illness; no pressure to return.

   C. Job transfer
      1. Help with a job transfer request.

II. Ineffective Incidents
   A. Poor follow-up
      1. Request for supplies; had to ask again 3 months later.
      2. Suggestion made to improve efficiency "never left the office."
      3. Supervisor asked to talk to another operator (by several other operators) about a problem; not done.
      4. Asked supervisor about service and equipment use; waited over 2 months for answer; had to ask again.
      5. Question asked about criteria to be used for evaluation; went to immediate supervisor and then to _____; took over 2 weeks for an answer.
      6. Question asked about mistake in calculation; after 1 week asked again and after 3 weeks gave up.
      7. Attempted to make report to supervisor; tried three times, but no response from supervisor; supervisor got information from someone else.
      8. Two incidents: rude customer reported, but no follow-up by supervisors involved.

   B. Ineffective feedback given
      1. No acknowledgment or praise for commendations received.
      2. Supervisor reprimanded subordinate but did not explain reasons for procedure.
      3. Feedback given to correct a judgment error from a supervisor to subordinate given in such a way as to stifle initiative.
      4. Feedback given to coworker at wrong time and place.
      5. Supervisor did not listen to or respond to a question about an evaluation.

   C. Job transfer and promotion
      1. Asked Personnel about transfer; after a month asked again; no attempt made to help from Personnel or immediate supervisor.
      2. Performance standards required are "artificial" barrier to promotion or transfer; jobs not advertised for bids as in other departments.
      3. Supervisor refused to discuss transfer, so had to go to another level to obtain recommendation; still nothing has been done by supervisor.

   D. Inappropriate use of channels
      1. Supervisor listens to gossip via "grapevine" and draws conclusions from what she hears—very unbusinesslike.

(continued)

TABLE 9.3. *(continued)*

E. Inadequate guidance or training
   1. Not enough guidance with new job, so employee reprimanded for poor work.

F. Overall dissatisfaction
   1. Stress by management on speed; no concern for courtesy and accuracy; can't combine high speed and helpfulness to customers.
   2. Two incidents: survey merely another reflection of ineffectiveness of communication in the office; survey vague, irrelevant, and no changes will occur.

TABLE 9.4. Communication Experiences

Please read the following descriptions of communication experiences found in most organizations. Then, in the left margin, place a check mark next to those descriptions that are extremely important to you in your organization. To simplify your task, check only five or six descriptions that most critically affect your performance on your daily job.

1. Role
   1.1 Clear or unclear, confused or not confused, informed or not informed about role in organization (e.g., job description is confusing).
   1.2 Differ or not on what your role should be (e.g., expectations differ).
   1.3 Did or did not perform role adequately (e.g., used or misused authority, did or didn't follow correct procedures).

2. Information Adequacy
   2.1 Presence or absence of information (e.g., was or wasn't informed).
   2.2 Amount of information adequate or inadequate (e.g., lack of sufficient verbal information or presence of redundant information).
   2.3 Timeliness of information adequate or not (e.g., message received too late to be used).
   2.4 Clarity or lack of clarity of information (e.g., message was understood or misunderstood).
   2.5 Usefulness or lack of usefulness of information (e.g., message was impractical).
   2.6 Accuracy or inaccuracy of information (e.g., message was or wasn't distorted or faulty or honest).

3. Proper Use of Language
   3.1 Correct or incorrect use of words (e.g., correct or incorrect use of jargon or terminology).

4. Feedback
   4.1 Presence or absence of feedback (e.g., did or didn't follow up).
   4.2 Amount of feedback adequate or inadequate (e.g., possible information overload).
   4.3 Timeliness of feedback adequate or inadequate (e.g., feedback not on time).
   4.4 Clarity or lack of clarity of feedback (e.g., feedback not understood).
   4.5 Usefulness of feedback (e.g., feedback was impractical).
   4.6 Accuracy or inaccuracy of feedback (e.g., feedback was distorted).

(continued)

TABLE 9.4. *(continued)*

5. Channel
   5.1 Presence or absence of channel (e.g., a needed channel was missing).
   5.2 Frequency of usage (e.g., sufficient or insufficient channel usage).
   5.3 Appropriateness of channel (e.g., the wrong channel was used).
   5.4 Quality of channel operation (e.g., the channel was not operating efficiently; the intercom was broken).

6. Participation in Decision Making or Problem Solving
   6.1 Presence or absence of participation (e.g., did or didn't accept or give input to decision making).
   6.2 Amount of participation sufficient or not (e.g., token amounts of input allowed).
   6.3 Timeliness of participation adequate or not (e.g., participation was allowed before decision was made).
   6.4 Effectiveness of participation (e.g., decision was more effective and resulted in higher morale).

7. Perception of Interpersonal Relationships
   7.1 Liking or disliking each other (e.g., personality clash).
   7.2 Similarity or dissimilarity of backgrounds (e.g., perceptions differ due to cultural differences).
   7.3 Degree of supportiveness of relationship (e.g., boss was strongly supportive of position).
   7.4 Hostile or friendly to each other (e.g., petty conflicts or fights).
   7.5 Degree of blocking or encouraging message flow (e.g., blocking downward or upward flow).
   7.6 Cooperative or uncooperative with each other or others (e.g., having good rapport with each other).

8. Personal Communication Competencies
   8.1 Good/bad listening (e.g., did or didn't listen).
   8.2 Good/bad speaking (e.g., ineffective nonverbal facial and eye behaviors).
   8.3 Good/bad writing (e.g., spelling errors or typos in written memos)
   8.4 Good/bad reading (e.g., insufficient time to read required documents).

9. Other (Please Specify)
   9.1
   9.2
   9.3
   9.4

PROVIDE AN EXAMPLE OF AN EFFECTIVE OR INEFFECTIVE COMMUNICATION EXPERIENCE FOR EACH OF THE DESCRIPTIONS YOU INDICATED WERE IMPORTANT TO YOU.

TABLE 9.5. Sample Critical Incidents

The material in this table represents verbatim responses to the questionnaire in one organization.

<u>Effective</u>

(5) Supervisors volunteered info that the Y employee had done an excellent job in catching up on the backlog of work on previous day. Used a low-keyed and sincere approach. Left no doubt that he was genuinely grateful for everyone's effort.

(18) Another company called for information. (2) My immediate supervisor took the call—which required a call back after the info was obtained (3) when the call back was made the person requesting the info was not available so a message was left. (4) I was advised of the situation so that I was able to intelligently and quickly handle the situation when I got the call. WHY EFFECTIVE? (2) It saves time. (2) Eliminates duplicated efforts. (3) It allows a better impression to a third party be they CRC or others. (4) Also gave me info and/or knowledge for future reference.

(20) About a month ago, top management came to our location to inform all staff about the company and where we were going. We were told good and bad points to expect during the next year. We were able to ask questions and a member of top management would answer. The questions were answered in a clear and knowledgeable manner.

(21) When—Jan. 24, Who—an agent from the previous shift, Why—the need to pass information not easily written, What happened—specific facts passed-on by this individual enabled me to perform my duties in a more efficient and expeditious manner, What—this person gave a brief yet accurate summary of actions he had taken. This summary allowed me to complete this joint task with a minimum of waste in time and effort.

(23) When—14 Feb.—lunch, Who—immediate supervisor and me, Why—we were alone at the lunch table, What happened—we just sat and talked about various things, totally informal. What person did—listen—reply honestly—was sympathetic.

(24) Wednesday, Jan. 13, Bill, Regarded a meeting I held with our Y agents regarding our procedures. Y agents were upset by secrecy of our new manual. I couldn't tell them about new proposals per my supervisor. Felt trapped in situation. Told them some of our "secrets." I didn't care to be involved in this type of approach again. They wouldn't give constructive methods for working. I was upset. Bill talked to me about the situation by calling me into his office. Gave me encouragement and pointers for this type of situation.

(29) After the holidays, a group of workers noticed an individual who was on vacation during Christmas. When he should not have been. It was presented to our immediate supervisor. He then said he would look into it, which he did. He gave us an answer within a couple of days. He has searched and talked with management and told them we were all concerned. He gave us the best possible answer he could in the position that he was in. It was all done in a very sincere and businesslike manner. We thanked him for looking into the matter and proceeded to go to the top management, not because of our supervisor, but because we wanted to hear from the horse's mouth. We felt that our supervisor could only do so much and get so much information—which he did—in fact, more than usual. But we were not satisfied with that and wanted more. We greatly appreciate our supervisor's efforts and kindness and helpfulness. He really went beyond the call of duty.

(continued)

TABLE 9.5. *(continued)*

Ineffective

(42) Received my paycheck which was for more money than usual. Inquired with immediate supervisor who advised me that I had received a merit raise. It would be more rewarding to be advised personally that your efforts are appreciated than to be advised only at the time you receive your paycheck.

(48) Team coordinator has no tolerance for opposite viewpoint. To accomplish a procedural change is impossible. If difference of opinion is expressed, it must be shouted for the longest duration to even be acknowledged. When acknowledged, the Team Coordinator never changes his viewpoint until ordered to do so by upper management. Then it is done grudgingly and with lots of grumbling. Yet, this Team Coordinator is thought to be supersmart by upper management.

(50) Feb. 14 X was very ineffective when explaining a new procedure. It went into effect 4 days ago. No one told us. It makes a job harder and it takes longer to drive the tickets. X explained it poorly, admitted he had not checked it out himself yet. Yet he expected us to know all about it and be able to do it, when it was not communicated to us in the first place. He is very ineffective as a team coordinator.

(53) Feb. 3 Brought to X's attention discrepancies on procedures regarding putting tickets in the problem file—very negative response from X. I insisted he present the issue to B—He never!! Feb. 8—Approached B with the issue, he agreed the procedure should be changed and said a bulletin to that effect would be issued immediately. Today is Feb. 17—we have seen no bulletin regarding the above procedure change!

(54) I went in to talk to my manager about putting in for a new job so I could go to a full-time position because I am going to be married soon. He kind of gave me the feeling that he was preoccupied with other things. I guess at a time when I need some definite answers. I get the same old excuses about waiting for the next quarter's budget, or we need to hear from the big guys, etc. I wish they would just level with us and not play games. This same person has helped me out at other times. But sometimes I wish our organization would get things together and level with all of its employees. The employees would be happier, thus creating a happier department and a great company to work for. This would boost the company far above if the morale of its employees were higher.

(70) Our supervisor called a meeting to present his ideas for a new plan for an ongoing program and to get feedback from his people on the new plan. After lengthy discussion, it was obvious that the near-unanimous opinion of the subordinates was that the new plan was very inferior to the old plan, and that the program would suffer if the new plan was implemented. The supervisor said, "Thank you for your opinions, but I think we will try the new plan anyway." He did, the program suffered, and we were all bitter and frustrated.

INTERPRETING THE RESULTS

In a sense, dealing with critical incidents is both easy and interesting. It is inherently more satisfying to read detailed reports than it is to deal with statistical data revealing the fact that 55% of employees say they do not get enough information about X. However, drawing meaningful conclusions from communication experiences is a great challenge. In fact, there are four obstacles to the effective use of communication experiences: (1) a low return rate, (2) difficulty in developing categories, (3) problems of ensuring anonymity, and (4) difficulty in deriving generalizations.

Note the Return Rate

As we pointed out earlier, low response rate is the greatest liability of the communication experience format. It is not so much of a problem when the communication experience form is the only questionnaire used in the audit or when the experiences are obtained orally. People also are more likely to write out detailed experiences if the form is filled out on a computer or via the Internet. However, when it is used in conjunction with other questionnaires, the response rate often drops below 33%. Many people fill out the rest of the questionnaire without answering the experience portion, leading us to conclude that people do not want to take the time to write. Low response rates make generalization more difficult.

Develop Categories

Our preference is to read the incidents until ad hoc categories come to us. This is a legitimate means of content analysis. It is, however, a slow process if many experiences are involved. Nevertheless, the extra time and effort needed are the prices to be paid for collecting very unstructured data. There are numerous ways that a common theme can be expressed. As a way of expediting the process of developing categories, refer to the list of themes in Table 9.4. These were used in the audit of a university, where hundreds of experiences were collected. This list is not meant to be an instrument in itself but merely to suggest some themes that may aid interpretation.

Maintain Privacy

In all audits, auditors promise individual anonymity. Keeping that promise is sometimes difficult when auditors' report specific instances for interpretation. A great deal of care must be taken to disguise the individuals. Nonetheless, there is still a likelihood that someone in management will know who was involved in the incident. In reporting the confidential results of an audit to a utility president, Downs used a disguised incident to support a generalization he was making, and the president quickly retorted, "I know exactly who that was, and let me tell you why that happened." He was correct too, even though Downs could not admit it. This situation reinforced the need to keep reports from detailing too much; otherwise, others are going to recognize them.

Derive Generalizations

The three observations that follow were taken from the summary of an audit of a telephone company.

1. Most of the effective incidents involved job-related situations in which praise and recognition were given.
2. Almost half of the ineffective incidents involved the lack of, or slowness of, follow-up by supervisors.
3. Other ineffective incidents focused on the giving of feedback. Respondents indicated that workers were corrected for errors in inappropriate ways, supervisors refused to listen to worker concerns about evaluations, and good work was not acknowledged by supervisors. Most of these occurred in Department B.

These observations point out some of the problems of interpreting data from critical incidents. First, grouping the incidents under some overall umbrella concept that makes sense is often a problem. Consider observation 3. Several different items were included under the general category of "feedback," even though they call attention to very different phenomena. Likewise, the term "follow-up" in observation 2 is rather vague. In addition, there is an apparent conflict between observations 1 and 3. Supervisors who give positive feedback are considered to be effective, whereas those who do not are considered ineffective. Or maybe some supervisors are being described in observation 1 whereas others are being described in observation 3. Which of these conditions really characterize the organization? We cannot tell from these observations, so we may need to check these findings against some questionnaire or interview data. There is also the tendency to report the data in quantifiable terms (e.g., "almost half"), so that counting the number of times a category occurs becomes all-important. This, however, is where a communication audit differs from a standard academic research project. Frequency of response can be very useful and should not be undervalued, but it is not always the standard by which the audit is to be judged. In the first place, the number of incidents is not likely to come from a representative sample of the workers. Position in the organization often gives one a unique view of the organization that cannot be shared by others. Furthermore, one truly perceptive incident may illustrate a great deal about an organization's operations. For example, in an analysis of an engineering firm that involved three departments, only one supervisor reported an incident that showed how employees in Department C believed they were always last in receiving communication. But this incident was so on-target that we later discovered that this perception revealed a root problem for some teamwork inadequacies.

CONCLUSION

In the total audit process, communication experiences can enrich the auditors' understanding of the organization. Table 9.6 illustrates some of the observations developed from an audit. However, in numerous audits in which we have used this method in con-

TABLE 9.6. Sample of Communication Experiences

Overview of Findings

Thirty-four employees provided us with a communication experience on the questionnaire in which they described an effective or an ineffective communication situation. Twelve of these responses reported effective communication experiences, and 22 reported ineffective communication experiences.

Since only half of the 67 questionnaire respondents provided a communication experience, it is difficult to generalize from this data. The experiences do, however, provide us with the following information:

1. The responses supported data from the interviews and clarified some areas on the questionnaire.
2. The majority of the responses were concerned with communication necessary or vital to doing the job.
3. The results of the effective experiences tended to indicate that an open, supportive atmosphere for communication exists at all levels.
4. The primary problems described in the ineffective communication experiences dealt with information sharing, dissemination, and timeliness.

Effective Experiences

Information gleaned from the communication experiences labeled "effective" tended to be best categorized as task-oriented. A breakdown of the responses is as follows:

A. Task-Oriented
1. A coworker accurately handled changes in personal schedule.
2. A telephone conversation with a coworker was accurate, purposeful, and cordial.
3. Upper management established policies and supported employees for abiding by policies.
4. Supervisor gave critical feedback to a subordinate that led to improved productivity.
5. Negotiations between speaker and management led to win–win situation.
6. (Two instances) Immediate supervisor gave supportive feedback and assignments.
7. A supervisor was open to suggestions or requests for help in getting job done.
8. An employee had an effective meeting with a supervisor.

Ineffective Experiences

The communication experiences that were labeled ineffective covered a wide range of problem areas. These areas included information sharing, timeliness of information, follow-up, promotion and transfer, evaluation/feedback, and general communication. Specific examples follow. Again, it is important to note that these are individual responses and may not represent general trends in the organization.

A. Information Sharing
1. A supervisor ignored a request for special information.
2. One person expressed a lack of understanding of what is going on throughout the organization.
3. One person believed upper management hoarded information from its meetings. This caused an uneasy feeling.
4. (Two instances) A worker withheld vital information from a coworker.
5. (Two instances) Instructions from top management necessary to perform job were unclear.
6. Worker did not receive all necessary memos to do his or her job.

B. Timeliness of Information
1. Information was mailed late by subordinate.
2. Employee received information from upper management late. This has occurred before and is frustrating.

(continued)

TABLE 9.6. *(continued)*

C. Follow-Up
   1. Person suggested to immediate supervisor that he or she create a memo index for easy future reference. Nothing has been done.
   2. Employee gave specific instructions to supervisor of another department regarding a mailing being sent out. The supervisor was then to pass on information to his or her people. Supervisor did not complete task.

D. Promotion and Transfer
   1. Immediate supervisor posted new job position opening, then the next day canceled the job—this caused frustration.

E. Evaluation/Feedback
   1. Worker unsure of how upper/middle management is evaluating his or her work and whether or not the evaluation is impartial. Causes strained relations.
   2. Worker receives no recognition or appreciation of work done.

F. General Communication
   1. Coworker did not clearly identify to whom a memo was being sent.
   2. Immediate supervisor handled an employee meeting poorly.

junction with interviews or questionnaires, we have found the communication experiences to be of less value than the other methodologies simply because people do not tend to write very much when they are filling out a questionnaire. On the other hand, it is highly desirable to obtain descriptions of specific behaviors to balance out the perceptual data obtained from standardized questionnaires. Furthermore, communication experiences are particularly useful in pinpointing specific problem areas that cannot be picked up by looking at statistical means across all respondents. Localizing a problem can be of value in auditing the total organization. In fact, sometimes one example can open up a whole interpretation of what is taking place in the organization. Not everyone has to report it or even to know about it for the example to give the auditor great insights into the organization. One way to ensure that communication experiences are collected from many and are explained in detail is to collect them during the interviews of an audit.

10

ECCO Analysis

Several methods discussed in previous chapters focus primarily on the perceptions and reactions of respondents to various communication phenomena. Most communication consultants, however, also advocate the exploration of the adequacy of the channels used in communicating throughout the organization. One way to assess adequacy is to have employees evaluate each channel. It is helpful, though, to provide some context for employees when assessing the channels. By focusing on actual internal messages, auditors are able to provide the context that avails them of useful information about channels. ECCO (Episodic Communication Channels in Organizations) analysis is a specialized questionnaire oriented toward *specific individual messages*. In this sense, it is very different from the previously described questionnaires, which focus on more global perceptions of communication processes and channels. Developed by Keith Davis (1953), ECCO is a versatile instrument that traces a particular message through the organization.

When using ECCO, auditors are able to judge the length of time messages take to circulate, the media usage for these messages, and the ways that different types of information are processed. Other questionnaires ask for an employee's response, such as satisfaction with the way the informal channel or grapevine works in the organization, but auditors have used ECCO analysis to plot the grapevine network and to see how particular messages actually flow through the organization. ECCO analysis's ability to reveal such information makes it very appealing as an audit instrument. *Our experience has shown that different types of messages are diffused or networked in different ways.*

Indeed, Davis (1953), following Jacobson and Seashore (1951), developed ECCO as a research technique to examine the spread of rumors through informal channels or the "grapevine." Davis's (1968) research grew, and as a major analyst of information channels he found that informal communication was frequently linked with formal channels. Specifically, in effective organizations, informal and formal communications were positively related to each other (Katz & Kahn, 1978). Tompkins's (1977) studies of NASA's Marshall Space Flight Center reinforced this finding as he observed that the practices of managing and communicating fused through an emphasis on both formal and informal communication channels. (We encourage auditors to read Putnam and Cheney's [1995] useful history of the instrument's development.)

One cannot help noting that references in academic literature to ECCO tend to be from the 1970s, and thus it would appear dated. However, ECCO technology has been used with consistent success in organizational audits, and therefore it is still an option worth considering. An Internet search shows that several consultants still list it as one of their technologies. Whether or not it is the best instrument to use depends not on the date of its origin, but rather on the auditors' purposes and plans for using other technologies. As we will discuss at the end of the chapter, relying solely on ECCO analysis has its limitations; however, when combined with other methods, such as interviews, observation, and surveys, ECCO provides insight into the message dissemination process.

DESIGNING THE ECCO QUESTIONNAIRE

There is a basic format for an ECCO log, but the actual questionnaire must be tailored to the client organization. A simple instrument, the ECCO log can be constructed easily and quickly, for it usually contains only four or five parts. These are illustrated by the examples in Tables 10.1 and 10.2, taken from actual audits.

The log breaks a message into several distinct parts. The respondents check off those parts that they know. Auditors can then determine how well a particular message circulated. This is important to know, because people often hear only bits and pieces of messages. In the example of the church in Table 10.2, some people had heard that a seminar was being offered, but many people did not know who was conducting it or who its intended audience was.

ECCO also tests the accuracy of the information being processed by asking respondents to indicate for each part whether or not they received information that differs in any way from the message stated on the log. These findings have great potential for checking inaccuracies in informal channels. Our experience, however, suggests that the auditor is much more likely to discover incomplete messages than inaccuracies. The following sections list the requirements for the effective use of ECCO methodology.

Choose the Messages

Whereas other audit questionnaires examine more global reactions to general types of information such as "personal feedback" or "information to do the job," ECCO focuses on whether or not respondents know a very specific message. This distinction is important. ECCO does not assess satisfaction with, or reaction to, a message: *its sole emphasis is on the process of circulating a specific message.* Since the diffusion process may differ for various kinds of messages, auditors generally construct several different ECCO logs, each one featuring a different kind of message. These are then administered serially through the organization. Bailey (1974), for example, circulated 15 different ECCO logs to audit communication in a church. Some messages may be work-oriented, but ECCO has also been one of the primary ways of charting informal channels (the grapevine or rumor mill).

TABLE 10.1. Rudolph Survey of Information Flow

Survey No. 1   (Confidential)   Your Code No._____

Prior to receiving this questionnaire, did you know the information in the box or any part of it?

(Message is divided into four parts.)

a)

b)

c)

d)

Please check one:

____ Yes, I knew all of it.

____ Yes, I knew part of it. If so, please list the numbers of the parts you knew.

____ No, I did not know any of it.

If your answer above was "Yes, I knew all of it" or "Yes, I knew part of it," please complete the questionnaire by providing the information requested below.

If your answer above was "No, I did not know any of it," you have completed the questionnaire. Please return the questionnaire to me or drop it in the information box. Thank you very much for your cooperation.

If you had the information in the box but the facts you heard were different, please write the facts you heard next to the associated number.

Question #1. *From whom* did you *first* receive the information in the box? Please place the source's code number (from your code sheet) on this line. Remember that by using the code number *you never identify* the specific person who gave you the information because each code number is assigned to several persons.

Question #2. *Where* were you when you first received the information in the box above? Please check one:

(11) ____ At my desk or other location where I carry out my job duties

(12) ____ Elsewhere in the room where I work

(13) ____ Outside this room but still working

(14) ____ Away from my unit-department but still working

(15) ____ Away from my unit-department but not while working (coffee break, etc.)

(16) ____ Away from the building and while not working for the organization

Question #3. How long ago did you first receive the information in the box? Please circle the approximate time:

Today	Yesterday	3	4	5	6	7 days ago
		2	3	4	5	6 weeks ago

(continued)

TABLE 10.1. *(continued)*

Question #4. By what method did you first receive the information in the box above? Please check only one of the following methods:

Written or visual methods		*Talking or sound methods*	
(20) ____	Personal letter from the company	(30) ____	Talking face-to-face, one-to-one
(21) ____	Letter, memo, or service program	(31) ____	Telephone
(22) ____	Annual report	(32) ____	Talking in a group
(23) ____	News	(33) ____	Organized meeting
(24) ____	Magazine	(34) ____	Overhearing others/rumor
(26) ____	Company film	(35) ____	Radio/TV
(27) ____	Public newspaper	(36) ____	Public speech
(28) ____	Company records		

Thank you very much for your cooperation. Please return the questionnaire to me or drop it in the information box.

Some specific criteria for the messages include the following:

1. They should be typical of the ones circulated in the organization.
2. All parts of the messages should be true and accurate.
3. They should be simple and straightforward. In the most desirable instances, they can be phrased in single declarative sentences. For example, the following message would be appropriate: "Greg Kessler has resigned as the Director of Organizational Development and will become the Vice-President of Personnel at Corporate Headquarters."
4. Since the ECCO log is used for the total organization, messages should be of interest or applicable to the entire organization.
5. For measurement purposes, the messages will have been released through a specific channel and will not have been widely known before the specific time of release.
6. To trace networks, the serial administration of messages must reflect both the upward and the downward flow of the messages. For example, in her investigation of a university administration, Sanders (1976) chose messages involving the resignation of a dean, a new requirement announced by the Office of Affirmative Action, and the movement of the Endowment Association to a new building.

Identify the Media

This section of the questionnaire must be tailor-made for the organization, as all possible channels need to be listed. Written media are often easily specified, but oral interactions may have to be classed more generally under headings such as "discussions during coffee breaks" or "interviews" or "meetings." Question 4 in Table 10.1 and Section D in Table 10.2 are good illustrations of how media can be arranged.

Set Up Categories for Reception Time

Organization members commonly complain that information moves too slowly in organizations. Of course, speed is relative and varies with the perspective of each employee. Actually plotting reception times allows auditors to determine how quickly information flows to each section and to compare the speed of different types of information flow. Auditors should modify the temporal scales to suit different needs; the scales can thus

---

TABLE 10.2. ECCO Log in a Church

A. Please check below the items of information you had by noon of the day you received this ECCO log (if you have received none, see Section B; if your information varies, see Section C):

_____ 1. Another "Bert Nash Seminar" for parents

_____ 2. Wishing to improve child-raising skills

_____ 3. Is now being held at Plymouth Church

_____ 4. On Monday evenings from 7:00 to 9:00 P.M.

B. I have received no information on the above subject.

Analysis

C. If your information differed from that listed in Section A, please write next to the associated number the information you have:

1.

2.

3.

4.

D. Please check the source from which you first received the information:

1.	_____ Church posters	9.	_____ The annual meeting
2.	_____ The "Plymouth Rock"	10.	_____ Word of mouth
3.	_____ Church bulletin board	11.	_____ Mail from the church
4.	_____ The "annual report"	12.	_____ "United Church News"
5.	_____ Announcement in worship	13.	_____ Church group meeting
6.	_____ "Coffee hour" conversation	14.	_____ Do not recall
7.	_____ Sunday worship bulletin	15.	_____ "Lawrence Journal World"
8.	_____ Local radio/TV	16.	_____ Other _____

E. Please check the appropriate time period in information:

1. _____ Before January 1

2. _____ January 1–15

3. _____ January 16–31

4. _____ February 1–14

5. _____ February 15–28

6. _____ After February 28

range from months to weeks to days. Keep in mind that respondents often have diffi-culty remembering exactly when they received messages; therefore, the categories need to allow plenty of leeway for differences. The reception time results on ECCO logs have consistently shown informal channels to be faster than formal ones.

List Potential Sources

The original purpose of ECCO analysis was to identify the communication networks as-sociated with specific messages; in order to do so, you must provide a space on the ECCO log requesting employees to identify the source of their information. The follow-ing is an example of such a request:

> From whom did you first receive the information? Please place the source's code number (from your code sheet) on this line.

As indicated in Question 1 of Table 10.1, each participant is sometimes given a codebook with every other person's name in it. The individual's code number differenti-ates between management and operators, between line and staff, and among different organizational levels and functions. For example, in Davis's (1953) original audit, "141116" meant, respectively, management (1), fourth level (4), line (1), belt factory (1), and Joe Smith (16) (p. 305). The chief reason for the code was to make tabulation easy; however, another important consideration was to make naming the source less per-sonal. The assumption was that people feel less threatened by writing down a number than a name. From the data concerning sources, it is possible to plot group interaction, directions of communication flow, types of information initiated by certain people or groups, and limited communication networks. If several ECCO logs are used, it is possi-ble to check the consistency of the network across messages.

Identify Location Possibilities

Because some auditors have wanted to know the physical location of the respondent when he or she received information, they have asked questions such as the following (Pacilio & Rudolph, 1973):

> Where were you when you first received the information? Please check one.
> _____ At my desk or other location where I carry out my job duties.
> _____ Elsewhere in the room where I work.
> _____ Outside this room but still working.
> _____ Away from my unit but still working.
> _____ Away from my unit while not working (coffee break, etc.)
> _____ Away from the building and while not working.

Auditors should consider carefully how such information would be used before adding such information to the ECCO log. You must always consider the question "What value does this information add to my understanding of the communication system?"

Knowing where someone is when information is received may give a picture of the level of formality of message reception. There is also some bias likely to be built in to employees' answers, however. For instance, in some companies there is an increasing emphasis on being accountable for work time. It is unlikely that someone would admit to receiving information "while not working" simply because it sounds more socially acceptable to say one was working at the time. Other organizations may encourage a culture of "downtime." Auditors should think about what kinds of answers are more likely to be given in a specific organizational culture and plan accordingly. The data has less value if the socially acceptable answers obscure what really happens.

ADMINISTERING THE QUESTIONNAIRE

On average participants can fill out an ECCO log in 3 minutes, thus allowing people to fill out the logs while in their workspace and with a minimum of interference to their workflow. Indeed, the easiest way to distribute the logs is to give them personally to the respondents or to distribute them by internal mail. If several logs are to be completed at once, however, response rates are improved by assembling groups in a conference room. Now that electronic media are commonplace, it is possible also to administer these logs through email, electronic bulletin boards, phone conferencing, or posting them online like any other questionnaire. The electronic means are particularly beneficial when participants are geographically dispersed.

For data from the logs to be useful, respondents must sign their names or sign code numbers identified with them. Auditors cannot plot the information flow without some means of identification. Using codes ensures confidentiality and makes tabulation easier. Naturally, some people are hesitant to use any form of identification that can be traced back to them. Rudolph (1972) suggests 11 guidelines for administering the questionnaire that may encourage people to include such identification:

1. Visit with the subjects when distributing and collecting the questionnaires.
2. Use as little of the respondents' time as possible.
3. Instruct the subjects on how to respond to the questionnaire prior to the first administration.
4. Learn as many of the subjects' names as possible and use them whenever given the opportunity.
5. Make a point of assuring the anonymity of each participant (if it seems necessary).
6. Impress the subjects with the importance of their individual answers to the success of the study.
7. Encourage questions about the project and attempt to answer them.
8. Allow an appropriate amount of time for questionnaire completion.
9. Develop employee interest and participation by requesting information for messages or communication episodes to be studied.
10. Make sure the participants realize that an "I don't know any of the information" answer is just as important as an "I know it all" answer.
11. Keep abreast of any developing problem with the instrument and be ready and willing to make necessary changes. (p. 7)

By engaging in these activities, auditors can do much to allay the fears of participants and encourage them to provide useful information.

ANALYZING THE DATA

The instrument is simple, and the analysis need not be difficult. The following steps have proved to be useful.

    1. *Screen the responses.* Like other questionnaires, this one will not be filled out completely by everybody. Some will be unsigned and therefore will not be useful.

    2. *Tabulate individual responses* so that a frequency distribution and percentages can be compiled. The subprogram FREQUENCIES has been successfully used for this (Nie, Hull, Jenkins, Steinbrennler, & Bent, 1975, pp. 218–219).

    3. *Arrange the data into predetermined groupings* such as work units, scalar levels, or functional divisions. Cross-tabulations can be useful in making these comparisons. Sanders (1976), for example, created 2 × 2 comparison tables for all variables. In this way she compared Department A with Department B on the frequency of receiving messages.

> A cross-tabulation is a joint frequency distribution of cases according to two or more classificatory variables. The display of the distribution of cases by their position on two or more variables is the chief component of contingency table analysis and is the most commonly used analytic method in the social sciences. These joint frequency distributions can be statistically analyzed by certain tests of significance, e.g., the chi square statistic, to determine whether or not the variables are statistically independent; and these distributions can be summarized by a number of measures of associations, such as the contingency coefficient, phi, tau, gamma, etc., which describes the degree to which the values of one variable predict or vary with those of another. (Nie et al., 1975, pp. 218–219)

    4. Since ECCO logs collect nominal data, one should *use nonparametric statistics for analysis.*

    5. *Compare units.* Some comparisons can be validly determined just by quick examination. However, there are also more elaborate and objective ways to make such comparisons. Davis (1964) devised the following formulas for determining the (a) receipt factor, (b) accuracy factor, (c) initiation factor, and (d) interaction factor. The formula for the receipt factor is

$$R = MR/SR$$

where *MR* is the number of messages received, *SR* is the number of ECCO surveys returned, and *R* is the percentage representing the receipt factor. Table 10.3 demonstrates how the receipt factors of various groups can be compared. Not only do the groups differ in terms of the two messages received, but in this instance it is fairly obvious that the two messages are processed quite differently. Salience of the messages is likely to be a factor in obtaining these results.

TABLE 10.3. Comparison of Units on Receipt Factor

	Message 1			Message 2			Message 3		
	SR	MR	R(%)	SR	MR	R(%)	SR	MR	R(%)
Sales	12	11	92	13	8	62	25	19	76
Personnel	10	9	90	10	8	80	20	17	85
Production Group A	46	45	98	40	25	62	86	70	81
Production Group B	33	30	91	33	15	46	66	45	68
Top management	12	12	100	12	10	83	24	22	92
Total	113	107	95	108	66	61	221	173	78

Note. R = MR/SR, where MR is the number of messages received, SR is the number of ECCO surveys returned, and R is the percentage representing the receipt factor.

The formula for the propensity of messages to be communicated accurately is

$$A = AR/MR$$

where MR is the number of messages received, AR is the number of messages received accurately, and A is the percentage representing the accuracy factor. Representative data are presented in Table 10.4.

The initiation factor is measured by the formula

$$I = IR/MR$$

where MR is the number of messages received, IR is the number of messages initiated, and I is the percentage or initiating factor. IR is obtained by tallying the answers to the question "From whom did one first hear the message?" The higher the initiating factor, the more active the person or group was in communicating the message to others. Con-

TABLE 10.4. Comparison of Units on Accuracy of Messages

	Message 1			Message 2			Message 3		
	MR	AR	A(%)	MR	AR	A(%)	MR	AR	A(%)
Sales	16	14	88	12	10	83	28	24	86
Personnel	18	15	83	18	10	56	36	25	86
Production Group A	30	25	83	28	19	68	58	44	76
Production Group B	45	36	80	18	9	50	63	45	71
Top management	12	11	92	11	6	55	23	17	74
Total	121	101	84	87	54	62	208	155	74

Note. The formula for the propensity of messages to be communicated accurately is A = AR/MR, where MR is the number of messages received, AR is the number of messages received accurately, and A is the percentage representing the accuracy factor.

struction of a table for the initiating factor (see Table 10.5) would be similar to those for the receipt and accuracy factors.

A rank order of the totals demonstrates that the president is initiating the communication of these two messages and that foreman B is also very active.

Another important aspect of communication is the interaction among different units in the organization. An *interaction factor* is computed by the formula

$$INT = RO/MR$$

where *MR* refers to the number of messages received in an area, *RO* is the number of messages received from outside that unit (this is obtained by identifying the unit of the source and the unit of the receiver), and *INT* represents the interaction factor, which is the percentage of identified messages. The number of messages received from outside the unit may be subtracted from the total number of messages received to obtain the number of messages received from within the unit. Table 10.6 presents data for the interaction factor.

Another possible use for these data is for the auditor to plot the actual linkages among the units being audited. For example, one could determine whether the 11 messages coming from outside Production Group A tended to come from one other unit or from many units.

6. *Plot networks.* It is possible to plot networks by hand from the ECCO analysis. Sometimes information flows through a single-strand channel, with one person telling a message to only one other person. Another pattern to identify is a cluster in which, for example, person A tells three people a message, and one of them passes it on to others.

Unfortunately, such charting can be time-consuming if many people are involved. To combat this problem, Walter Stewart (1982) of Ohio University has designed a computer program to make the task quicker and more complete. Called the ECCO Analysis Program, it can process data from organizations with more than 1,000 employees. Fur-

TABLE 10.5. Comparison of Individuals on Initiation Factor

	Message 1			Message 2			Total		
	MR	IR	I(%)	MR	IR	I(%)	MR	IR	I(%)
President	4	15	375	3	2	67	7	17	242
Foreman A	9	2	22	9	3	33	18	5	28
Foreman B	19	17	89	25	7	28	44	24	55
Sales manager	50	5	10	40	6	15	90	11	12
Personnel manager	58	8	8.6	35	9	26	93	14	15
Unidentified	2								
Total	140	46	33	112	27	24	252	71	28

Note. The initiation factor is measured by the formula *I* = *IR/MR*, where *MR* is the number of messages received, *IR* is the number of messages initiated, and *I* is the percentage or initiating factor. *IR* is obtained by tallying the answers to the question "From whom did one first hear the message?" The higher the initiating factor, the more active the person or group was in communicating the message to others.

TABLE 10.6. Flow within and between Units

	Top management		Sales		Personnel		Production Group A		Production Group B		Total	
	N	%	N	%	N	%	N	%	N	%	N	%
Within	8	89	11	79	0	0	19	63	22	76	60	71
Between	1	11	3	21	2	100	11	37	7	24	24	29
Totals	9	100	14	100	2	100	30	100	29	100	84	100

Note. N, the number of messages received; %, the percentage of the total number of messages sent.

thermore, it has been validated against hand-computed networks. Stewart's program increases the utility of ECCO as an audit technique simply because it reduces the time and energy necessary to analyze the data.

7. *Check media usage.* It is easy to prepare a frequency distribution to differentiate the usage of each channel listed on the ECCO log. The channels can then be rank-ordered to get a sense of how widely they are used. Additional information can be obtained by comparing different units' frequency of usage. Compute a table for each message featured, similar to the one shown in Table 10.7. On the ECCO log, one can begin to determine the compatibility of a message to given channels. Of particular importance is plotting how the informal channels work in this organization.

8. *Check the message's locus of receipt.* The procedure for determining this is much like the preceding one. The auditor simply lists all the options and then computes the frequency of location for each unit being audited.

9. *Note the timing of each receipt.* Again, a frequency distribution can demonstrate how quickly messages are circulated. To make this information particularly useful, it can

TABLE 10.7. Comparison of Units' Channel Usage

	Top management		Sales		Personnel		Production Group A		Production Group B		Total	
	N	%	N	%	N	%	N	%	N	%	N	%
Telephone	0	0	1	20	6	29	0	0	2	.05	9	8
Informational interaction	2	17	1	20	8	38	22	69	30	77	63	58
Organized meeting	10	83	1	20	7	33	4	13	1	25	23	21
Memos	0	0	1	20	0	0	0	0	1	25	23	21
Organization house organ	0	0	1	20	0	0	6	18	5	13	12	11
Totals	12	100	5	100	21	100	32	100	39	100	109	100

Note. N, the number of messages received using a specific channel; %, the percentage of total messages received using a specific channel.

be related to the channel used. For example, some auditors have learned that the informal channels are often faster than the formal ones.

DRAWING CONCLUSIONS

The adaptability and flexibility of ECCO analysis allow many different focal points, so an auditor must be selective. The previous discussion has already suggested areas that can be audited beneficially. Nevertheless, the following findings from other audits may be instructive. ECCO has been particularly useful in analyzing the informal channels as Davis (1964) did. Marting (1969) found no significant differences either between line and staff employees or between hierarchical levels. Knippen (1970), however, found that employees at higher levels had significantly more information than those at lower levels in a retail chain store. In his audit of branch banks, Lee (1971) discovered that the informal channels primarily flowed downward and were slower than the formal channels.

Second, information blockage has been pinpointed. Davis (1964) was able to specify that certain management levels were blocking downward communication in a manufacturing group. In another audit, Christie and Oyster (1973) described how clique ownership of information restricted the flow of informal messages. Similarly, Davis (1964) identified some functional groups that were consistently isolated.

Channel adequacy has also been assessed. For example, Bailey (1974) noted that the two messages received by the fewest number of respondents were the only two received through Medium A. This finding would lead one to believe that this channel was not very effective in disseminating information generally.

During the 1990s, as a class exercise, Downs traced the patterns among departmental graduate students to discover how information was processed among them. Two liaison individuals were identified, and it was determined that location of offices was a major reason for their being central to the communication flow. Later, when one of the individuals changed offices, she no longer was central to the communication network. Perhaps the most frequent use for ECCO analysis has been to examine roles and network structures. Bailey (1974) found three different communication networks operating in a church. Sanders (1976) contrasted the differences among functional and scalar groupings of administrators. She described precisely how they processed types of information.

ADVANTAGES OF ECCO ANALYSIS

The simplicity of the ECCO instrument is appealing. It does not take much time either to develop or to fill out the questionnaire. Respondents generally find it easy to answer right at their workstations with minimal interruptions. This means that ECCO logs are also inexpensive to administer.

The simplicity and quickness of ECCO analysis allows several logs to be administered over a period of time, thus overcoming the snapshot impression associated with longer questionnaires. Easily adaptable to field settings, it can generate large amounts of data about different aspects of communication in a short time.

The ECCO log's brevity makes it feasible to include all employees in the survey. In fact, if one is going to obtain an accurate assessment of how the message spreads, most employees should be included.

LIMITATIONS OF ECCO ANALYSIS

Perhaps ECCO's greatest weakness is the high nonresponse rate. Even though the questionnaire is simple and short, many people simply refuse to fill it out. Their reaction may be no different to other questionnaires; however, there have been some unique reactions to the ECCO methodology. Comments from potential respondents in one organization indicated that they did not want to identify sources. In fact, several protectively said, "We can't give you that information." These were people high in the organization, and for some reason they felt threatened by the likelihood of identifying the sources, even though the message had been released publicly and they were promised anonymity.

Nonresponse creates a problem for analysis. If 30% do not answer, as happened in one audit, severe limits are placed on any network construction or unit comparisons.

Also, respondent honesty is questionable at times. Although people have been generally open, we have experienced situations in which people did not like to admit they had not heard important information. We have toyed with the idea of testing truthfulness by using a false statement, but the risk is too great because we would be giving people false information. In a sense, the ECCO log is a communication channel that not only tests what people know but also informs them of things that they did not know.

Memory is also a limitation. How does one treat the data when there is obviously a mix-up? For example, in an audit of a university administration, Sanders (1976) circulated a message from the Office of Affirmative Action. However, a number of people "remembered" receiving this information in a memo from the top executive. Upon checking, it was determined that the executive had never sent such a memo. Consequently, the respondents must have been confused or forgetful. Whatever the reason, the data were wrong and any network analysis built on them would have been misleading.

Choice of specific messages is limiting. Although one does try to choose typical or representative messages, there is no way one can assuredly generalize to all messages. Even using 15 messages, as Bailey (1974) did, does not ensure that one really understands how other messages will be processed. Furthermore, the type of messages investigated may not be the most important type. For example, the most crucial messages in an organization are those sent to particular people to enable them to perform their jobs. Since the messages on an ECCO log have to be distributed to all people being audited, specific performance-related messages are often precluded from the study. Finally, ECCO not give the comprehensive overview of organizational communication that is grasped by either of the questionnaires reviewed in previous chapters. Therefore, it may be wise to use it as a supplement to interviews, observations, or other questionnaire.

CONCLUSION

We have described the basic ECCO methodology and pinpointed some of its applications as well as its inherent limitations. It is a valuable audit tool, particularly in tracing the dissemination and networking of a particular message. ECCO covers many of the major elements in the communication process such as sources, receivers, messages, channels, timing, and space. It also has the benefit of being economically practical to administer and is relatively unobtrusive concerning employees' time. Auditors can adapt the ECCO methodology to any organization to collect data about information flow. We find, however, that it is most useful when used in tandem with other audit methodologies.

11

Diagnosing
Communication Networks

D. Thomas Porter
Allyson D. Adrian

To what extent do employees share with each other information about effective or ineffective communication episodes involving customers? Through what channels, and with what effect, is such information exchanged? These are the kinds of questions communication auditors investigate by studying the communication networks in companies (Hargie & Tourish, 2000, p. 309).

The history of studying network structures has a rich and worthy heritage. For example, one can trace the various networks of scholars through which network analysis developed (Susskind et al., 2002). Gestalt theorists who were fleeing Nazi Germany came and planted the seeds of network analysis in the United States (Scott, 1991). Germans such as Kurt Lewin, Jacob Moreno (who left before the Nazis took power), and Fritz Heider differed in the specifics of their theoretical pursuits, but each contributed to the future development of network analysis and each relied on gestalt theory, which stresses the organized *patterns* that *structure* thoughts and perceptions. These organized patterns were seen as "wholes," or systems that have distinct properties from the parts and yet establish the nature of the parts. While commonplace today, this construct of "wholes" was a legitimate paradigm shift in how we consider systemic phenomena. The field of communication saw much network analysis research and development being conducted by Michigan State University faculty and students; their interest focused on the diffusion of innovations (Susskind et al., 2002).

Thus far, most of the methods described in the book have been concerned with questions of attributes, that is, how individual people view the organization. Network analysis taps into a completely different kind of data and thus requires different kinds of questions, particularly questions concerning relations (Scott, 1991). A communication network can be defined as "interconnected individuals who are linked by patterned flows of information" (Rogers, 1995, p. 308). Because one studies the *relations* among people—even the *patterns of relations*—what emerges from the data is the communication structure at work. This communication structure may be quite unlike the organization structure depicted on an organizational chart.

Generally speaking, the actual communication structure is often unrecognized, even by veteran employees. Why? Consider the potential complexity of any communication network. In a company with merely 100 people, there are potentially 4,950 links. (We compute the number of possible links using the formula $N[N-1]/2$, where N is the number of people in the company.) In larger organizations, the potential links are only possible to analyze with computer-aided algorithms. Indeed, in the past, network analysis was often considered expensive and impractical because of the difficulty of tracking all the linkages and analyzing the patterns. This has changed today, however, with the advent of computer packages such as UCINET (Borgatti, Everett, & Freeman, 1995) and GRADAP (Group Definition and Analysis Package; *www.assess.com*), both of which are relatively user-friendly.

The most basic unit of analysis is the communication link between two people. A talks to B about the company newsletter; B talks to C about job cuts. Links can be unidirectional, such as when A sends messages to B, but B sends no messages to A. Or the links can be reciprocal, as when A and B engage in two-way communication. Links can even be transitive, as when A talks to B, B talks to C, then C also talks to A.

When conducting network analysis, the auditor identifies groups based on the communication proximity in networks. *Communication proximity* is the measure of whether two people have personal communication networks that overlap (Rogers, 1995, p. 308). Individuals who are closer in proximity belong to the same *clique*. Personal communication networks are comprised of individuals who are connected by patterns of communication flows to one person. Thus, every person in the company has a personal network. These personal networks are interconnected, which in turn creates the communication structure at work—the structure about which most communication audits are concerned.

A host of other terms are used to describe people in the network. People who are central to a network are called "*role stars*" (Brass, 1995). *Liaisons* link two or more groups to which they do not belong, whereas *bridges* link two or more groups by virtue of belonging to them (Brass, 1995). *Gatekeepers* act as the single link between parts of the network, and thus control the flow of information. *Isolates* are people who have no connections, or perhaps only a few, with other people. These different terms help one to map the organization's communication structure.

WHY STUDY NETWORKS?

The basic rationale for using network analysis is that it helps auditors understand information flow (Porter, 1988). Network analysis can help one ascertain where information flow is being blocked, identify who is blocking it, and even suggest how to implement new communication structures to facilitate greater flow by building new work teams (Stohl, 1995). Information flow is vital to healthy organizations. When information overloads the communication system, people make decisions prematurely, inaccurately, or not at all. Communication costs are enormous, particularly given their oblique linkage to productivity. Accordingly, some of the most difficult-to-acquire resources are often wasted due to poor understanding and use of an organization's actual communication structure. What is the core goal of network analysis? To find that actual communication structure.

Network analysts assume that it matters who talks to whom at work about what topic. By empirically mapping who talks to whom with what frequency and about what, we almost always see a different picture of the organization than the one portrayed by the organizational chart. Mapping who communicates with whom even gives us a different picture than simply asking with whom do people work on tasks. Why does the communication picture matter? Consider some of the following questions that have been answered using network analysis.

Do Employees Share a Common Understanding of the Organization's Mission?

Mission statements provide the direction and rationale for a company's work. Sometimes organizations want to know how people understand the mission simply so they can know whether the mission is fulfilling its purpose. Contractor, Eisenberg, and Monge (1996) analyzed semantic networks to assess whether employees had a shared interpretation of the mission statement. They asked employees about (1) the extent to which other employees actually agreed with them and (2) the extent to which other employees perceived they agreed with them. They discovered people with higher roles in the organization had increased levels of perceived agreement, even where none existed. Those with greater tenure had greater levels of actual agreement, but did not perceive that others shared their view of the mission. People in close communication proximity did not necessarily share interpretations of the mission.

Why Do Some People Embrace or Reject an Innovation?

Scholars agree that communication networks play a vital role in employee attitudes about innovations (Rogers, 1995). Burkhardt (1994) found that employee attitudes and use of a data-processing computer network were directly affected by the attitudes and use of individuals in their communication networks. Likewise, Rice and Aydin (1991) found that hospital employees who communicated with one another or who shared a superior–subordinate relationship were more likely to share similar attitudes about new information technologies. Employee attitudes about email are related to their communication relationships with their supervisors and closest coworkers (Fulk, Schmitz, & Ryu, 1995).

Why Are Some People More Satisfied with Their Work?

A host of factors have been found to be responsible for levels of work satisfaction. Communication, though, plays a strong role in employee job satisfaction (A. Downs, 1991; Orpen, 1997; Pincus, 1986; Ticehurst & Ross-Smith, 1992). Pollock, Whitbred, and

Contractor (1996) found that employee satisfaction was predicted by the satisfaction of people in their communication networks. The satisfaction of their communication linkages was more important even than the job characteristics or employee dispositions.

Why Are Some People More Committed to the Organization than Others?

Organizations are often interested in data that shows their employees' commitment levels. Again, communication variables play a strong role in fostering employee commitment (Adrian & Ticehurst, 2001a). Sometimes, though, employees' loyalty to a team or division negatively affects their commitment to the larger company (Hargie & Tourish, 2000). Hartman and Johnson (1989, 1990) found that employees with cohesive connections were likely to have similar levels of commitment. Understanding the strength of communication ties at various levels may help auditors understand why some people are more committed to their company than others.

As one can see, network analysis asks important and unique questions. The answers to these questions can be critical to a successful communication audit. Nonetheless, numerous questions remain to be asked. For instance, Hargie and Tourish's (2000) questions at the beginning of this chapter raise issues about how communication with clients becomes a source for internal conversation. You may realize at this point that there must be more to analyzing networks than simply counting the frequency of contacts, and you would be right. There are numerous ways in which communication linkages vary, and those difference affect information flow in significant ways.

WAYS OF DESCRIBING COMMUNICATION LINKS

Strength of Ties

Multiple terms are used, but one of the most important descriptions of communication linkages is how strong or how weak the link is. Strong ties indicate closer communication proximity; weak ties indicate less communication proximity. Granovetter's (1973) classic study of getting a job in the United States found that people gained more information from those with whom they had weak ties or less communication proximity. Those with whom they had strong ties (family, friends) were unable to pass on the new information that yielded jobs. Studies in U.S. organizations have found that weak ties are crucial to passing on information and adopting new innovations throughout the entire organization (Rogers, 1995). On the other hand, strong ties play a role in making people feel comfortable adopting new technologies (e.g., email). Fulk and Boyd (1991) found that more cohesive (stronger) ties positively affected employee attitudes and use of email systems. Fulk (1993) explained the importance of cohesive ties by arguing that when strong ties are present, employees give greater support and assistance using the technology. Rogers (1995) suggests that "there is a 'strength of weak ties' component in networks that convey information about an innovation, and a 'strength of strong ties' in networks that convey interpersonal influence" (p. 311). So if auditors are interested in how employees reacted (or *are* reacting) to a change effort, understanding the degree to which strong and weak ties are present in the communication network is indispensable.

Density

Furthermore, the density of communication networks affects how people receive and react to new information. If you viewed each link between two people as a line, then you could count the number of lines as a proportion of the maximum number of lines possible—$l/[n(n-1)/2]$—where l represents the number of lines present. In this way, you can compute the density of a network (Scott, 1991, p. 74). Like strong ties, dense networks are more supportive (Papa, 1990). Their role in adopting new ideas is less clear. Some people have found that dense networks are more averse to making changes and taking risks (Papa, 1990). Others find that dense connections help people feel more comfortable with innovations (Albrecht & Hall, 1991), and facilitate openness to new communication technologies in particular (Fulk, 1993).

Complexity

We have already stipulated that all links are not the same: some are stronger than others. Some communication links are also more complex than others. For example, some employees only interact regarding a single topic or function; Putnam, Phillips, and Chopman (1996) called this a "uniplex linkage." If employees talk about multiple functions, however, they form a multiplex network (Putnam et al., 1996). Multiplex linkages are generally more stable, pass on more information, and tend to be more influential and supportive (Albrecht & Hall, 1991; Stohl, 1995). Many organizations introduce team building to create networks with more multiplex linkages (Stohl, 1995).

Centralization

Sometimes auditors want to assess the degree of centralization because centralized networks have a higher degree of vertical differentiation, lots of isolates, and few liaisons. Decentralized networks allow more participation and information sharing among a greater number of interconnected people (Putnam et al., 1996, p. 382.) In the United States, we often assume decentralized networks are more democratic and that organizational members have a greater voice in their destinies at work (Rosenau, 1992). In order to determine the degree of centralization, however, one must rely on formal positions listed on the organization chart and then compare them to actual communication patterns. Formal networks are an important source of information for the communication auditor, though by no means are they the only ones that should be considered.

TOPICAL NETWORKS

It is all too easy to think of an organization in terms of a single, static, communication network. Nothing could be further from the truth. Researchers continue to find that networks vary dramatically, depending on the topic of interest. Thus one cannot assume that the network that emerges for daily work tasks is identical to the one surrounding a new innovation or even the network for social support (Albrecht & Hall, 1991). Auditors need to do more than demonstrate that a single network exists: the challenge is to identify all the relevant networks. (There are few organizations that can be understood well by *one* network; hence, the plural form of network.) By tracing *semantic networks*— those based on vocabularies and interpersonal relationships—one can see new dimensions to communication flow (Monge & Eisenberg, 1987). Furthermore, employees may perceive either feast or famine where certain messages are concerned. For instance, they may receive no information about the company's relocation or downsizing initiatives, but a glut of information about benefits and compensation. Message content is every bit as important as interaction frequency in creating a picture of the communication map. Though it makes our job more complicated, the reality is that we as communication auditors need to consider both kinds of networks: the formal and the emergent.

So we conclude that whom one talks with at work matters because it affects one's own attitudes and behavior. *Information only becomes knowledge in the hands of people who interpret it.* In some ways, communication networks reflect the communication filters with which people come into contact on a regular basis. Strong communication links often result in strong interpersonal influence—that is, propinquity undergirds interpersonal attraction. Although it may sound dry and rather dull to say the purpose of conducting network analysis is to identify the information flow in the communication structures, do not be fooled. Understanding the communication structure of an organization provides insight into the very essence and richness of organizational life.

This chapter provides a plan for using techniques designed for network analysis and applies them to ongoing "real-world" organizational communication audits. (For a review of technical work on "traditional" approaches, see Moreno, 1934; Bales, 1950; Barnes, 1972; Shaw, 1964; Monge & Day, 1976; Monge & Contractor, 2001.) These techniques give the auditor several advantages.

Traditional approaches to examining communication structure take one of three forms. First, ECCO analysis, discussed in Chapter 10, is useful for some studies but does not always meet the needs of a comprehensive communication audit.

Second, communication diaries or logs theoretically cover all messages in the system. Because their administrative logistics call for every organizational member to note every received or sent message and a variety of associated characteristics, employees soon tire of this assessment process, and the authenticity of collected data becomes quickly suspect.

Third, traditional network analysis (which also takes several different forms) gives detailed descriptions of individuals' information flow, but it too has inherent limitations. For one thing, it requires a *census* to be conducted; sampling communication links within traditional network methodologies simply will not work. A census requires *everyone* to fill out the appropriate data collection forms. Moreover, all it takes to invalidate the whole data set are a few people on vacation, or just one reluctant key individual who avoids filling out the form. For example, in a recent audit, a manager of an important unit refused to be interviewed and did not fill out the demographic data on a questionnaire; therefore, no analysis could be made of his entire unit. Realistically, it is almost miraculous if response rates are as high as 90%; yet validity suffers considerably when even a small (5%) proportion of employees fail to respond.

In addition, traditional network analysis is limited because it gives only a generic view of communication flow. In an audit of a university, respondents were asked to indicate first their network of "formal" communication and then their network of "informal" communication—not exactly the most concrete terms around. Abstract and vague questions create abstract and vague answers, and result in random numbers. On the other hand, many organizations would profit from an assessment of information flow on a *topic-by-topic* basis. For example, a communication flow about potential downsizing may be blocked internally, but the flow may be glutted with information about compensation and benefits. Traditional network analysis would detect neither problem.

In contrast, the approach to network analysis in this chapter relies on noncensus data collection procedures and identifies several message-specific communication networks. Furthermore, the validity of this approach is dependent upon retrieving a random sample, not a census-level data set. *Statistical theory holds that procedures that use a truly random sample of organizational members are more valid than even a network analysis with a 90% return rate.*

Our approach to networks also provides communication structure analyses for a number of different message topics selected by the client organization. Finally, it provides an empirically derived pictorial map of *how* information flows on a *given* message topic. Such information assists managers in identifying blocks in the communication system on one topic while discovering gluts on another. As a result, the techniques presented here make it easier to get to the three essential points of communication network analyses: (1) understanding an organization's communication structure, (2) providing a data base from which systematic changes can be made in communication structures, and (3) taking advantage of this new understanding and change to improve the flow of messages within the system.

CONDUCTING A COMMUNICATION NETWORK STUDY

Although audit interviews and surveys give a glimpse of information flow structures, only a direct, *dedicated* assessment of these networks allows one to:

1. Identify *where* information flow is blocked or overloading a communication network.
2. Identify *who* is blocking or overloading the flow of information.
3. Construct *new* structures to reduce information blocks or overloads.

Interpreting network results is always easier if auditors have conducted audit interviews and surveys that provide a framework for understanding and framing the network data. To conduct an effective communication network analysis one must (1) plan data collection carefully, (2) collect data in a logistically efficient manner, (3) analyze data so that the conclusions are scientifically defensible, (4) interpret the data in a qualitatively integrated manner, and (5) integrate the results into the final plan for organizational communication change and development (Porter, 1988). We focus now on the first four elements of a successful analysis, leaving the final communication plan to the discussion in Chapter 14.

Plan Data Collection

Planning plays a central role in collecting data for a communication network analysis. One needs to resolve four issues before designing a form and collecting data. One must identify (1) *who* is to be studied, (2) an appropriate *sampling* method, (3) *what message topics* are important, and (4) *which work groups* are to be assessed. Unless they make careful, strategic decisions regarding these issues *before* collecting data, auditors will find that they have collected unreliable or biased data. So what? Why does that matter? Such "data" often invariably leads to intractable and organizationally tragic errors, both in terms of interpretation and in terms of application. Only after making these other decisions should auditors set about designing the data collection form (DCF).

First, consider who is to be studied. What constitutes the network? Although the answer may seem obvious at first, the question can be vexing. For example, are part-time workers, contractors, and consultants part of the network? Consider security or janitorial personnel and temporary clericals contracted via an independent company. Their involvement in the organization could be critical, yet their assessments of the communication flow are rarely considered in communication audits. Furthermore, how should external communicative contacts be treated? Messages to and from customers, sales representatives, advertising executives, consultants, and the general public are clearly part of an organization's communication system. Too often auditors assume "important" communication links are limited to the formal, internal organizational structure (Scott, 1991). Yet collecting data from external individuals can be a logistics nightmare. If auditors wish to assess external contacts or temporary internal personnel as part of the communication structure, they must accommodate data collection from them also. Otherwise, it is not uncommon for a data set to be full of references to messages *to* these individuals, yet void of data *from* these individuals and how they view messages in the organization. Therefore, make sure that reciprocation is as high as possible; for every response from work group A about its communications with work group B, one needs information about how B sees communicating with A.

Second, choose whom to sample. Defining relations in the organization is actually quite tricky (Scott, 1991). There are issues of reciprocity, for instance. That is, John may consider that he and Sara have a strong communication link; however, Sara may not recognize the same communication link. Choosing a sample is further complicated by the fact that choosing a representative sample of *employees* does not ensure that one has chosen a representative sample of *employee relations* (Scott, 1991).

By one estimate, the amount of data lost through sampling is equal to $(100 - k)\%$, where k is the percentage of employees included in the sample. Thus, one only gains an accurate picture of the organization by including everyone in the network analysis. If auditors sample 10% of the people, they have lost 90% of the information. Even including 50% of the employees means one has lost 50% of the information. Why does sampling make such a difference in network analysis as opposed to regular surveys and interviews?

The answer is that auditors are interested in matters of *relations*. As indicated above, they need to assess relations rather than individual perspectives. The statistical rules that govern sampling individuals do not apply for relational data based on a sample (Scott, 1991). So what can you do?

Several sampling options are available.

1. You can take a positional approach and group people based on their roles and structural positions. The assumption is that people who fill similar roles have similar attributes. For instance, you could group all the employees who make key decisions and use them as the sample (Scott, 1991).

2. You can use a reputational approach and use a list of nominees produced by knowledgeable informants (Scott, 1991). Auditors tell their participants that they want to talk to people who are involved with certain topics or processes; the informants recommend employees based on their knowledge of how the employees meet auditors' criteria. The obvious danger in this method is that informants can intentionally or unintentionally bias the sample through their choices.

3. You can choose a snowball sample. In a snowball sample, you ask each participant to recommend another participant. The advantage to snowball sampling is that auditors are implicitly drawing on the actual networks. By allowing the sample to emerge, auditors may also succeed in following the emergent networks

4. You can also choose a random sample and focus on several message-specific communication networks, rather than trying to map the entire communication structure. This choice has merit in that one does not claim to be sampling the entire organizational network, but rather focuses on emergent, semantic networks (Monge & Contractor, 2000). Because topic-dependent networks are so important, and random sampling proves to be statistically defensible, this choice is the one we use for examples in this chapter.

Third, identify message topics that are key concerns for the client organization. By identifying specific messages, one can identify influential communication linkages, as well as information blockages or overloads. Most messages communicated by people in organizations center around the following:

1. How well the person does his or her job
2. Job duties
3. Organizational policies
4. Pay and benefits
5. Specific problems faced by management
6. Promotion and advancement opportunities in the organization
7. How the individual's job relates to the whole operation
8. How organization decisions that affect one's job are made
9. How job-related problems are handled

10. The organization's mistakes and failures
11. How technological (or social) changes affect the job
12. Job-related complaints
13. Reporting what an employee does in his or her job
14. Asking for work instructions
15. Evaluating the performance of superiors/subordinates/peers (Porter, 1979, 1985)

While this list provides a useful guide, auditors should modify it to match the client organization's particular semantic idiosyncrasies. Nothing is more dulling to the senses of a respondent than a "canned" untailored DCF. In addition, because this list serves as just a guide, the topics are intentionally vague. The final list of message topics should be as specific regarding the audited organization as possible. For instance, if the organization recently acquired another company, it might wish to identify information blockages and overflows that arise as a result of the consolidation. One could add the item "the acquisition of Mervis Industries." As one can readily see, the selection of message topics and the use of the organization's particular wording significantly affect the usefulness of analyses. The more specific the message topic, the more specific and useful derived conclusions and recommendations can be.

Fourth, identify the actual groups of people. In many audits one will be interested in communication between departments or units—or some other official grouping. If so, one needs to think about the necessary group identification. Which groups of people should be communicating with what other groups? What are the relevant departments or units that should be in contact communicatively with each other? The identification of these work groups could come from the official organizational chart—or perhaps more intelligently, from problem areas identified from interviews or surveys in other parts of the audit. In either case, the work group identification should be exhaustive *and* mutually exclusive. Employees should be able to recognize the work group categories and identify themselves as belonging to one and only one group. If one finds out through pilot testing that a significant number (greater than 5%) of respondents work in more than one work group, one's list of work groups is not mutually exclusive and the network will be much harder if not impossible to trace. If one's list does not cover all work group areas for all respondents, then the list is not exhaustive. *Both* of these criteria must be met. If they are not met, then a key advantage of this approach to network analysis will not accrue: the identification of interunit communication blocks and gluts.

Examining networks between groups may be particularly valuable since our audits have revealed a common problem involving interunit communication across departments.

Collect Data

Auditors collect data in several ways. Auditors can observe interactions personally, use data collection forms linked with computer software, or design their own collection forms.

Personal Observation

For instance, Kilduff and Funk (1998) did a network analysis of a large Japanese high-technology company by relying on intensive participant observation. They collected no surveys, but rather they observed data about (1) how many times pairs of people talked during one week at the beginning of summer, (2) how many times each pair talked during one week at the end of summer, (3) the total number of conversations involving each pair during one day at the beginning of the summer, and (4) the total number of conversations involving each pair one day at the end of the summer. Kilduff and Funk (1998) discovered the existence of enduring subgroups—that is, their observations allowed them to see communication relationships that were stable and ongoing. They were also able to see how the informal communication structure (in this case, conversations) compared with the formal organizational chart.

The disadvantage of participant observation is that the external consultant cannot always observe without disturbing normal communication interactions. As an external person, it is difficult to step in and be a "participant" for a few days. It is also possible that as an external observer one can miss contextual cues meaningful to employees. Observing a few days at a time is definitely better than only observing once; however, the potential remains for missing the rhythms of daily life or the processes that center around one's topics of interest. Participant observation also focuses almost exclusively on face-to-face interaction and misses the importance of electronic communication.

Using a Data-Collection Form (DCF)

As an alternative to participant observation, auditors may design a communication form. Here, modern computer technology provides help. If auditors use UCINET, they can access data-collection forms online. Anyone interested in using UCINET can download free trial copies at *www.analytictech.com*.

Auditors may also design their own forms. If they do, their overall goal should be to develop a data collection form that is aesthetically pleasing, easy to fill out, and complete in detail.

On the first page auditors should ask each employee to identify the work group to which he or she belongs. In addition, one may ask any relevant demographic questions such as sex, length of employment, job classification, or age. Let the employees know the purpose of the network analysis. If auditors are collecting network data as part of a larger survey, they should tell employees how this section differs from the other parts of the survey instrument. The directions should emphasize the necessity of checking one, and one only, work group; otherwise, the data from the individual respondent is worthless. A common format for the forms entails listing a set of message topics and a list of work groups. Employees indicate how much or how often they communicate (sending and receiving) with other work groups.

Figure 11.1 contains an example of a typical form. This particular form was designed for a communication network analysis of 10 work groups. The respondent is in-

Listed below are a series of message topics about which the company regularly sends and receives messages. For each message topic, indicate how often communication (sending or receiving) occurs. When responding, please use the following rating codes:

WORK AREAS

If you communicate (sending or receiving) with the work area:

Never, print a "1"
Seldom, print a "2"
Occasionally, print a "3"
Periodically, print a "4"
Daily, print a "5"

Be sure you have put a number (1, 2, 3, 4, or 5) in each and every space.

MESSAGE TOPIC:

	President's Office	Corporate Staff	Marketing	Los Angeles Sales	Chicago Sales	Cleveland Sales	Accounting and Finance	Indiana Manufacturing	New York Manufacturing	Personnel
1. Pay and benefits	( )	( )	( )	( )	( )	( )	( )	( )	( )	( )
2. Promotion and advancement opportunities	( )	( )	( )	( )	( )	( )	( )	( )	( )	( )
3. Specific problems faced by management	( )	( )	( )	( )	( )	( )	( )	( )	( )	( )

... continue list of Message Topics as desired

FIGURE 11.1. Sample data-collection form.

structed to indicate how often he or she communicates with each work group about each message topic. The auditors who designed the form asked people to respond using a 5-point scale, where 1 = Never and 5 = Daily. The rating scale used here is arbitrary, but it is useful as long as respondents understand it and as long as it goes from low to high degrees or amounts of communicative contact. If possible, use a verbal referent for each point on the low–high continuum; it will reduce respondent confusion. This is particularly important with small scales (e.g., "1–5" vs. "0–100"). Auditors could also use a scale ranging from 0–100, or ask people to estimate the number of times they talk in one time period (e.g., a day, a week, or a month, etc.).

The responses provide the auditor with data that quantifies how each work group is connected communicatively with every other work group. From an analysis of these responses, a mapping of the communication structure can emerge. The auditor can see how informal communication compares with formal structures, and identify where communication is blocked (or overloaded) about "specific problems faced by management," or "pay and benefits," or any other subject put on this message topic list.

Assess the Data

Once auditors have collected the data, they must make two preliminary judgments before data analysis can begin. They must assess the data set for its sampling adequacy and its reliability.

Sampling Adequacy

Auditors need to collect data from an adequate number of employees in each work group identified in Step 1. If everyone in the organization received network surveys, auditors need data from at least 50% of the employees *in each work group*. With less than 50% representation, communication linkage data must be interpreted cautiously. On the other hand, if auditors randomly selected respondents from each work group to fill out the survey, they need data from at least seven to 10 representatives from each work group of 15 to 20 people. When these criteria are not met, the sampling adequacy of the network data set prevents all but the most crude statistical analyses.

Reliability

The statistical value of "reliability" ranges from 0.0 to 1.0, where 0.0 indicates no consistency internally or over time and 1.0 indicates perfect consistency. Two factors affect a communication network data set's reliability (see Porter, 1978, for a technical paper on network reliability). First, the agreement of respondents across work groups about how often or how much they send or receive information affects reliability. If the President's Office respondents say they communicate with Corporate Staff "daily" and Corporate Staff respondents say they communicate with the President's Office "periodically," there is an important inconsistency to be resolved; there is low reliability about the communicative link between the President's Office work group and the Corporate Staff work group. Therefore, one can have little confidence about the quality of this linkage estimation. Serious discrepancies occur when there is greater than a 20% differential between work group linkage values. For example, if the message topics are scaled on a range from 1 to 5, a differential greater than 1.0 (5 × .20) between the work group linkage values indicates a serious lack of reciprocation. While a problem for the network analyst specialist, such reciprocation "deficiencies" are important findings for the auditor. Organizational implications can be profound when one group, for example, perceives "high" contact and the other does not.

Additionally, the number of respondents within a work group also affects reliability. For example, consider two work groups: the Los Angeles Sales group with 12 respondents and the Chicago Sales group with 92 respondents. The 92 respondents will be more reliable over time than the group of 12 respondents. It is somewhat similar to a classroom test. In this case, each respondent is equivalent to a multiple-choice test item. The greater the number of test items, the greater the consistency over time. Assuming all other factors are equally internally consistent, a 20-item test will be less reliable than a 100-item test. If one makes a single clerical error on the 20-item test, it constitutes 5% of the total score. If one makes a similar error on the 100-item test, the effect is almost negligible.

Thus, errors of reliability in network data can be attributed to two sources: (1) the degree to which work groups disagree about their linkage strength (link reciprocation) and (2) the proportion of people who fail to respond to their DCF. When work group A says it communicates with work group B "occasionally" and work group B says it communicates with A "periodically," there is error in the reporting of their linkage strength. When work group C fails to be represented adequately or does not report contact that in fact occurs, error is also introduced. In order to provide estimates of reliability for network analyses, the following formula is useful:

$$\text{Reliability} = \frac{2rP^2}{1 + r}$$

where r is the correlation of reciprocation and P is the proportion of total survey forms returned.

For example, consider an average correlation of .72 between work group linkage values. In other words, if we took the linkage values of work groups A through G (seven groups), constructed correlations between these two sets of values (e. g., A's links to C and C's links to A), and averaged these seven correlations, we would have the correlation of reciprocation ($r = .72$). If 100 people were sampled and 92 returned forms, the proportion of forms would equal .92(P). Thus the reliability of this data set would equal the following:

$$\text{Reliability} = \frac{2(.72)}{1 + .72}\,(.92)^2 = \frac{1.44}{1.72}(.8464) = .71$$

In this formulation, reliability is a function of the degree of reciprocation (average correlation between work group linkage values) and the proportion of respondents providing input. The P value serves to adjust the reliability estimate according to the absence of information (a source of measurement error). Squaring the P value emphasizes the exponential effect of missing information on the resulting picture of the organization's communication network.

In most cases, a reliability coefficient of .65 or higher is acceptable. If .65 is not reached, auditors should try to collect a greater proportion of responses—that is, they should follow up by getting more people to cooperate and return their survey forms.

Compile and Analyze the Actual Network

Once auditors are confident of the data set's adequacy and reliability, they can begin the analysis. To do so they need to construct a geometric map of how work groups are connected communicatively; fortunately, computers now make constructing these maps relatively easy. UCINET uses a program called KrackPlot (Carnegie-Mellon University, 2003) to evaluate communication proximity statistically. The program uses multidimensional scaling and simulated annealing to compute the networks. One can specify different colors for different "nodes" or people. Figure 11.2 illustrates one such network map. In the figure, the width of the lines corresponds to the strength of the relationship: wider lines represent stronger ties.

Figure 11.3 illustrates another output for a given message topic, the "acquisition of Tandem Industries." In the mapping, the closer the dark circles, the closer the communicative linkage. Figure 11.3 shows, for example, that the Accounting work group and the

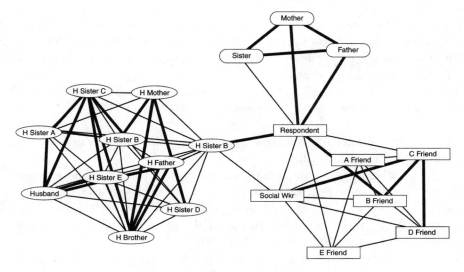

FIGURE 11.2. Communication matrix.

Human Resources work group are very far apart communicatively on the acquisition of Tandem Industries; in other words, these two work groups had little communication contact on this message topic.

The procedures used to create Figure 11.3 come from a statistical technique called "smallest space analysis." For a complete technical description of how to execute the statistics described in the example that follows, see Norton (1980). We use Norton's actual data here to illustrate how smallest space analysis is used for communication network

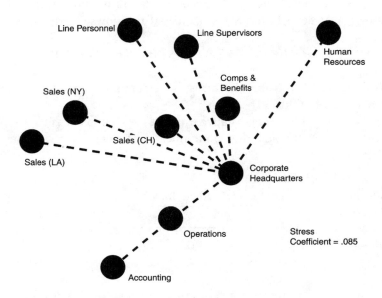

FIGURE 11.3. Information flow analysis.

analyses. Auditors have many options for calculating networks now, and most of the time they do not need to know the statistical operations to run the computer programs.

To show how these statistics operate, however, consider the example in Figure 11.3 and smallest space analysis (Porter, 1988). Assume that there are communication linkages between four work groups: (1) the Los Angeles Sales Group (LA), (2) the Chicago Sales Group (CH), (3) the New York Sales Group (NY), and (4) the Corporate Headquarters (HQ).

The rank of their average linkage values would look like the "rank table" in Table 11.1 (Norton, 1980, p. 312, Table 4).

The rank table weighs interactions so that a visual cofiguration of these work groups matches the numerical values provided by the work groups.

Next we *arbitrarily* place the work groups in a two-dimensional space (Dimension I and Dimension II). Table 11.2 illustrates what the initial geometric coordinates table might look like (Norton, 1980, p. 313, Table V).

If the initial visual placement of the work groups is fairly close to the relationships reflected in the rank table, fewer adjustments (iterations) are necessary to reach a "best fit"—that is, the fit between the communication link data and the visual map of that linkage data.

Next we compute all possible distances between the four work groups using the Pythagorean theorem for right triangles. These geometric distant are calculated for each relationship (e.g., between HQ and LA) by the following equation (Norton, 1980, p. 313):

$$d_{ij} = \frac{1}{2}[(X_{ia} - X_{ja})2 + (X_{ib} - X_{jb})2]$$

where X_{ia} is the coordinate for the first location in Dimension 1, X_{ja} is the coordinate for the second location in Dimension 1, X_{ib} is the coordinate for the first location in Dimension 2, and X_{jb} is the coordinate for the second location in Dimension 2. For example, the distance (d_{23}) between CH and NY is calculated as follows (Norton, 1980, p. 314):

$$d_{23} = \frac{1}{2}[(8.00 - 3.20)2 + (3.00 - 5.60)2] = 5.46$$

Once this is done for all possible distances, we create a distance table like Table 11.3 (Norton, 1980, p. 314, Table VI).

The goal is to get these *visual* distance estimates as close as possible to their numerical source: the LA, CH, NY, and HQ communication linkage values. To see whether or

TABLE 11.1. Rank Table

	LA	CH	NY	HQ
LA	—	12	13	14
CH	4	—	23	24
NY	2	6	—	34
HQ	1	5	3	—

TABLE 11.2. Coordinates Table in Two-Dimensional Space

	Dimension I	Dimension II
LA	4.00	3.00
CH	8.00	3.00
NY	3.20	5.60
HQ	2.00	3.00

not these distances are sufficiently accurate, a "stress test" is calculated (Norton, 1980, pp. 314–316). The amount of stress tells whether these arbitrary dimension points are useful and how much to adjust them to get an acceptable fit. The initial coordinates are adjusted by creating a correction set of new coordinates (c_{ij}) such as those in the following calculation (Norton, 1980, p. 316):

$$\text{If } i = j, \text{ then } c_{ij}^{*(t)} = 1 + \sum_{k} \frac{d_{ik}^{*}}{d_{ik}}$$

$$\text{If } i \neq j, \text{ then } c_{ij}^{*(t)} = 1 - (d_{ij}^{*}/d_{ij})$$

For example, the correction adjustment for HQ would be 3.91 (instead of 4.00 in the initial configuration):

$$HQ_{44} = 1 + \frac{2.00}{2.00} + \frac{5.46}{6.00} + \frac{2.86}{2.86} = 3.91$$

Carrying out the correction adjustment for all possible distances gives the new set of coordinates for Dimension I and Dimension II listed in Table 11.4 (Norton, 1980, p. 317, Table XI).

Once these new coordinates are used for LA, CH, NY, and HQ, creating an accurate picture of their communication relationships becomes possible.

These new averages then can be placed in the appropriate places in a "table of relationships" like the one in Table 11.5. The numbers in the upper right half of the table represent the average rating between the particular work group combinations. For example, the rating of 3.15 between the President's Office work group and the Personnel work

TABLE 11.3. Table of Calculated Distances

	LA	CH	NY	HQ
LA	—	d_{12}	d_{13}	d_{14}
CH	4.00	—	d_{23}	d_{24}
NY	2.72	5.46	—	d_{34}
HQ	2.00	6.00	2.86	—

TABLE 11.4. **Adjusted Coordinates in Two-Dimensional Space**

	Dimension I	Dimension II
LA	4.00	3.00
CH	7.99	2.94
NY	3.08	5.67
HQ	2.16	3.01

group indicates that the strength of their communication link is somewhere between "occasionally" and "periodically." Please remember, of course, that there is no magic to these numbers. They have meaning only when compared to the other numbers in the table. Assessing the relative strength of these numbers is a major value of smallest space analysis.

The next step is to rank-order the strength values in the upper half of the table in Table 11.5. This means assigning a "1" to the largest or strongest communication link, a "2" to the next strongest, and so forth. The lower left half of the table in Table 11.5 contains these ranks. For example, the strongest communication link (4.78) is between the Chicago Sales work group and the Indiana Manufacturing work group. Note the rank of

TABLE 11.5. **Sample Table of Relationships and Rank: "Hiring a New Vice-President for Manufacturing Operations"**

Work group area	President's office	Corporate staff	Marketing	Los Angeles sales	Chicago sales	Cleveland sales	Accounting and finance	Indiana manufacturing	New York manufacturing	Personnel
President's office		4.14	3.78	3.98	3.75	4.21	4.25	3.79	3.81	3.15
Corporate staff	10		2.75	2.58	2.49	2.67	2.01	2.65	2.71	2.99
Marketing	17	29		4.01	3.73	3.89	2.11	3.12	3.32	1.75
Los Angeles sales	12	33	11		1.51	1.45	3.55	4.51	4.55	1.34
Chicago sales	18	34	19	40		2.02	3.41	4.78	4.66	1.47
Cleveland sales	9	31	14	42	36		3.47	4.52	4.23	1.32
Accounting and finance	6	37	35	20	22	21		3.01	2.78	1.97
Indiana manufacturing	16	32	25	5	1	4	26		1.43	3.95
New York manufacturing	15	30	23	3	2	7	28	43		4.22
Personnel	24	27	39	44	41	45	38	13	8	

Note. The values in the upper half of the table are average rating values between the particular group areas, where "1" = "never communicate" to "5" = "communicate daily." The values in the lower half of the table are the rank order of the values in the upper half of the table.

"1" in the table. The weakest link (rank = 45) is found between the Cleveland Sales work group and the Personnel work group (linkage value = 1.32). These ranks function to weigh the strength values in order to obtain a geometric configuration of how these numbers fit together. In other words, these ranks tell us what work groups are linked most closely communicatively. Without these ranks, smallest space analysis cannot assess whether or not the geometric map of the communication structure is accurate.

Interpret the Data

Until auditors give some meaning to the geometric map of the communication structure, they have only data, not information. They need to give some meaning to the data in order to make intelligent, scientifically defensible recommendations to the organization. Thus the emphasis in Step 4 is on giving meaning to the numbers and their corresponding geometric maps.

Auditors should use three strategies to interpret data from a network analysis. First, examine the numbers for statistical and organizational problems. Second, inspect the visual map of communication relationships (e.g., Figure 11.2 or Figure 11.3) for "surprises," for it is in these surprises that one learns more about the client organization and its communication flow. Network data can enrich findings that auditors gather from surveys and interviews. Network data, in addition, have a special characteristic to reflect aspects of organizational life unable to be "seen" using other methods. Third, generate specific recommendations not only about the overall communication flow, but also about communication relationships between specific work groups.

Examine the Numbers

Technically examining the numbers falls into the preanalysis stage of interpreting data. Because some interpretation is necessary even as one determines sampling adequacy and reliability, we want to discuss it again here with an example. As you examine the numbers, look for a "red flag," for example, discrepancies in reciprocation values. Returning to the example in Figure 11.3, perhaps the Los Angeles (LA) Sales group reports that it communicates with Chicago Sales an average of 3.5 (on a 5-point scale). Chicago, on the other hand, reports that it communicates with the LA Sales group an average of 2.4. There is a serious discrepancy here—serious nonreciprocation.

Auditors could interpret the unacceptable anomaly in several ways. There could be a simple problem of sampling adequacy. Perhaps one of the sales groups was not adequately sampled either because there was an insufficient response from one group or because nonrandomly selected respondents from one group were more (or less) eager to report communications with the other work group. On the other hand, the LA Sales group may, in fact, communicate more with Chicago than Chicago wants to admit. For whatever reason, Chicago thinks the connection is not as strong. Needless to say, without qualitative data from the interviews or surveys, it would be difficult to figure out which interpretation is correct. This example highlights the need to collect multiple forms of data if one hopes to turn that data into information—that is, to triangulate your audit methodology wherever possible.

Examining the numbers for sampling adequacy is critical. As we emphasized several times in this chapter, auditors must sample each work group adequately in terms of numbers of respondents and respondent representation. If only 4% of the LA Sales work group provides communication strength ratings, but 11% of the Chicago Sales work group provides ratings, then by definition auditors will have a more accurate picture of Chicago's communication links than LA's. If at all possible, auditors should follow up with LA to increase the group's respondent rate.

In addition, an examination of key demographics from the first page of the DCF can be used to assess the other side of sampling adequacy: respondent representation. For example, if the work group Personnel is composed of 63% women but only 48% of its respondents were women, the communication strength values will be biased toward male perceptions. This imbalance may not matter on one topic, but it may matter on others. Therefore, you must follow up with additional efforts to balance the analysis of respondent data with known organizational demographics.

As a final check, auditors should also examine the numbers for strong and weak communication links. For example, they should inspect those three or four work groups with the highest communication relationship values. Table 11.5 indicates that the LA, Chicago, and Cleveland Sales groups have close connections with the manufacturing work groups of the organization. As the specific message topic being traced in Table 11.5 was "Hiring a new vice-president for Manufacturing Operations," these strong communicative links make sense.

In contrast, Corporate Staff and these same work groups have relatively weak communication links. Perhaps Corporate Staff, like many corporate staffs, is out of the mainstream of key decisions. Often corporate staffs are viewed and treated as decision implementers, not decision makers. Qualitative data collected elsewhere in the audit can assist in deciding which interpretation makes more sense.

Although these data inspections and follow-up procedures may seem tedious, they are critical nonetheless. Respondent under- or overrepresentation will affect conclusions. Without taking time for data inspection and appropriate follow-up procedures, auditors will not know how, or even whether, unfortunately, their conclusions were affected. There is no point in wasting the client's time and resources on collecting communication network data if those data lead to faulty conclusions. And they will—without detailed data inspection and appropriate follow-up action.

Look for Surprises

Surprises come in a variety of forms. First, look for closeness where communicative distance is expected. Second, look for distance where communicative proximity is expected.

The geometric map in Figure 11.3 illustrates several of both types of surprises. For example, consider the communicative distance between Accounting and Corporate Headquarters. The acquisition of a new company should directly involve Accounting; yet, relatively speaking, the communicative distance between the two groups is large. In addition, consider the relative noncentrality of Operations. While Corporate Headquarters should be in a communicatively central position (and it is), Operations should also be centrally located.

Some distances are not surprising. Tandem Industries was located physically nearest Chicago, and, as such, Chicago Sales is "communicatively close" to Corporate Headquarters on this message topic. An alternative interpretation here may be that Chicago Sales is also closest physically to Corporate Headquarters (30 miles). Resolution of the correct interpretation would come from other communication audit data sources.

It is also clear that Human Resources, on this message topic, remains relatively isolated. Perhaps Human Resources needs to be more communicatively close, given the significance of adding a union company to a predominately nonunion holding company (the client, organization).

Some of the communication linkages are strong and should be strong. For example, the closest work groups communicatively are Line Person and Line Supervisors. This is as it should be. Some of the communicative relationships are relatively weak and perhaps should be. For instance, the linkage between Line Personnel and Accounting is weak and has no reason to be stronger, relatively speaking. While these latter interpretations are not surprises per se, they do confirm the validity of the geometric representation—an important feature if we expect the client organization to take the results of the network analysis seriously.

Generate Recommendations

Generating recommendations results from "examining the numbers" and "looking for surprises." From examining the numbers in the example, auditors could generate at least two recommendations. First, auditors learned from interviews that poor reciprocation between Chicago and LA Sales was due to Chicago Sales thinking of itself as superior to LA—that is, Chicago accounted for 76% of sales of the primary product line and was closest to the action at Corporate Headquarters. The auditors' recommendation was:

> "Transfer two key personnel from Chicago to LA to 'help' LA increase sales and reduce the competitiveness between two groups that should be cooperating."

From the numbers auditors also found Corporate Staff had weak communicative connections to a large proportion of the other groups. From interviews the auditors found that Corporate Staff personnel believed they were "left out of several key decisions and that the President's Office and Accounting thought Corporate Staff should be left out." They also learned that Corporate Staff were required to implement aspects of acquisition decisions and held accountable for that implementation. The auditors' recommendation was:

> "Inform Corporate Staff of decisions regarding acquisitions as they are being made. Otherwise they cannot be held accountable for the decision results."

From looking at the surprises, auditors could make at least two further conclusions. The visual map in Figure 11.3 showed that Accounting and Corporate Headquarters were communicatively distant. From the additional climate survey auditors found much lower job satisfaction in Accounting. From interviews they learned that Accounting personnel were suffering from an acute sense of job insecurity. Preliminary investigation of the client organization and interviews with Corporate Headquarters personnel disclosed that the client was suffering from severe fiscal stress (cash flow), yet it was committed to a growth-through-acquisition/diversification program. The auditors' recommendation: None.

The fiscal parameters of the client were beyond the auditors' communication expertise and were deemed to be the true cause of problems, not communicative distance per se. In other words, business problems were causing communication problems, not communication problems causing fiscal stress.

From the visual map of communication relationships auditors also found Operations was out of the communicative mainstream. Analysis of the demographics of Operations personnel revealed almost all respondents had been in their positions less than 1 year. From follow-up interviews auditors learned that Operations was a new organizational entity and did not, as first suspected, suffer from a high turnover rate. Recommendation:

> "Since Operations is a new organizational entity and is left out of key decisions regarding the acquisition of Tandem Industries, Operations and Corporate Headquarters should be housed physically in the same building."

Although one could certainly derive more recommendations from both the numbers and the visual map, these recommendations illustrate three principles. First, they reflect all the available data sources. None of the recommendations presented here could have been made without qualitative data from other sources—for example, interviews. Second, the fact that there is a communication disturbance does not mean that there are communication-related reasons for such a disturbance. It is better at times to admit that and simply back away. Third, the recommendations reflect simple sense. Too often it takes complex diagnostic tools to bring about commonsense recommendations. And sometimes common sense becomes apparent only when auditors have "data" to support it.

In summary, interpreting the data comprises three strategies: examining the numbers, inspecting the visual map for surprises, and generating recommendations. The goal of interpreting communication network data is to give meaning to the numbers. We need information, which is data given meaning, to integrate the recommendations into the overall strategic plan for organizational communication change and development, which is discussed in Chapter 14.

CONCLUSION

An auditor's goal in communication network analyses is to understand the underlying structure of an organization's communication flow. To accomplish this goal, data must be (1) collected in a well-planned and logistically defensible way; (2) analyzed in a scientifically and pragmatically justified way; and (3) interpreted in a qualitatively integrated manner. The success of these steps depends on integrating all data sources into recommendations, considering at all times the client's needs—from data collection to recommendation integration—and involving the client in the entire process. Without client involvement, not only will many recommendations be irrelevant and misleading, but also the client will not "own" them and the analysis will become "just another consultant's report on the shelf." As an auditor, one has an ethically driven, professional responsibility to see that this does not happen.

D. Thomas Porter, PhD, School of Mass Communications, University of South Florida, Tampa, Florida.

12

Focus Group Interviews

Government Organization T had a Unit A comprised of 450 people. After collecting survey data from the people in Unit A, and conducting personal interviews with many of its members, we still needed to know how the interdependent units throughout Organization T—that is, Unit A's internal "customers"—reacted to Unit A. To do so, our communication audit needed to incorporate an additional methodology not yet discussed: the focus group. To collect the necessary information—or perspectives—we interviewed eight internal "customers" for 2 hours in a group setting. The insights we gained from the perspectives expressed in that group completely changed our understanding of Organization T's operations and Unit A's role within the organization. The organizational members' interactions in the focus group provided a different kind of data and a different picture of the organization than we had been able to obtain previously using both quantitative and qualitative methods. Auditors should value the focus group as an additional resource for gaining perspective in a thorough communication audit.

Basically, a *focus group* is a collection of 6–15 people, led by a moderator, who engage in an intensive exploration of some general questions or concepts planned by the auditor. Because it has become the research methodology of choice for so many people and because it sounds so easy to do, it can easily be misused. Nevertheless, well-conducted focus groups can contribute a great deal to our understanding of an organization. A focus group is a special kind of interview, and the prescriptions covered in Chapter 5 apply. The big difference is that this interview involves a group, not an individual, and thus the focus is not on confidentiality but on how members' perceptions build on one another.

HISTORY

Focus group interviews are adaptable to many situations. During the 1990s the popularity of focus groups as a research methodology soared as people became interested in in-depth qualitative data. Almost no U.S. political or marketing decision will be made without first testing the public's reactions to that decision in focus groups. A search of the World Wide Web in August 1999 yielded almost 6 million references to focus groups.

Originally, focus groups were used extensively for making *marketing decisions*; that continues to be one of their most important uses. While most of them continue to be conducted in face-to-face group settings, some are now conducted via the Internet. A Web search in 2002 revealed many companies who claim to conduct electronic focus groups.

The following list suggests some of the ways focus groups have been used:

1. Testing website usability.
2. Naming a product and a university class.
3. Testing brand image and differentiation.
4. Designing credit cards to appeal to certain demographic groups.
5. Designing logos for organizations.
6. Deciding on packaging in terms of color, design, shape, and so on.
7. Choosing the design of a book.
8. Testing reactions to popular songs and predicting hits.
9. Obtaining reactions to potential news anchors.
10. Restructuring individual parts of a national magazine.
11. Brainstorming new uses for a product.
12. Determining why a new product failed in a particular regional market.

Political usage has also increased to the extent that the government now uses focus groups almost as much as businesses do. Politicians use them to sample opinions about any political issue relevant to a campaign. For example, a political candidate wanted to know how his divorce would affect people's reactions to him, so he retained a firm to conduct focus group interviews in his state to investigate campaign issues, including reactions to his divorce. While citizens often complain that public policy is determined too heavily on the basis of what politicians learn in focus groups, the fact that they are used so thoroughly and so effectively testifies to the credibility of their results. Many governmental agencies also base their decisions on the data obtained from focus groups. For example, the Environmental Protection Agency has used focus group technologies to evaluate products and to enlist the aid of trade associations.

Focus groups are also suitable for analyzing many aspects of *organizational communication*. We have used focus groups to investigate a number of different communication issues. For instance, we have used them extensively to make recommendations about warnings that manufacturers should put on a product. This area is not often covered in basic organizational communication literature, but it is a very important aspect of communicating in our current legalistic society.

Also, manufacturers often want to anticipate reactions to their advertising. In one case, we picked five commercials about similar products and ran focus groups to discuss customers' reactions to the manufacturer's TV commercials versus their reactions to those of the competition.

The previous examples concerned the organization's external communication with its customers—a common type of communication explored in focus groups, though auditors often overlook it. Focus groups, however, are also extremely useful for assessing the organization's internal communication. For instance, how do people within the organization perceive interdepartmental communication? Once a manager wanted to know about the communication among four of his departments. Consequently, a focus group enabled us to provide concrete examples of where communication was perceived to have broken down.

Similarly, once Downs needed to know how managers would react to the proposed implementation of 360-degree feedback. He tested employee reactions in a focus group by exploring each aspect of the design. He was thus able to help the organization anticipate both positive and negative reactions to the new process and therefore to plan useful modifications to its implementation.

Indeed, one of the strengths of focus groups is that they provide much-needed insights for planning the implementation of new processes and plans. Even training programs can be viewed as new projects needing to be implemented. For example, we once tested the elements of a training program on a group of managers as part of the crucial development of the training program. The "test" differed from traditional testing procedures in that the focus group allowed managers to share their reactions to the training process and to build on each other's reactions, rather than relying on an external observer's assessment.

Only recently have auditors begun using focus groups in their communication audits. They can be tremendously useful in understanding organizational communication issues from the perspectives of the participants. Furthermore, the communication interaction within the focus group provides the auditor with added insight that would not be gained in interviewing employees one-on-one.

NATURE OF THE FOCUS GROUP INTERVIEW

One of the distinguishing characteristics of the focus group is that it taps _qualitative data_. Whereas auditors often want to quantify the answers they get in interviews and questionnaires, the auditor's use of a focus group gives him or her an opportunity to explore in depth the scope of reactions to a given person, procedure, or concept. It is important to note that the auditor should be trying to discover the _range of responses, not consensus of the group_. As the example at the beginning of the chapter illustrates, in conducting the focus group we were looking for understanding of Organization T's perspectives, not necessarily Organization T's agreement in the form of a single perspective.

Listed below are some of the ways this qualitative research technique can be used in conjunction with an audit:

1. The interview focuses on subjective experiences for the purpose of ascertaining interviewees' definitions of the situation in which they were involved (Merton, Fiske, & Kendall, 1961, p. ix).
2. It can be conducted as a preliminary step to determine what needs to be surveyed or quantified. In other words, it could be an initial part of an audit.
3. It is often used as a means to secure information to interpret the results already

obtained from a quantitative analysis. For example, in most of our audits, we find people's answers running the gamut across the entire scale for most items. We can quantify the experience, but we cannot know "why" they answer as they do. The focus group is an excellent forum for exploring "why." Additionally, we often compare surveys with a benchmark year so that we can demonstrate changes, but we do not know always *why* the changes took place. The focus group helps discover that information.

4. Some people have used the focus group as their primary means of collecting data for an audit, but this can be dangerous if a biased group is used. In analyzing a university, a number of people volunteered to be interviewed as a group, and the results could have been stacked in their favor had we just relied on them. Group selection is very important.

5. It uncovers differences in perspectives as well as the factors that influence these perspectives. For example, top management may have different views than the nonmanagers do. Salespeople may have different perspectives than the accounting employees do. They work for "different organizations" even if the name is the same (Krueger & Casey, 2000).

ADVANTAGES OF FOCUS GROUPS

The popularity of focus groups is well deserved; as a resource, they can be an exceedingly useful way of accumulating information. Furthermore, focus groups have some very special advantages over other data-gathering techniques. These advantages include (1) efficiency, (2) free association, (3) reliability checks, (4) economy, (5) flexibility, (6) speed, and (7) participant satisfaction.

The greatest advantage of a focus group is its *efficiency* in collecting information. In just 1–2 hours the auditor can obtain a great deal of information from a number of respondents.

They also give respondents a chance to talk freely—even to *free associate*—without the restrictions imposed by systematic questioning. Furthermore, "The interaction in a focus group is multiplicative, with each respondent becoming a richer source of information than he or she would be alone. This happens because one interviewee's statement serves as a crystallizing accent and as a springboard for additional comments and ideas [by others]" (Downs, Smeyak, & Martin, 1980, p. 396). Since different members of the group have different levels of knowledge, they learn from one another. Furthermore, "as a part of group dynamics, interviewees may be challenged and forced to defend their views with a spontaneity that becomes valuable research data in itself" (Downs et al., 1980, p. 396).

A corollary to the multiplicative nature is that the focus group provides some quality control and *reliability checks* as participants provide some checks-and-balances for the opinions of one another. As in a personal interview, the in-depth responses of focus group members can be explored in detail and offer greater understanding than can be acquired through most written survey techniques. However, the multiplicative interaction makes the focus group even more valuable in this regard than the personal interview. An auditor may want to understand in great detail a communication process involved in decision making. In interviewing employees separately, one can piece together elements of the process, but in the focus group one can actually iron out the details of the process in order to get a composite explanation.

In terms of costs, focus groups are more *economical* than large survey projects. Eight people can be interviewed in 2 hours, whereas individual interviews would certainly take more time than that. Processing a survey would take several days. Furthermore, focus groups can be analyzed without elaborate data-processing requirements. Whereas we have always remunerated people in focus groups outside the organization, we have never had to pay anyone while doing a communication audit.

Focus groups give the auditor great *flexibility*. Indeed, "The study design can be modified while it is in progress" (Debus, 1990, p. 2). They also allow for probing that is not possible with questionnaire responses.

Focus groups offer *quick results*. Depending on the number of groups run, one can generate conclusions soon after the group interaction. Those conclusions may include observations of interactions between some of the key liaison individuals in the organization.

Finally, focus groups tend to be *enjoyable communicative interactions* for the participants. We have never facilitated a group where people felt they were not contributing something. Indeed, we have conducted many focus groups where the group wanted to stay and visit after the interview was officially over.

CHALLENGES OF FOCUS GROUPS

Since the focus group is a qualitative research technique, much attention has been paid to its potential pitfalls. Academic researchers do not always agree on what is or is not acceptable. Nevertheless, the following disadvantages are mentioned as potential difficulties. One will note, however, that some of them are not inherent weaknesses of the focus group technique, but rather are weaknesses in the way they are used.

First, *realistic interpretation* of focus group data is a key challenge. Comments must be interpreted in context as auditors try to get a "feel" for the organization and as they try to draw out the subtle, complex aspects of organizational processes and relationships. As a qualitative research technique, the focus group "is highly dependent upon insight and interpretation . . . [and is] susceptible to subjective bias on the part of the researcher" (Debus, 1990, p. 3). This, of course, is the bugaboo of all analysts—that is, researchers making certain that they find what they want to find. Given the fact that one is not trying to count the number of people who say one thing or the other, but rather trying to discover the range of responses, auditors have considerable latitude in selecting what is relevant to a given conclusion. If the qualitative auditor has only marginal experience or is not careful about objectivity, it is possible to let the biases sway too heavily.

Second, small sample sizes often make it *difficult to generalize* to a large population—but focus groups should not be analyzed as if they were quantitative studies anyway. The important element is to use them to get insight into the organization. It is difficult to assign statistical meaning to focus group data, but an auditor can certainly gain understanding of the processes involved in the organization.

Third, the advantage of the multiplicative interaction also creates a disadvantage: a *lack of depth*. The interviewer is not able to explore each person's thinking, background, and experience in the depth that he or she might in a personal interview. Each respondent's information is revealed in a much more piecemeal fashion. Similarly, a limited number of questions or topics can be explored in the allotted time. Presumed pressure for socially acceptable responses often distort the reality of the way people describe the way they feel. People have ideas of what it means to be politically, religiously, or organizationally correct, and this mind-set limits what they say publicly. Yet what people actually think can sometimes be gaged by whether or not they want to continue to participate in organizational projects and processes. For instance, one of us participated in a focus group in a church concerning its sponsorship of free meals for the homeless. After several years, members had noted that it was not just the homeless who were coming, but "regular" people who just wanted a free meal. Members of the church were reluctant to articulate their resentments about these "freeloaders": no one wants to sound like an ogre. But concerns about freeloaders have caused the number of volunteers in this program to dwindle. Even when people will not say what they truly feel, they register their feelings by abandoning the process.

Fourth, each group develops its own dynamics which form a unique *group personality*. Some produce good discussions and some do not. In terms of group dynamics, individuals within the group can sometimes create problems by talking too much or by so dominating the discussion that the group experience has limited value. Again, this is not an inherent limitation of the focus group, but it can be a common occurrence.

Fifth, *confidentiality* is totally lost. One can assure privacy in a personal interview; one can only ask all participants to respect their fellows' privacy in the focus group. Some people are inhibited from sharing, knowing that someone from their own organization could publicize what they say on a given topic.

Sixth, since most focus groups occur with a *time limit* of 1–2 hours, there is not enough time to probe everything that the moderator might wish to probe. Furthermore, it may not be possible to probe topics as systematically as the moderator might wish. Much depends on the group interactions.

Seventh, *interpretation* is a key challenge. Comments must be interpreted in context as auditors try to get a "feel" for the organization. The fact that there are often differences in perceptions presents the auditor with some important filtering to analyze.

Eight, it is altogether possible for a consultant to encounter a situation where the climate is so emotionally charged in an organization that a group discussion might *aggravate the conflict*. We have never encountered a problem with a focus group in this regard; nevertheless, it is a consideration when choosing to use focus group interviews rather than individualized interviews (Krueger & Casey, 2000).

Even though there are some disadvantages associated with focus groups, please note that most of these are not inherent to the process. Like other methods, the effectiveness of the focus group may be influenced by the skill of the auditor. That is why examining the protocols and suggestions for facilitating a focus group are so important.

FOCUS GROUP PROTOCOLS

Keep the Objectives in Mind

The first step in any assessment process is to analyze your objectives and identify the organizational issues that you wish to understand more thoroughly. Everything flows from this initial statement. In planning the interview, ask yourself "What do I want to be able to say at the end of the focus groups?" Be as specific as possible.

Developing your objectives will ordinarily lead to a concrete list of questions to ask or topics to explore. Designing these questions will be an important part of your planning. The following are some sample questions we have found successful.

> What forms of communication at ACME have been particularly helpful to you?
> What influences your commitment to this organization, either negatively or positively?
> If you had the opportunity to be CEO for a day, what would you do?
> How do you think the communication across departments could be improved?

Solicit Respondents for the Focus Groups

An auditor has an advantage over the people who do market or political research because organizational members may expect to participate and do so willingly. In some market research, no-shows are a constant problem.

Determine the number of people to be interviewed, and thus determine how many groups will be needed. There are no hard-and-fast rules to be followed here. A major consideration is to balance out the numbers of people surveyed versus those given in-depth interviews. Auditors must also consider the geographical locations to be represented. In some of our work, we have tried to make certain that each major geographic region (or local site) of an organization was represented.

Determine the composition of the group. The composition of a focus group may vary, of course, with the purpose of the project. At times, auditors may desire very different points of view to be shared. Thus, a very diverse group is warranted. In a state government organization that had employees dispersed geographically, we selected people from different geographic areas who might meet in central locations for the actual discussion. In that case, we wanted the diversity of perspectives that came with geographic location.

On the other hand, you want the focus group to engage in a true discussion—not simply to express a random series of unrelated views. "To obtain the most valuable qualitative information, participants should have some unifying elements out of which true discussion can grow" (Downs et al., 1980, p. 401). In our opening example about Unit A, we selected people who were Unit A's in-house customers or clients. These people were supervisors or managers from the other units. This made sense because they were people who would have a good view of the interdependence of the organization's units and the need for interactions. They shared a common level of responsibility that enabled them to have a good discussion.

In some cases, we have asked for volunteers; however, one must be careful because volunteers may neither be representative of the organization nor desire to discuss the issues at hand. Indeed, volunteers may have a specific agenda to pursue that non-volunteers do not and would not endorse. *Auditors should be aware of the bias that can be introduced to the data by relying solely on volunteers.*

In summary, there are three rules of thumb to be considered in determining the composition of the group. First, consider people's status in the organization because including managers and nonmanagers in the same group can inhibit the exchanges. Second, select a group with some common experiences (or levels of responsibility) in the organization to facilitate productive interactions. In this way, auditors can avoid the problem of some participants feeling "lost" because they lack the experience of the others. Third, make certain that focus group membership includes representatives from most major units, geographical regions, or division of the organization.

Call Potential Participants

Have a liaison in the organization call each potential participant and explain what a focus group is and why this person is being invited. This contact provides legitimacy for the forum and may allay fears people have about being selected to participate. The grapevine may construe all kinds of purposes and motivations for the meeting; the liaison can counteract those messages to some extent by talking directly with the potential participants.

Choose a Length for the Focus Group

Participants need to know how long they can expect to be in the group. Furthermore, the facilitator can plan how long it will take to accomplish the purpose. If 10 people, for example, come in for an hour, then theoretically that gives each of them 6 minutes to talk. Can interviewers realistically cover the materials they want to know in 6 minutes per individual? If not, then a longer period may be necessary. The size of the group has a direct bearing on the length of time that it should meet for.

Arrange the Group Setting

The two most important considerations of meeting place are (1) ease of assembly and (2) an environment that facilitates interactions. In terms of convenience, a logical place to assemble is generally a meeting room in the organization itself. This enables members to take the shortest amount of time away from work. However, if different geographical areas are to be represented, then a conveniently located hotel meeting room may be better.

In terms of facilitating interactions, arrangements must be made to (1) ensure privacy for the participants, (2) make them comfortable (e.g., with good chairs and refreshments), and (3) enable them to see one another and interact freely. Arranging comfortable chairs around a table permits people to see one another and interact without interference. If the facilitator sits at the table, this also reduces some of the feeling that this person will ask all the questions or structure the entire discussion. Debus cautions against "designating status in the seating arrangement" (1992, p. 14).

Schedule Carefully

This is one of the hardest parts of assembling a focus group from within an organization. Work demands change constantly, and even people who want to contribute may not be able to attend because of sudden changes in his or her work schedule. Time demands vary from organization to organization. Check whether early mornings or late afternoons offer the greatest flexibility for organization members. In one organization, we even provided lunch and conducted the focus group for 90 minutes while people ate. That was the only time the group could get together, and the free lunch became a bit of an inducement for participating.

Determine the Number of Groups to Conduct

There is no magic formula for determining the number of groups to conduct. Auditors may use such criteria as including a percentage of employees, having one employee per company division, or by deciding to continue to enlist more participants until reaching saturation, "the point when you have heard the range of ideas and aren't getting new information" (Krueger & Casey, 2000, p. 26).

FACILITATING A FOCUS GROUP

Moderating any group appears deceptively simple to onlookers. In truth, one can easily keep any group talking for 1–2 hours if that is all that is expected. On the other hand, generating useful data from 6–15 people for 2 hours requires considerable group skills and mental acuity. *In some ways, the facilitator is the most important determinant of the success of a focus group.* Facilitators must be so alert that nothing gets by them, and they must always pace the groups to accomplish the desired objectives. Facilitation is a role that combines the best skills of communication, psychology, leadership, and decision making. Listed below are some of the specific challenges for moderating a group.

Stay Focused on the Objective

There will be plenty of digressions by the group, side conversations, and explorations of interesting topics other than the ones the facilitator wishes to hear. Therefore, remember your purpose and be guided by it. One of the best ways of staying on track is to have a thorough topic guide that outlines what is to be covered. Having PowerPoint slides or another visual aid is another way to keep groups focused on specific topics. Note, however, that the reins must not be too tight because excessive control inhibits free interaction.

Orient the Group

First, thank the members for participating, and then explain the general purpose for conducting the interview. Respondents will generally be motivated by the potential for them to have an impact on their organizations, so explain to them how important the auditor's mission is and how essential their participation is.

Second, it is necessary for the facilitators to establish their own credibility at the beginning of the session. Facilitators should introduce who they are and why they are there.

Third, even though group members may work for the same organization, people will need an orientation to each other. Therefore, take a short time to let them identify themselves. They may also ask again how they were selected.

Finally, most organizational members probably have not participated in focus groups before this experience; therefore, they will need some orientation as to what it means to participate fruitfully in such a group. They should be encouraged "to discuss without having to raise their hands or take turns talking. They should also be assured that they can feel free to agree or to disagree" (Downs et al., 1980, p. 404).

One particular point needs emphasizing. Most groups feel that their inherent purpose is to come to consensus, and there will be powerful strains on the participants to try to do so. *Explain to them from the outset that focus groups are designed to tap a range of responses and that achieving consensus or agreement is not the objective.*

Control the Pace of the Group

Few things stifle a group as much as the feeling that nothing is being accomplished. Keep on top of the discussion, nudge it gently in constructive directions, and constantly give people a sense of progress. Although facilitators seek to pursue topics fully without bogging down, recognizing when to change topics is an important assessment skill.

Control does not mean that the facilitator dominates or stifles different points of view. There is indeed a fine line that one must tread in order to "strike a balance between friendly permissiveness and business-like-directness" (Downs et al., 1980, p. 404). A good auditor must constantly judge what is being accomplished by the discussion. If some aspects of the discussion are irrelevant, redirect the conversation in a friendly and relaxed manner. One of the best ways of controlling the process is to keep visible the careful plan that facilitators have for the discussion. A plan must never become a straightjacket, but it should reflect your best planning for the topics that need to be explored. Furthermore, just as we pointed out regarding individual interviews in Chapter 5, control does not mean that the discussion must follow a strict agenda or that the topics must be discussed in a particular order.

Deal Sensitively with Group Problems

The fact that facilitators want to have lots of group interaction makes it very likely that problems involving group dynamics will occur. Listed below are some of the greatest challenges.

Domination of Discussion

The same individuals may be the first to comment on any topic, and they may even try to keep the discussion oriented toward their points of view. Their behavior can have a negative impact on others in the group. Such behavior certainly does not enable the facilitator to accomplish the purpose of the focus group: to get a range of responses. You may have to deal with them by directly inviting different people to speak. You may also deal with them by using their statements as invitations to different points of view by asking, "Do others agree with that?" Sometimes you may even have to call attention to the fact that different opinions are welcome.

Domination also occurs because a person is simply verbose. Compulsive talkers talk on and on. Frequently, it is difficult to follow these people because their descriptions are random. The important strategy to deal with them is to be directive, ask closed questions, and probe for specific or concrete information. Do not hesitate to cut these people off.

Wallflowers

Shy individuals often remain silent, voice only agreement with what others say, or are perfectly content to make observations in a self-deprecating way. Fortunately, not many of these people volunteer for focus groups in the first place. However, if facilitators do encounter wallflowers, they can draw them out by asking them directly for their opinions or experiences. Sometimes they can motivate a wallflower by demonstrating the value of the person's prior contributions.

Tendency toward Compromise

For some reason people who disagree publicly in groups often want to ameliorate such differences by changing their minds and working toward a compromise. Perhaps they see this as being "good team players" or perhaps they simply see conflict as dysfunctional. Keep reinforcing the idea that the focus group is not meant to arrive at consensus or a decision that everyone can support. Exposing differences is key to the successful understanding of the organization. Keep probing for differences while suggesting it is okay to disagree.

Persistent Negativity/Positivity

Occasionally, a group member is negative about everything in the organization. In fact, our research has demonstrated that dissatisfied employees tend to be dissatisfied generally. In many audits, for example, we have found that some dissatisfied people tend to be dissatisfied about almost everything in the organization. When a person is negative continuously, you must refrain from reacting defensively or from fully discounting the person's opinions. But once again, some of their reactions may be diffused by asking, "Do others feel this way, too?"

People who make only positive comments can also conceal the truth. Probe thoughtfully, suggest that most things could be improved, and make people feel that they are not bad people just because they can offer constructive criticism.

Digressions

Some respondents persistently make irrelevant comments that easily lead the group off the topic. This could be caused by the participant's (1) need to grind a particular ax so the same topic always keeps coming up, (2) poor listening ability, or (3) inability to follow a discussion. Without correcting the person directly, you can use transition phrases to bring the group back to the topic. "As we were probing a moment ago . . ." or "That's interesting, but the basic question is. . . ."

Probe in Depth to Cut Through Superficial Opinions

Unlike a questionnaire, a focus group allows you to uncover the reasons behind an opinion rather than just to discover the existence of the opinion. Do it sensitively. Some typical probing questions might include:

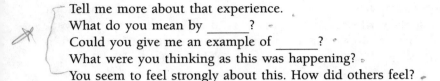

    Tell me more about that experience.
    What do you mean by _____?
    Could you give me an example of _____?
    What were you thinking as this was happening?
    You seem to feel strongly about this. How did others feel?

If Bill suggests that he does not feel the performance review system is equitable, that can be valuable information. That information becomes even more valuable, however, if you can determine what experiences have led him to that conclusion and also what he means by "equitable."

Take the time to probe individual reactions. Bill may find the feedback system to be inequitable; Mary, on the other hand, says she likes it because it gives her good feedback. You also need to probe her individual experiences. A good facilitator will note quickly that there are two different dimensions being addressed by their comments: equity of reward and feedback. Therefore, the facilitator may need to break the discussion apart so that others can talk first about equity and then about the nature of the feedback.

One caution is warranted here. Never ask for "sensitive information that should not be shared in a group or could be harmful to someone if it is shared in a group" (Krueger & Casey, 2000, p. 25). Remember that these are people who have to work together in the same organization after the consultant has gone home.

Use Controversy Positively for Effect

In most focus groups, conflict occurs naturally because people's experiences and outlooks differ. However, occasionally participants all seem to verbalize the same point of view. Because facilitators realize that they get the richest data when people disagree and have to explain the reasons for their disagreement, they may try to spark some controversies. Some state an extreme position to see if anyone will disagree. Others may ask a leading question—not normally a good research practice but sometimes useful if one is a skilled facilitator who knows the limits of the practice. In the era of "political correctness" people are often reluctant to reveal their true feelings because someone will hit them with criticism or even a lawsuit. The fear factor inhibits controversy, but more importantly it keeps facilitators from finding out the truth about the organization's people. One may even have to address this point very directly and perhaps with humor.

Sometimes controversies are articulated, discussed, and the group is left agreeing to disagree. Since some controversies cannot be resolved, there are limits to the time that should be spent on them. The facilitator wants to know the range of responses and why they occur. Once this information is obtained, the group should move on. Pace the progression.

Involve All Members

One of the most important duties of facilitators is to ensure that everyone has opportunities to participate. Recognize that each person may have more to say about one topic than about another one. Nevertheless, the challenge is to make certain that everyone stays involved. Call on people. Rotate the discussion. Follow one person's comment by questioning others and asking, "What other points of view about this are there?" or "You look as if you might have something to say about that—do you?"

Because of position or credibility, some people become quickly known as the *experts*. Others begin to defer to them. This can easily happen when members from the same organization know the positions of all other members. There is a tendency not to tread on someone else's turf. Sometimes that individual can give valuable information that explains a given area beautifully. But because people behave on the basis of their beliefs, it is also valuable to know the opinions of others.

A special problem occurs when the expert can correct the misinformation of other groups, and that does occur. Not all viewpoints are valid. And we have heard some participants say, "Well, I certainly never knew that." Such interactions are part of the multiplicative nature of focus groups.

Choose a Variety of Techniques to Prompt Discussion

While the focus group is a group interview, it is not just a question-and-answer session. Build discussion so that you are not necessarily always asking the questions. Keep people interested by using some common techniques that facilitators draw upon.

Visual Aids

A picture of the actual building may evoke comments revealing people's feelings about the company. Showing one word on a screen is a nondirective way of probing for people's definitions and feelings. For example, in analyzing one organization, we used a PowerPoint display and alternately showed the name of the organization and the names of several different units on the screen. Our objective was to get participants to describe their reactions to their organization and then their reactions to its individual units. Our visual aids communicated subtly to the participants that we had a plan. In another instance, participants were asked to give their impressions of several communication systems in the organization. Finally, they were shown the entire list and asked to identify which ones they liked best.

Laddering

With this technique, the line of questioning starts at a general level, but each answer leads to more specific probing. For example, facilitators might start by asking how the organization has changed in the last year. If one of the differences is a greater emphasis on productivity, then the meaning of productivity is probed along with the resultant behaviors associated with it (Debus, 1992, p. 32).

Pictures/Cartoons

Some facilitators have people describe what is going on in the organization by drawing a picture and sharing it. Sometimes, facilitators get people to draw a picture or cartoon or to write a caption for a cartoon, such as Dilbert. "After each participant has drawn a picture, he or she is asked to hold it up for others to see and then describe it" (Krueger & Casey, 2000, p. 51). The real benefit of any such participatory exercise, of course, is in the explanations given in the discussion.

Role Playing

It would be highly unusual to have people actually play roles for any length of time in a focus group. However, role plays can be incorporated by asking people to demonstrate briefly the opinion or attitude of others. For example, by asking a supervisor in Unit A to say what he thought a supervisor in Unit B would say about Unit A, you could obtain some interesting data about interdepartmental communication. We have actually done this in focus groups. The role plays present opportunities for further discussion—for example, "What would this mean if someone in Unit A said it? What would it mean if someone in Unit B said it?"

Metaphors

This is like the old parlor game that asked, "If one's friend were a car, what kind of car would he or she be?" The answer reveals how one thinks of the friend. Some auditors use this method for their assessments. For several years, Clampitt would give people several metaphors and ask the people to choose which would apply to their organization. Sample metaphors might be "circus," "zoo," "military unit," "hospital," "school," or "basketball team." Discussions during this exercise can be insightful as well as entertaining.

Script Writing

If one were to tell a story about this company, what would it be about? Who would be the main characters? The heroes? The villains (Debus, 1992, p. 32)?

First Impressions

Sometimes one can get interesting diagnostic information by asking people what they first think of when they hear a word or see a picture. For years, we used this technique not in focus groups, but rather in management training.

Concrete Experiences

While perceptions are important, good facilitators can also get members to reveal some of their personal experiences. In that way, the focus group collects some of the critical incidents covered in Chapter 9.

ANALYZING THE FOCUS DATA

What is the real data that auditors have at the end of the focus group? This is the most important question that needs to be part of the initial plan. The most obvious data will be the observations and notes that the facilitator makes during the group interactions. Since facilitating the group requires full attention, however, it is often impossible to take all the notes that one might want to take. Yet facilitators can enhance these notes in two ways.

First, we recommend, just as we recommended for personal interviews, that another person be retained as the note taker during the entire exercise. Not participating verbally in any way allows this person to take copious notes about what is said, even writing down verbatim comments. The note taker could also see some analytic strains not immediately available to the facilitator.

Second, making an audiotape of the interactions is not only unobtrusive, but it can provide you with a means of obtaining verbatim comments. It is also beneficial to listen to the conversation more than once. It is amazing how much we miss with just one hearing. Taping also allows the entire audit team to take part in the analysis. Moreover, many researchers like to have transcripts made of the interviews so they can be cut and pasted easily. Software now exists that facilitates creating transcriptions from the tape. Furthermore, there are even computer software programs that will analyze the data for particular themes. If the facilitator does decide to record the conversation, he or she should make this fact known to the focus group participants and should explain what will be done with the recording.

You need to reconcile the time, energy, and money needed to have note-taking assistance with the overall objectives of the audit. While we do believe in using verbatim comments to help explain ideas, good facilitators or analysts may not need a full transcript because they can pick up the main trends from listening to the discussion.

The main form of analysis for focus group data is content analysis, using one of two methods. First, auditors immerse themselves in the data and let *ad hoc categories* develop spontaneously from their consideration of the data. In this case, we often type a label for a theme and then list all the comments made that are related to that theme. After doing this for each theme, it is possible to write a general definition for that theme. Second, if, objectives are clearly identified, auditors arrange the comments to fit those *pre-planned categories.*

AVOIDING COMMON ANALYTIC PROBLEMS

1. *Minimize the statistics.* There is sometimes a tendency to quantify the data such as by noting that "60% of the focus group participants. . . ." This is the wrong approach because the people were not necessarily selected on a representative sample basis anyway. Keep in mind that in focus groups auditors are trying to find the *range* of responses that help them make sense of the organization. Sometimes a few comments can provide keys for understanding the organization.

2. *Focus groups are designed to probe the depths of what is thought or felt or experienced.* It is easy to examine comments at their face value without probing the subtleties of what was actually meant. Too often we note that people are dissatisfied with X without teasing out the reasons why.

3. *When several focus groups are used, one needs to look at the themes that cut across the groups* and not just report on the groups individually. It is easy to focus on single discussions; it takes greater skills to see the larger picture that emerges across group discussions. Synthesizing these themes adds value to the picture that emerges and helps one think about crafting the final report.

4. *Objectivity is never a deterrent to realistic understanding.* There is always the tendency to let the auditor's biases guide the analysis. As outside observers, auditors cannot get away from the fact that they bring an external—or objective—understanding to the situation. Yet, in the focus group, one strives to represent the subjective understandings of the organizational members—to present their views of the organization and its processes. Staying faithful to that goal keeps auditors from imposing their own views too heavily.

5. *Prioritize and limit what is covered.* Not everything said in a focus group is important. If auditors become aware of certain important themes, they should limit their analysis to these.

PREPARING A FINAL REPORT

Given the current popularity of focus groups, it is entirely possible that someone might conduct a communication audit using only this data collection technique; however, triangulation with other methods is probably more common. In these instances, auditors combine focus group data with data from other interviews and questionnaires. It is an important analytical skill to be able to reconcile the differences in the data that can be accumulated. However, the final report will have the following eight sections whether focus groups are used alone or in conjunction with other methods: (1) Executive Summary, (2) Background, (3) Objectives, (4) Methodology, (5) Disclaimers (e.g., explaining the limits of the qualitative research), (6) Findings, (7) Conclusions and Recommendations, and (8) Appendices (e.g., Facilitator's Topic Guide, Stimulus Materials) (Debus,

1992, p. 55). We mention the final report here because no auditor should ever lose sight of the final report when considering the data. We will reserve our full discussion of those final reports, however, for Chapter 14. Simply know that as auditors examine and synthesize data, they should simultaneously be thinking about how the data relate to the larger report.

CONCLUSION

We consider focus groups to be one important tools for audits because of their considerable and unique strengths. If auditors desire qualitative data that gives in-depth information in an efficient manner, then the focus group can be a valuable tool for collecting information that explains how an organization works. Their effectiveness, however, depends on the skills of the facilitators. They must be people who plan meticulously, listen analytically, probe thoroughly, analyze objectively, banter good-naturedly, and report truthfully.

13

Final Analysis and Interpretation

Collecting data using the methods described in Chapters 4–12 can be interesting and creative. The process of data collection can be scientifically planned to meet rigorous research standards. There are general rules to be followed concerning the sampling of respondents, the design of questionnaires, and the strategies of interviewing. By following these rules, the auditor can be confident of creating a quality audit product to this point. Nevertheless, the audit is incomplete without a conversion of data into conclusions through skillful interpretation. And that is where the real fun and the ultimate learning about the organization begin. Furthermore, in contrast to the data collection procedures, no one has been able to delineate completely and specifically how interpretation ought to be performed. Therefore, this chapter describes the general amorphous nature of interpretation, suggests a process that facilitates effective interpretation, and identifies some common issues and problems. Because some aspects of interpretation were discussed for individual methodologies, this chapter will focus on a general diagnosis when all data from all resources are brought together.

NATURE OF INTERPRETATION

Once a professor made a presentation to a group of executives on her research in international business. Afterward an executive from IBM asked her to explain one part of the results. When she replied that she could not explain it without doing more basic research, the whole room erupted in laughter, and the executive turned to the person next to him and said, "Spoken just like a true academic!" Many years of graduate education not only impart knowledge but also, perhaps inadvertently, condition us to be "reasonable," to be extremely cautious about saying anything definite, to accommodate multiple points of view, and to feel uncomfortable about taking a stand. This well-intentioned humility is a welcome relief from a tendency to "shoot from the hip" without real facts to back up one's claims. Nevertheless, such caution can cause problems at the interpretation stage of an audit because it generates a fear of being wrong—that is, of not having complete documentation so the overly cautious auditor cannot really say anything definitive.

Yet, *to interpret is to try to make sense of, or to understand, something in a particular way*; as understanding increases, the auditing process becomes worthwhile and valuable. The following description of the process of interpretation by Weick and Daft (1983) offers useful perspectives to consider. Interpretations:

1. are like trying to construct a reading or manuscript that is foreign, faded, full of ellipses, incoherences. . . .
2. inform and modify that which they are intended to explain. Interpretations interpret interpretations rather than events.
3. utilize special knowledge, sympathy, or imagination.
4. are like acts of translation from one language to another.
5. focus on elapsed action . . . [which] precedes cognition.
6. are quasi-historical.
7. construct environment rather than discover it.
8. are reasonable rather than right, which connotes a position of certainty. (pp. 74–78)

At first glance, these views of interpretation appear to be negative. They suggest that interpretation is not a very exact science. Such lack of definition may seem weak and inconclusive in a culture that values certainty and exact definition. Nothing is further from the truth for the knowledgeable professional auditor. Nevertheless, implicit in these statements is the notion that different auditors may interpret the audit data differently. Indeed, the auditor who is particularly trained in networks and structures may view the problems as being caused by ineffective organizational structures. The auditor with expertise in interpersonal communication might perceive deficiencies caused by imperfect interpersonal relationships. Admittedly, selective perception takes place among the auditors. This is nothing more than saying that auditors, like everyone else, have communication filters influenced by what they know and by what they think is important. This point is taught in Communication 101. What we apply depends on the theoretical and experience cards we are dealt and the choices we make about those cards.

Having dealt with many audit teams, we know that people of goodwill, of high levels of knowledge, and of considerable experience will still have different interpretations of what is going on in the organization they are analyzing. Those discussions can be frustrating, but they can also be extremely helpful in making all auditors aware of the complexities of interpretation. Furthermore, if the auditors are competent, their different interpretations will contribute much to a fuller understanding of the organization. This does not mean that the one auditor should back away from his or her interpretation. What really separates better interpretations from poorer ones is the "degree to which the interpreter had knowledge or imagination to provide a plausible rendering of events that might have generated the present display" (Weick & Daft, 1983, p. 75).

In summary, the process of interpretation requires the construction of an answer that makes practical sense, rather than the discovery of the one "right" answer that already exists in the environment. Adopting this frame of reference frees auditors to *develop their own systematic approach to interpretation.*

Most people have pet systems for developing solutions to problems. Many of us were trained in the five steps of Dewey's legendary reflective thinking pattern:

1. Define the problem.
2. Analyze the problem.
3. Set up criteria for a solution.
4. List alternative solutions.
5. Choose a solution.

This pattern has had a profound influence on organizational and group decision making because it offers a linear process that seems to make intuitive sense. One of its greatest contributions has been its emphasis on defining the real problem before being solution-oriented.

A similar interpretive process for reaching conclusions in communication audits was developed by DeWine et al. (1985). The following example illustrates the six steps in their process.

1. *Problem identification.* Employees indicate they have insufficient information about personnel policies.
2. *Set an objective.* Employees should more fully comprehend the policies relative to their jobs.
3. *Proposed method or solution.* Two changes would address this problem: (a) development of a Policies and Procedures Manual; and (b) distribution of the manual to all employees.
4. *Reality.* Limited resources within the Personnel Department make the development of a manual unlikely. Therefore, a modification of the idea may be implemented.
5. *Implementation.* A representative small group of employees should meet with the Personnel Director to identify issues that need clarification. These employees can then begin to work on parts of a manual.
6. *Evaluation.* Once the recommendation is implemented, effectiveness could be assessed by: a survey 6 months later; discussion of the policies in employee appraisals; or questions about new policies in the organization newsletter.

The particular system that we have found useful is similar to those advocated by the reflective thinking process and by DeWine et al. (1985), with some important modifications. Basically it involves eight steps:

1. Synthesize all data.
2. Develop focal areas.
3. Identify and define problems.
4. Identify organizational criteria for success.
5. Consider the organization's stages of development.

6. Form tentative conclusions.
7. Finalize the conclusions.
8. Make client-centered recommendations.

In the discussion that follows, each of these steps will be described in detail, along with some of the problems inherent in each.

Synthesize All Data

Whereas Dewey (1930) and DeWine et al. (1985) both start their analyses with problem identification, our interpretive process actually begins with a close examination of all the data collected. Few aspects of the auditing process are more challenging or more troublesome than integrating the results of qualitative and quantitative analyses. In some ways, the synthesis process is as much intuitive art as science. Experience will help you refine your own synthesis process, but the following sections list some of the guidelines that we have found useful.

One of the reasons why we avoid opening with "problem" identification is that it often connotes that auditors are searching only for negative information. Synthesizing all data will probably reveal more positives than negatives about an organization. If the situation were too negative, the organization probably would have ceased to exist.

Use Data from All Instruments

Unlike the researcher who knows exactly how information is going to be used from the start, an auditor does not know exactly how information will be used until after it has been collected and examined. Ostensibly, all data may yield significant information about the organization. On the other hand, auditors know from the start that much of it will have to be discarded as unimportant. Decisions concerning data's importance can only be made after a thorough examination.

A common problem at this point is the tendency to rely too heavily on data from one method at the expense of the other methods. Auditors sometimes rely too heavily on questionnaire or quantitative data simply because they feel more comfortable dealing with numbers. The attitude seems to be, "If I can count it, I am on safer ground." *Not everything that is important can be counted.* Favoring one data set to the exclusion of others is not necessarily good auditing technique, so one should look for ways that the different findings reinforce or contradict one another.

Reconcile Contradictions

Resolve differences by searching deeper into the reasons that the methods yielded different kinds of information. Presumably, the auditors have developed an accurate description of the organization; therefore, contradictory information may be accounted for by the differences among the methodologies.

For example, once one of our strongest survey findings was that subordinates perceived upper management negatively. Their evaluations of management on trust, sincerity, encouraging differences of opinion, concern for employees' welfare, and recognizing outstanding performance were significantly low. Yet the interview data did not support this negative view. The conclusion from the interview data was that although subordinates did not see superiors as much as they might have liked to, they understood the demands under which upper management was working. In the case of such contradictions, it is necessary to decide which interpretation is more representative. In this particular example, upper management may have come off worse in the questionnaire because it was the one item that all employees had in common; thus negative comments about it were magnified. But because the interview data suggested that employees had some appreciation of upper management's problems, we tempered our conclusions.

Welcome Different Points of View

We all have communication filters, and sometimes those filters can become blinders. Seek out different points of view from team members and avoid knee-jerk attempts to defend one's own point of view. It is always interesting how two people, for example, can listen to the same employee interview and "hear" different things. When those differences occur, they should be considered and respected. Once when Downs was poring over data from an audit, Adrian walked up from behind, glanced down, and immediately identified one of the most crucial findings of the audit—one that Downs had not observed at that point even though he had been immersed in the data.

One of the great differences in interpretation comes because auditors have very different perspectives over definitions of what "effectiveness" is. In those instances, a major consideration needs to be given to organizational criteria for effectiveness.

Avoid the Halo Effect

A "halo" refers to the tendency for one thing to become so big or so important that all other estimates are somewhat biased by it. For example, when auditors work in teams, members sometimes tend to emphasize the information that they personally obtained, and that information becomes more important to them than other types of information. Two auditors once conducted an interview that was particularly enlightening and enjoyable to them. In the group analysis sessions, they let that one interview bias their every observation; in fact, that is all they wanted to talk about. When this dysfunctional pattern was pointed out to them, they finally began to consider other information more objectively. It takes considerable self-discipline to overcome such a halo effect.

Use Other Auditors' Work Carefully

Audit teams frequently divide up the analyses so that people work from summaries written by other people. Make certain that these summaries are complete, using verbatim comments whenever possible. After the first round of interviews in one audit, all summaries were given to an interviewing team of three people. The team quickly learned that the initial summaries were too sketchy and that the other auditors' understanding of what had been written during the interviews was different than the team's interpretations. Consequently, a quick training program was implemented, and all summaries were rewritten to be more explicit and more usable.

Keep Negative Information in Perspective

This was mentioned earlier, but it is worth repeating. The ultimate objective of an audit is a realistic appraisal of the organization's strengths as well as its weaknesses. There is a common tendency, however, to focus almost exclusively on the negative: tackling problems seems to be more interesting, more challenging, and maybe more glamorous. Therefore, the negative must be kept in perspective with the positive. Also keep in mind that most organizations must work fairly well to be able to stay in existence.

On the other hand, another potential problem (although less common) is the tendency to downplay the negative. It is not uncommon for beginning auditors in particular to be intimidated by managers or to want to please the managers by emphasizing the positive. This tendency must be overcome. Although it may be interpersonally pleasing, it damages the realism, and therefore the value, of the audit.

Develop Focal Areas

One disconcerting characteristic of most audits is the sheer amount of information generated. When one combines data from several of the audit instruments covered in this book, the result can be information overload. The essence of a general communication audit is to search for as much information as possible; then, when the information is obtained, some important analytic and interpretive questions, such as the following, have to be answered:

What are the needs of the organization?
What areas are really important?
What gives the most useful diagnosis of the organization?
Of all the things that might be mentioned, what are the areas that can yield the improvement for management?

Such questions lead to the beginning of a focus for interpreting the data. Chapter 4 discussed many areas to explore, but not all are equally applicable for every audit. Therefore, we present three suggestions that may be helpful in developing important focal areas.

Brainstorm

If there is an audit team, it should spend time discussing the results and what they mean. There will be disagreements, and these consume some time, but the time is not necessarily wasted. Remember that the nature of interpretation is *constructing a case, not discovering a case*. Therefore, these discussions can be invaluable in refining one's thinking. Even when conducting audits alone, we have found it useful to discuss some of the findings with trusted colleagues. Presenting the ideas to others forces us to refine and clarify our insights. Sometimes we actually do not know what we think until we are forced to express it.

Allow Time; Do Not Rush

Interpretation requires an incubation period. All the information needs to be digested and integrated, and this cannot be done quickly. If a team is involved, group discussions are important. Progress may seem slow sometimes, but the process is important.

Remember That Not All Problems Are Communication Problems

Communication may indeed be the process by which organizational problems are solved, but not all problems are necessarily communication problems. If employees are dissatisfied with their benefits, for example, communication is not likely to change that. Or consider the plight of one of the best plant managers with whom we have worked. He developed a thorough team approach in a new plant. Within 5 years it was a showcase in his large international organization. One innovation had been that employees were paid for what they knew, not what they did. The system encouraged employees to train for several jobs: each time they learned a new one, their salaries could advance. The system worked so well that management and employees thought it effective. However, the plant manager could see a problem looming on the horizon. So many employees liked their jobs that there was little turnover. However, as people got to the top of their pay scales and learned all the jobs associated with that team, there was nothing else they could do to earn more. Therefore, the plant manager fully expected the organization's next great challenge to be the dissatisfaction of the longer term employees. He planned to keep the communication channels open and did discuss this problem with employees, but this problem is potentially so complex that it cannot be defined merely as a communication problem. The implication of recognizing noncommunication issues for the auditor is profound. In a communication audit, one must stay with what one knows and be honest about the findings: do not try to force everything into a communication framework, but rather acknowledge when issues require noncommunication expertise.

Another example may reinforce this idea. In 2001 the United States was undergoing a major economic challenge, particularly after September 11. We audited the same company three times that year, twice after September 11. One of the greatest concerns communicated to us was job insecurity. We reported the problem to management, but given the state of the economy there was no way that all employees could be assured of job security. We did discuss strategies management could use to communicate about this, but there were company units that were actually insecure because of the business environment—and ultimately had good reason to feel insecure because a loss of business meant a loss of jobs.

Identify and Define Problems and Strengths

"Problem definition by its very nature is an ill-defined, complex, and ambiguous problem in its own right" (Kilmann & Mitroff, 1977, p. 150). As auditors examine all the data they begin to *sense* problems. Then, after this intuitive sensing, comes the necessity to identify more specific areas. The actual process of defining a problem is an *exercise in creativity*. There are decisions about how best to express the problem and what terms best represent the essence of the auditor's insights. At the beginning auditors often have a nebulous notion about what is wrong. Somehow they must work through this vagueness to refine their grasp of the problem.

It has already been pointed out that problem definition is linked to concepts of organizational effectiveness—that is, the problem is a gap between current practice and an expected or desired level of performance. But the gap must also be in an important area for it to be considered a problem for the entire organization. In defining problems, there are four errors that can be made:

1. Not discovering a problem that actually exists.
2. Identifying a problem that does not exist.
3. Trying to solve the wrong problems.
4. Failing to probe deeply enough to understand the problem.

Each of these errors can be addressed in the following ways.

Make Your Search Comprehensive

A communication audit is generally more like a fishing net than a fishing line in that auditors are trying to "catch" as many problems as possible. To do so they cast a wide net by making the area covered as general as possible so as not to miss anything. This is why several methodologies are desirable. The "catch" must be examined comprehensively. Some problems will grab your immediate attention, but do not let them deter you from examining more subtle areas.

Determine Whether an Observation Really Is a Problem

If auditors do not do this, there is a likelihood of *solving the wrong problem*. For example, we normally expect problems to occur if organizational roles are not clear. In one organization, we found widespread disagreement about a certain manager's role. We asked whether or not this led to any real communication problems. After much discussion, we concluded that it did because this influential person was violating a number of organizational values. In another instance, we discovered a lack of communication between two units in the same department. We presumed that they *ought* to be communicating, but actually the organization was not suffering as a result of their lack of communication because there was no strong task interdependence between the two groups. Consequently, we had to admit that their decision not to communicate was not a problem. Similarly, in a network analysis, having certain people described as "isolates" sounded bad, but it turned out that these people neither wanted, nor needed, to be integrated into the organization. Hence, the lack of communication did not cause a problem.

Test Different Ways of Characterizing Problems

Kilmann and Mitroff (1977) propose the following methodology for problem definition:

1. Formulate several, if not many, different definitions of the problem situation.
2. Debate these different definitions in order to examine critical assumptions, implications, and possible consequences.
3. Develop an integrated or synthesized problem definition by emphasizing strengths or advantages of each problem definition while minimizing the weaknesses or disadvantages.
4. Include in the definition process those who are experiencing the problems, who have the expertise to define problems in various substantive domains, whose commitment to the problem definition and resulting change program will be necessary for that program to be successfully implemented, and who are expected to be affected by the outcomes of any change program that attempts to solve or manage the perceived problem. (p. 150)

This methodology contains excellent suggestions for guaranteeing a sensitive analysis of the organization. Step 1 requires breaking up some of the cognitive maps developed from first impressions of the organization. Furthermore, managers who employ an auditor often have a definite problem in mind. In such cases, it takes a kind of self-assured discipline to explore problems in ways that differ from management's viewpoint. In other words, an auditor should consider management's definitions without being swayed by them. Finally, of all the previous steps, Step 3 is probably the most difficult to achieve, but trying it can liven up the auditors' meetings. In a communication audit of a university, five auditors spent many hours sharing insights and hammering out problem definitions. The process is tiring but is very fulfilling when the synthesis finally occurs.

Probe the Nature of the Problems Fully

Probe as deeply as one can into the root causes of the problem. Every problem has subproblem roots, tributaries, or contributing factors (see Figure 13.1). Most of us start by defining problems superficially, but it is a mistake to end with a superficial definition. And although it may be wise to keep our explanations to others simple, we certainly should not be willing to leave our understanding of problems simple. For this reason, the communication analysts often work with liaison members from the organization, testing out ideas and refining definitions.

For example, when one finds, as we did, that the communication climate in a manufacturing plant has deteriorated in recent months, one obviously wonders why? We found that a "poor climate" was really a symptom of several other factors affecting relations in the plant. It was important to note those contributing factors because they were part of the problem. Several things that had happened to reduce employees' identifications with the plant were pinpointed: a 50% increase in output that strained workers, a new hiring policy, and a recent reorganization. The relevant communication factors were extracted for each. At the end, we had a very specific understanding of the problems that had reduced the health of the communication climate.

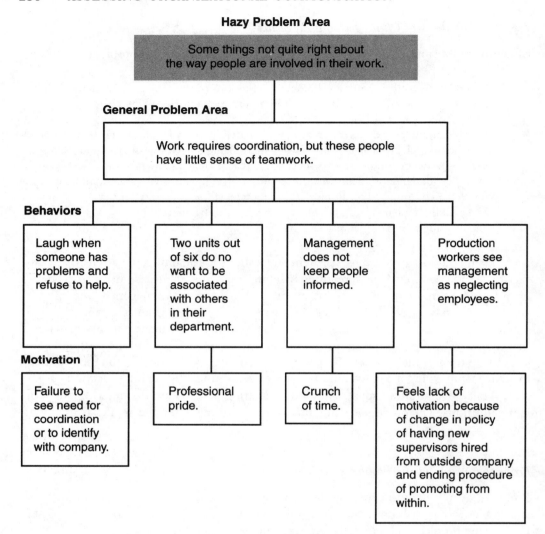

FIGURE 13.1. Probing the nature of a problem.

We have defined problems as the gap between current performance and the performance that is desired. Although the identification of effective criteria is implicit in the definition of a problem, it is useful to make these criteria explicit.

Identify Criteria of Organizational Effectiveness

Defining organizational effectiveness is wickedly difficult; the major hurdle to solving such problems is the need to formulate the problem (Cameron & Whetten, 1983, p. 268). Different theories lead to different measures of effectiveness. The best criteria for assessing organizational effectiveness vary with all of the following:

1. whose perspective is used,
2. the domain of activity on which the judgment is focused,
3. the level of analysis being used,
4. the purpose for judging effectiveness,
5. the time frame being employed,
6. the type of data (subjective or objective) being used for judgments, and
7. the referents against which effectiveness is judged. (Cameron & Whetten, 1983, p. 268)

Although effectiveness is a loosely defined concept, it is absolutely necessary for the auditor to discover the referents against which effectiveness is being judged in the client organization. Organizations are political/business arenas in which competing interest groups vie for control over resources. Perceptions of effectiveness reflect the demands made by critical constituencies. For example, in one audit we discovered a case in which management had invited professional workers in two units to participate in determining space arrangements in a new facility. Management considered the participation a demonstration of its effective communication. However, employees in both units were very angry because not all of their advice was taken. They characterized the communication as ineffective. One representative said, "They should not have asked us if they were not going to take our advice." As an auditor, how does one reconcile these different interpretations?

There can never be, nor is it desirable to have, one simple approach to effectiveness. Knowing that there is not one *right* answer can have a freeing quality; on the other hand, it also can increase the tension to discover what is really important about organizational communication. The discussion that follows pinpoints several of the referents against which effectiveness can be judged. In each case, the assessment of gaps in effectiveness is the basic means of identifying a problem, that is, a problem occurs when there is a difference between what the organization wants and what it actually has. In making these comparisons, auditors may be wise to make their judgments descriptive. For example,

> The elements of the process are twofold: (1) the presence of objective measures that compare actual behavior with some kind of standard, and (2) the communication of the standard, the measure, and the judgment to the recipient. (Filley & Pace, 1976, p. 67)

Finally, every auditor will have his or her own ideas about the nature of effectiveness and the antecedents for it. People in the company will have their own ideas, as well. Whose point of view *should* prevail? Whose *will* prevail? If the auditors have strong credibility and can construct a strong case, they will receive much consideration. But no company can afford to neglect its own driving forces.

Organizational Comparisons

In the final audit reports, managers often want to know how their organization compares with others. They apparently believe that if others are doing better than they are, they must have problems. Such "norm-referred appraisals" take place when a judgmental interpretation compares one organization with other comparable members (Filley & Pace, 1976, p. 67). These comparative judgments give a basic frame of reference for effectiveness, and that is why the data banks for the ICA and Communication Satisfaction (ComSat) Questionnaires, discussed in Chapters 7 and 8, might be useful tools. Obviously, what one knows about other organizations offers some comparative standards. However, auditors should be cautioned against comparing different types of organizations too readily or comparing organizations that operate under different circumstances. Within the same large company, for example, the communication within a Florida plant differed in some significant ways from that in a Minnesota plant. In this case, regional differences had to be taken into account. Recently, we have contrasted manufacturing organizations with service organizations (Clampitt & Downs, 1993) and public with private organizations (Cook, Patterson, & Downs, 1996). The differences in the ways these types of organizations develop can be dramatic. How do we account for those differences in our interpretations? How do we even recognize what those differences are? We find that such analyses often rest with intuitions that come from a great deal of experience. That is, one has to draw on experiences beyond what one finds in a single data set.

Internal Organizational Comparisons

Similarly, one way of identifying problems is to make comparisons among units within the same organization. If one unit has more success communicating than another unit does, we look for ways of improving communication in the second unit. For example, when several plants in the same large organization were audited, the comparisons among them became useful tools for offering suggestions to the individual plants. The reasons for the communication successes of Plant A allowed us to make suggestions for Plant B. In most audits, we make similar comparisons among shifts, work units, managerial levels, and pay classifications. This is a means of identifying exactly where communication problems are.

Comparisons with Stated Goals

Much has been made about the importance of goal setting in appraising individuals. It does not take much imagination, therefore, to realize that the same process can be useful at the organizational level. The problem is that these goals are rarely stated specifically or explicitly at an organizational level. More often, they are vague encouragements to "emphasize communication." However, if the auditors search, they may find definite goals. During an audit of a service organization, the chief executive handed the audit team a statement of values and goals for the organization and asked that the audit be oriented toward how well the organization was achieving them. "Communicate clearly and appropriately" was one of the values. In the audit results it ranked lowest of the 12 values listed. This procedure helped in the definition of problems.

In such cases the noncongruency between goals and performance is in itself a problem. In a European organization, we compared the audit results with their mission statement and their core values. The data revealed that two aspects of the mission had been achieved, but the degree of implementation of teamwork and coordination were still viewed negatively by the employees.

By using a priori goals as standards of effective communication, the auditors and organization members agree on the definition of "good" communication in advance. "Thus, it escapes the arbitrariness of an externally imposed standard" (Filley & Pace, 1976, p. 68).

Benchmarks as Comparisons with Past Performance

One standard for effectiveness is to ask, "Where are we today relative to where we were?" This book began by recommending periodic audits because then the auditors can work from a sense of progress over time. In one audit it was significant to discover that the ratings of communication climate had gone down significantly in a manufacturing plant. We probed vigorously to discover that increased pressure to be productive had actually precipitated tensions and created a feeling among employees that they were not being informed of what was going on. Furthermore, increased demands on the managers' time had made them less accessible. It was, therefore, not only the auditors who were comparing the present with the past: the employees registered their reactions on the same basis.

"Change score analysis" over time is useful because it prompts a thorough examination of why changes for the better or for the worse occur. In making these interpretations, however, the auditor is challenged to look at the total system and to avoid making simplistic cause–effect inferences. We have now conducted nine audits of the same organization at 1- or 2-year intervals, and it has been fascinating to plot the trends. Furthermore, the CEO has become interested in developing a historical sense of what happens to make scores go up or down. For example, what observations could auditors make from the following actual data collected over time from the same organization? Employees evaluated the areas on a scale ranging between 1 and 7, with 1 representing high satisfaction and 7 representing high dissatisfaction.

Factor	2001	1999	1997
Communication climate	3.4	3.1	3.7
Interdepartmental communication	3.6	3.3	3.9
Personal feedback	3.1	3.1	3.6
Relationship with supervisor	2.0	2.3	2.6
Corporate perspective	3.1	2.9	3.5

Although comparisons with past performance give some insight into the organization, auditors still need to analyze the data in terms of outcomes and comparisons with other organizations. Organizational improvement may not be sufficient if rival organizations are improving or producing more.

Outcomes

Chapter 4 dealt at length with outcome variables such as satisfaction and productivity because they are key ways of measuring communication success. Unless there are severe environmental crises, many people tend to view inadequate communication as a root cause for either morale or productivity problems and to see improved communication as a means of solving these problems. In this arena, the question is, "What works?" If something is not working well, change it. Again, we must direct attention to the fact that *many variables other than communication affect productivity and satisfaction*; nevertheless, the auditor can look for direct links between organizational communication and organizational outcomes. In fact, relating internal communication processes to job satisfaction, productivity, and commitment has become our primary emphasis in audits.

Desirable Characteristics

Communication effectiveness is often judged in terms of normative ideals, that is, those that are assumed to be characteristic of properly functioning organizations. For example, since the ComSat Questionnaire assesses eight communication factors, auditors often assume that the employees should be satisfied with each one. Consequently, one way to measure effectiveness is to rank-order all factors in terms of what employees find most satisfying. When we did this in one audit, we found, for example, that the means for all eight factors fell in the satisfied range. However, the mean for the Personal Feedback factor rated lowest. In fact, the mean score fell close to the midpoint, "neither satisfied nor dissatisfied." Since feedback is one of the most important types of communication and since it was ranked lower than less important types of communication, we concluded that the organization was not providing it as effectively as it should.

The same ranking pattern can be used with any audit instrument. All individual questions in each section of the ICA Questionnaire were rank-ordered in an audit of a chemical plant to determine what relations were not as effective as others, what channels were not as effective as others, and so on. The most effective ones were identified as strengths; the least effective were mentioned as potential problems.

The value of these "content-referenced evaluations" depends on a proven connection between behavior and outcomes and on the recipient's acceptance of that connection (Filley & Pace, 1976, p. 68). When a certain form of communication has been demonstrated to lead to a desired goal, controlling the communication assures that the goal will be achieved. Its chief limitation is that different contingencies allow other alternatives of communication behavior to achieve the same goal.

Tailor the Interpretation to the Organization

Consider the Stage of Organizational Development

Although organizational comparisons have merit, every auditor must be sensitive to differences among organizations. Research studies comparing types of organizations usually report some similarities but also pinpoint some major differences. These differences reinforce the contingency approach to organizational communication that advocates viewing each case as unique. One area of contingency that we have found to be especially important is the organization's stage of development, or its organizational age. Greiner (1972) maintains that organizations evolve through various stages of development, and each growth area creates its own crisis. He points out that it is important to know what stage of development the organization is in and to realize that each new solution breeds new problems in the long run. In other words, the organization never stops evolving.

One Size Does Not Fit All

One important implication of the evolutionary perspective for the communication auditor is that the same rules of communication do not apply equally to all organizations. For example, interactive patterns are much simpler in small organizations than in large, well-developed organizations. The president of a successful insurance company reminisced about the early days of the organization when he had access to everyone. With success had come more demands on his time, and with greater numbers of employees had come a reduction in the time he could spend with any one of them. He was no less competent in communication as the organization grew, but circumstances dictated changes. Similarly, we audited a manufacturing organization that had a successful and profitable history. However, a new plant manager decided to modernize it through improvements. Within a year, the plant experienced an increase in productivity of 50% as the organization moved from one stage to the next. Nevertheless, the new creative approach led to a crisis in leadership, and some employees experienced difficulties. Nevertheless, as objective outsiders we could forecast that in time the plant manager's innovations would be helpful. The problem was the transition period—a time that is probably always going to be somewhat painful for an organization.

As a final example, an audit of a consulting firm again revealed the importance of keeping the evolutionary perspective. This nationally known company had been developed by one man and was still family-controlled. As it grew, the founder decided to move toward professional managers. The audit was conducted during a transition phase. It was helpful to interpret its findings in terms of the organization's evolution from a one-man operation to a firm with a diversified approach to management. Some communication problems arose because of sudden changes in management and moving part of the staff to another location. In assessing the current communication practices, we also had to be cognizant of where the organization was heading.

Consider the Influence of National Culture

Economic globalization has focused a great deal of attention on culture. We cannot assume that people from different cultures are necessarily alike. Hofstede (1980) challenged the "silent assumption of universal validity" characteristic of management studies published in the United States (p. 373). His Value Survey Module is a popular measure of cultural values that contrasts cultures on four dimensions: individualism, uncertainty avoidance, power distance, and masculinity. Downs et al. (1996, 2002) have demonstrated how organizations in different cultures may put different emphases on what is important.

With all the emphasis on the advantages of diversity in hiring for organizations, there are also some problems. We once worked with an organization that had substantial percentages of Eastern Europe and Hispanic immigrants working with a local workforce. The groups had difficulty getting along because they did not understand each others' languages, traditions, and humor. One day a misunderstanding led to a mistake that caused the company to trash several thousand pounds of produce. The influence of culture was very evident in this lack of communication.

Cook and Downs (1999) audited communication in an organization in China, where it was particularly important to know something about their unique culture. In this case, we did many interviews before giving out a questionnaire because we needed to know more about how Chinese workers in this organization thought.

The final point to be made about culture is that cultures are constantly changing. These changes are accentuated thanks to economic globalization and the transporting of people from one culture to the next.

> The conception of business activity as essentially based on local or national markets, with a degree of permanence reinforced by local standards and distinctive technology which will change only slowly, is displaced by the paradigm shifts of globalization. The integration of markets and technology allowed by deregulation and facilitated by telecommunications and improved transport suddenly means that more businesses are up against world standards, and that breakthroughs in products and processes can occur everywhere at once. As companies attempt to internationalize, they quickly learn the paradox of globalization: that the world is composed of many cultures. They must begin by coming to terms with this pluralism. (Clark & Clegg, 1998, p. 60)

Auditors must never be satisfied with old depictions of a particular culture. They must also be cognizant that generalizations about organizational communication made in the United States do not necessarily apply globally. This requires heightened awareness on the part of auditors to know what those generalizations are and to recognize subtle differences in communication assumptions across cultures.

Form Tentative Conclusions

If there are a number of ways that a problem can be phrased, there are even more ways that improvements can be suggested. These different solutions will have relative weaknesses and merits that need to be examined.

Look at the Implications of Your Conclusions

Particularly, relevant costs should be examined. For example, one of the most widely advocated solutions to communication problems is to hold more meetings. Meetings can be important communication vehicles that offer excellent communication opportunities; however, when one computes the employees' downtime and salaries, the cost of any meeting may determine how useful it is. Furthermore, if employees believe that they already go to too many meetings or that their current meetings waste time, more meetings are not going to solve a problem. In another instance, formalizing job descriptions was touted by an auditor as the answer for solving a problem involving ambiguous roles. Although clear job descriptions can be useful, many managers resist having formal, explicit job descriptions because they are too restrictive and cause other kinds of problems. Therefore, in this case, management would have rejected that suggestion. An otherwise good communication vehicle may not always be acceptable when one considers people's reactions, time pressures, or costs.

Check Your Assumptions

Although assumptions are implicit in everything we do, we often have difficulty stating them. Furthermore, when we are able to state them explicitly, we do not always like what we hear. For that reason, analyzing your assumptions at both the problem identification and the conclusion stages can facilitate a greater understanding of the interpretive process.

Kilmann (1984) advocates a process of "assumptional analysis." When different conclusions are given for the same problem, the analyzers are divided into teams, with each team discussing one of the conclusions. Each team's assignment is to make a list of the assumptions underlying the conclusion. After this is accomplished, the teams regroup, reveal their lists of assumptions, go through a process of challenging the assumptions, and finally prepare a matrix of assumptions divided into "certain/uncertain" and "more important/less important" categories. They then begin to synthesize the assumptions in order to improve their conclusions.

Use Your Intuitive Powers

Intuition is not something to be avoided; in many ways, it is akin to creativity. Interpretation requires mental leaps from data to conclusions, and this requires that one go beyond mere descriptive statements. *Insight is probably the most important contributor to the success of any audit.* Conclusions can never be determined exclusively by mere counting procedures.

Beware of the False Cause–Effect Trap

Just because one thing precedes another in time does not mean that the first thing caused the other. And just because auditors are conducting a communication audit does not mean that a lack of communication caused all the problems. It is common to think of correlations and regressions in terms of causality, but the causal relationships may not exist. We have emphasized throughout this book that organizations are complex. Any conclusions drawn about the organization must reflect an understanding of that complexity. Tom Porter (1986) coined the term "cauffective" to help deal with these cause–effect problems.

> This "need" to separate myopically causes from causes and, more importantly, to attribute cause "or effect" to events can be disastrous. This is particularly true with communication in

organizations. Too many communicative acts are both cause and effect and neither. . . . To say a given act is the "cause" is clearly subjective assignation. With systematic events, "cause" is simply the "effect" of a previous "cause," ad infinitum. . . . Cauffective acts are the best way by which to conceive of communication in the organization. (p. 5)

Interpret Strengths as Well as Weaknesses

Problems are often more fun to work on than are the strengths of the status quo. Nevertheless, auditors can get as much insight into the organization through what works well as through what its problems are. Auditors should not fail to incorporate the strengths into their understanding of the organization.

Finalize Your Conclusions

The interpretive process described here should lead to basic conclusions about the organization. The conclusions should be general statements, amplified with specific rationales explaining why the auditors think they are true. They should also cover only the most important items; do not try to cover everything in the conclusions.

The following examples were drawn from conclusions in two independent audits, one of a business and the other of a police department.

> *Example 1*: Results indicate an inconsistency between the statement of values by upper management and the ways these values are perceived by staff. Upper management espouses a belief in an open culture and is very concerned that company values are incorporated into company and employee behavior. However, many employees did not feel that these were effectively carried down through the ranks. (A rationale was then provided.)

> *Example 2*: Employees reported that information going up the organizational hierarchy often stagnates because of the filtering of information by their superiors. Furthermore, there was the perception that, though procedures required workers to report formally up the hierarchy, they rarely receive feedback via similar formal channels.

> *Example 3*: Technology is not being fully utilized for communication at ACME. Employees either do not have access to or are not aware of the capabilities of using e-mail to communicate with others in the organization. Management was viewed as not utilizing this medium as a means to communicate with employees.

Make Client-Centered Recommendations

One temptation of auditors is to substitute their own values for those of the organization or of management. This is a grave mistake. The recommendations should always address the practical realities of the organization. Is a recommendation practical or workable? Is it desirable? And is it cost-efficient? As auditors, we seek answers to these questions in preliminary discussions with managers. Because they know the situation far better than we do, we have tentative discussions with them in which we explore one another's thinking. This is basically a form of process consultation (discussed in Chapter 2). It also leads directly into the final phase of the audit: feedback.

We cannot emphasize too much the need to integrate the client's perspective into the recommendations. Recently we addressed groups of consultants (auditors) on two separate occasions. In both sessions, there was a heavy dose of whining about managers who would not accept the consultants' proposals. The truth is, however, that outside auditors and consultants do not have the same vested interest in an organization's survival as do the organization's members, who will naturally be more cautious in what they implement. Auditors need to factor in these different vested interests when they make recommendations and must recognize that acting on the recommendations will affect many peoples' lives.

The abilities to conduct research, to analyze cases, and to conduct thorough and valuable audits are the chief skills developed during an auditor's training. Such skills translate into good consulting if—and only if—the auditors also develop good interpretive skills that enable them to make useful interventions. And part of being a good auditor is remembering that the client will always be the one who defines what is "useful."

RELATION OF THEORY TO AUDITS

Basically, interpretation is a process of constructing theory about organizational communication. "The fate of all theory is to be either ignored or improved" (Mackenzie, 1986, p. 12). Many readers may consider this a shocking statement, but it represents the reality of theoretical development. In no organizational discipline do scholars have enough "theoretical truth" to predict exactly. In fact, there are many theories about organizational design, organizational behavior, and communication, and each theory focuses on different elements and relationships. Furthermore, each one is (or should be) undergoing constant development. Mackenzie (1986) exemplifies the proper scholar by claiming that his theories are the best that he knows today but "this belief is tempered with the awareness that when it is examined in 1992, it will be found wanting just as the 1976 version looks primitive when viewed in 1984" (p. 12). Nevertheless, one must use whatever theory one has at hand.

The ultimate test of any theory is whether it works—that is, whether it is usable and relevant when applied. In this sense, communication theories have been applied with great success in communication audits. Furthermore, the fact that theories are incomplete does not deter our attempt to understand as much as we can from our current theoretical perspective.

Since there are many theories, the auditor seeks to be so well informed that theory can be used judiciously. Consider the example of "openness." Most sources we know encourage openness in communication. It is supportable by theory and by research studies. But "openness" has no absolute meaning, and experience teaches that certain forms and certain amounts of openness can be detrimental. It simply is not always wise to expose everything one is thinking. "Openness" is always a matter of degree. Therefore, we must ask how what we know about open communication can be used to the best advantage.

Furthermore, the state of our art is such that no umbrella theory of communication exists. Therefore, each problem in the organization may require auditors to use different kinds of theories, always watching for their contradictions and inconsistencies. Research has taught us much about the use of channels, supervisory–subordinate relations, and other communication phenomena, even if the findings have not been developed into full-blown theories. In reviewing the communication research on feedback and on the relationship of communication to productivity and satisfaction, we find a great deal of information has been generated in all three areas. Knowing that information helps us interpret communication audit data, even though no definitive explanation of any of those three areas exists. One of the joys of conducting communication audits is that we get to test and form and reform our organizational communication theories.

CONCLUSION

When it comes to interpreting communication audit data, good auditors need to possess four important attributes: (1) skill in data collection, (2) familiarity with current theories and research, (3) the motivation to seek greater explanatory and predictive insights, and (4) a practical orientation that "organization does matter but it needs to be seen as contingent on strategy" (Clark & Clegg, 1998, p. 103). Resist those who want to advocate the "proper" way to organize as if it contains the secret of success. These four attributes supply auditors with the skills they need to interpret usable conclusions about the organization. Once the interpretation stage is completed, the auditor is ready to prepare the final report.

14

The Final Report

The data have been collected, and the interpretation has been made. Throughout these processes, the managers have been interested observers and participants. Now it is payoff time: the final feedback report is the most important step in the entire audit. This report is the reason the audit was conducted; all the hard work has led up to this moment. Therefore, this final phase should be accorded great care. This is not just another report; it is *the* report—the one opportunity that the auditor has to discuss the issues and make important points.

Furthermore, although it marks the end of an audit, it is not necessarily the end of the relationship. In fact, it often is the beginning of a longer term relationship if the auditor is to help the organization implement solutions to problems. The nature of that relationship depends in large part on the reaction to this report. Therefore, we cannot overemphasize the importance of this final report. This chapter explores the options for preparing the most effective report possible and provides specific guidelines for communicating the report.

The final report must be a superb form of communication about communication. This is often a real test for communication scholars. Auditors who propose to audit communication practices also need to be able to practice what they preach.

This final communication is doubly important because those who listen to the message may expect the report to concentrate on problems identified with them—a fact that often makes managers nervous. Or they may not have great expectations of what a communication audit can provide for them—a fact that makes them resentful of the time and money spent on the project. The following example illustrates the attitude that one person had toward the report. In 1995 we did an audit of the corporate headquarters of a company in Great Britain. We had arranged a 3-hour block of time with the top six managers to present our report. After the report ended, one of the managers said aloud for everyone to hear: "When they asked me to block off 3 hours to hear a report on communication, I thought there was no way I could sit here that long to talk about communication. I was prepared to excuse myself at any moment. But this discussion has been fascinating. Thank you and thank _____ [the director of communication] for arranging it."

PREPARING THE REPORT

Although there are several considerations in preparing an effective audit report for the clients, all of them must be interpreted with one overriding consideration in mind: *effective feedback requires sensitivity to the client's abilities to process the information in the report.*

Feedback affects performance. That is the general conclusion drawn by Downs et al. (1984) in their review of research studies. This point is true for organizations as well as for individuals. However, the research also cites many instances in which feedback has had either little impact, or even a negative impact. Therefore, the dominant consideration for designing the report is determining how the feedback can be given effectively to *these people under these circumstances.*

Stay within the original boundaries set at the beginning of the audit. Review the expectations announced by the organization's representatives, as well as the benefits that you promised. What were the selling points you used to get the client to agree to the audit? These become the ultimate criteria for judging what goes into the report. Furthermore, make certain that the report covers all stipulations of the consulting contract, either formal or informal.

Manage the Message

Choosing what to present in the final report and how to present it often takes a great deal of consideration. The end product should be a complete and professional document. (See Figure 14.1 at the end of this chapter.)

Be Thorough

At a minimum the report should include the following:

1. Statements of purpose.
   a. Identifies major thrusts of the diagnosis.
   b. States the limitations of the audit.
   c. Describes the particular client system concerned.
   d. Provides historical background for the study.
2. Review of the procedures for data collection.
   a. Includes copies of all the instrument used.
   b. Describes the sampling techniques for collecting responses.
   c. Indicates the formats used in collecting data.

3. Summary of raw data obtained for each question.
   a. Includes separate sections for each kind of data. For example, summaries from interviews and questionnaires may be written separately.
   b. Reports information in a descriptive, nonevaluative way.
   c. Pinpoints any problems with data, such as absences of responses.
4. Description of analytic procedures.
   a. Describes statistical manipulation of raw data.
   b. Summarizes results of the analysis.
   c. Provides narrative descriptions of tables.
   d. Amplifies results with relevant examples or details to make them meaningful to the client.
5. Conclusions about strengths in, and obstacles to, communication.
6. Recommendations for future development.

Arrange the Report Systematically and Attractively

As with all other management communication, the physical arrangements of the report affect receptivity to the presentation. This report must be as professional in appearance as possible. Keep it physically attractive, typed with lots of white space. Arrange headings for easy reference. Start each section on a new page. Place the entire report in an attractive loose-leaf notebook. Leave the pages loose for maximum ease of reference but have dividers that clearly mark each section. Use charts and graphs to add explanatory power. Certain key statistical data will stand out more if they are presented using some type of graphic display.

Limit the Number of Conclusions

Don't try to tell everything you know; choose the essential findings. Do not "fight a battle on every front" (Brache, 2002, p. 219). Some of the criteria for making the choices include the following:

1. Keep the conclusions to the agreed-on purposes of the audit.
2. Relate them to the goals of the organization.
3. Choose only the most important findings. Even some areas that are significant statistically are not meaningful organizationally.
4. Emphasize those problem areas where change is possible.
5. Be prepared to rank-order the areas of concern in terms of their importance.

Build Cases

Remember that the report is basically an exercise in case building. Most audits obtain more information than it is possible to comprehend in a short 1- to 2-hour report. It is essential to demonstrate the connections among your data so that you build a strong case for each conclusion. It is imperative also to go beyond numbers. For each conclusion draw supporting data from each method used. Furthermore, a *descriptive example* is one of the most influential ways of giving feedback (Nadler, 1979).

Keep Areas Needing Improvement and Areas of Strength in Perspective

Auditors should remain neutral, objective, and realistic. The report should be insightful, conveying the best overall estimate of the state of the organization. The tendency to focus only on problems has been discussed before in detail; however, it should be especially avoided in the report. Care should be taken not to overwhelm clients "with negative findings that leave them with disproportionate feelings of helplessness and, therefore, unable to act" (Levinson, 1972, p. 496). The most negative reaction to an audit report we have witnessed erupted because the managers felt the auditors were actually enjoying pointing out the negatives and had become overly obsessed with them. A viable organization is going to have many strengths, and these should be recognized in the report. Such a balance will increase the auditor's own credibility and make people more receptive to the total feedback presentation.

Remember also that sometimes there are positive and negative sides to the same feature. In one organization, all data indicated that "communication relationships between supervisors and subordinates are quite positive." However, we also concluded that "the extent to which supervisors know and understand the problems faced by subordinates was one area of dissatisfaction—with 36% indicating dissatisfaction on the survey." Pointing out both sides raises questions, but it also increases the likelihood that the audit is fine-tuned, valid, and accurate.

Emphasize Variability in Responses

When a teaching assistant once told a student that she could read with rapt attention for an hour or more, the student countered that she could not possibly do this because research showed that the average attention span was 10 minutes. For that student, the average had come to represent the total reality; he disregarded individual differences. This tendency is both unfortunate and misleading in terms of representing the organization. Averages do not represent any particular individual—we must never lose sight of that fact.

One reason that we provide frequency distributions for answers to questionnaires is to show the variability of responses. If there is a 1–7 scale for questions on a questionnaire, it is likely that the responses will cover at least a spread of 5 points on most questions. Why is this important? Sometimes we forget that averages do not tell the whole story, that they hide individual cases. For example, if the average response to a question was 3.4, there may still have been a number of people who answered 1 and some others who answered 5. These individuals need to be remembered.

Maintain the Anonymity of Respondents

Since anonymity should have been promised in the initial stages of the audit, it should be maintained. Care must be exercised to avoid revealing information inadvertently. Specific examples need to be disguised. If critical incidents are reported, positions as well as names may need to be camouflaged.

Even the presentation of numerical and statistical data must be reviewed. If demographic data are presented, it may be undesirable to break down answers into groups of fewer than 10 people because someone may be able to guess how an individual answered. Consider our dilemma in the audit of an airline. A high-ranking manager in this airline had five subordinate managers reporting to him. Each of them indicated great dissatisfaction with the same aspect of communication. To report the responses on the questionnaire in a normal frequency chart would have told him exactly how each subordinate had answered. To prevent this, we had to report the results in a different, nonquantitative way. The findings were described narratively as "most" respondents feeling a certain way.

Note Limitations

Every assessment will be limited in terms of completeness or in the ability to generalize what can be drawn from the data. Although there is no need to be apologetic or defensive, these limitations need to be clearly spelled out to remind both the auditors and the managers how the data can be utilized.

A common limitation that needs to be acknowledged is the fact that many audits are based primarily on perceptual data. Unless they have done extensive observation, auditors rely on what people tell them about the organization. One hopes these perceptions are valid, but sometimes they are contrary to the truth. For example, we interviewed people who said they had not had a performance review in a year, but later we discovered signed reports that indicated that they all had had reviews during the past year. In another instance, people said they had not been informed of a change, yet in actuality an information sheet explaining the change had been included with every single paycheck. When such perceptual/reality disparities are discovered, however, the disparity in itself may constitute a communication problem.

Another common limitation is the underrepresentation of some units. In a recent audit, only one person from a unit returned a questionnaire, and no interview could be arranged with the manager of that unit. Therefore, what could be said about communication either in or with that unit was restricted by lack of data.

Make Well-Developed Recommendations

The rationale for audits includes not only reinforcing what the organization does well but also forecasting problems and pinpointing beneficial *ways to change*. It is in the latter area that recommendations become important. If there are significant problems, the auditors may have the insights and expertise to point out corrective actions. Recommendations must never be made cavalierly but with the recognition that the well-being of the organization is at stake.

Keep Recommendations Consultative

In keeping with the process model of consulting, make tentative recommendations that essentially comprise areas for discussion. Since the managers will have to implement any new changes, they will provide important input as to what may or may not be effective. For example, one group of auditors wanted to recommend more training, and they were taken aback by the CEO's statement that he had spent millions of dollars on training and had never seen any results from it. His comment led to a useful discussion of the kinds of training that might be effective.

Consider Cost Implications

We have stressed the importance of outcomes throughout this book. There are many outcomes that are important to organizations, including productivity, satisfaction, commitment, corporate citizenship, customer satisfaction, and stockholder satisfaction. Sometimes, the bottom line is often forgotten by auditors who have specialized in personnel, human resources, or organizational communication. Money is just a given—it is always there. Nevertheless, every proposal has monetary implications: costs and rewards. Philip Clampitt noted in an unpublished interview with us that one of the biggest problems he saw with organizational communication auditors is that they "do not value the dollar value of communication. Until they do, they cannot promote effective communication." In a similar interview Sue DeWine (1996) recommended *Costing Human Resources* as a book that directly ties communication and human resources to the bottom line.

Auditors may not be able to compute the actual costs of a proposal, but they should be aware that manpower, downtime, social activities, publications, meetings, and training are expensive items. If there are several potential solutions to a problem, expense should be an important consideration. In one audit, the plant manager talked about the need for training the supervisors, but the production schedule made it unlikely that they could take off even 3 hours a week. Training would have been costly in terms of instruction, but the important cost to the plant manager was the fact that the supervisors would be unavailable to their subordinates during the training.

Assess Priorities

The 20/80 rule so adaptable to personal performance reviews is equally applicable to audit recommendations. Essentially, it requires one to assess priorities in selecting the 20% of those things an organization may do to improve that will achieve 80% of the improvement desired. In addition, it would be wise to eliminate any recommendation that does not have a high probability of success.

Examine Auditor Values and Biases

Harold Leavitt (1972) observed that we all define problems according to the solutions that we have available. Some consultants seem to have the same proposal for any problem. One prominent writer saw participative management as the ultimate solution. Others recommend meetings, quality circles, or training as standard solutions. In a sense, these recommendations fit the auditors' biases, but do they *always* work?

Although we can never get outside our own values, we can ask ourselves whether the organization should be bound by these values and to what extent can we frame solutions consistent with organizational values and with the customers they serve. One of the best ways to bring these to one's own attention is through discussion of the recommendations with other experts or with people in the organization.

Remember That Perfection Is Illusive

As Greiner (1972) has pointed out, every solution carries within it the seeds of new problems. This thought is not meant to paralyze actions or discourage making recommendations. It does, however, suggest, that for every recommendation, it is important to anticipate what new problems may be encountered. If we change an organization's structure, for example, we take something away from those with a vested interest in the current structure. Will that change create more problems? A public utility learned that lesson the hard way. The new structure looked good on paper, but it caused many serious problems once it was implemented. An advertising agency was sold reengineering to replace its departments in 1995. This was a very popular concept, touted in magazines, newspapers, and academic studies. Frankly, the managers were enjoying the reengineering changes very much. But the reengineering came to a dramatic halt within 6 months when some key clients informed the company that their work was not being done properly and that they would take their business elsewhere unless the company went back to the old way of doing things. The agency restored its departments.

Perhaps the best way of illustrating this point, however, is to look at the companies that were praised so highly in the book *In Search of Excellence* (Peters & Waterman, 1988). If that book were being written today, those same companies would not be described. Many of them do not even exist any more.

COMMUNICATING THE REPORT

Thoughtful preparation of the written report thoroughly acquaints an auditor with the material that should be presented to the clients. But being well informed is not enough to ensure a successful interaction with the client about the report. Consequently, the following discussion suggests ways of maximizing the potential for success.

Choose an Appropriate Report Context

There are basically two options: to give the report to a group of managers all at once or to give it first to the manager in charge of the audit. Organizational politics are typically involved, so we usually follow whatever method the organization prefers. Our preference is to brief the top manager first, then brief the management group later, and finally to prepare a short report for all employees. This order of presentation allows the greatest flexibility in dealing with the managers' responses. In a variation of this method, a group of auditors of a university once prepared a general report for the management group and then met individually with the deans to give each one a report tailored to his or her particular domain.

Use Multiple Channels

A combination of oral and written reports can reinforce one another. The oral report permits the auditor to set expectations, to explain the report, and to highlight what is most important. The written document can be more detailed, for managers can examine it in depth at a later time. Under no circumstance, however, should one submit a written report without taking the opportunity to present it orally first. The oral report gives managers a chance to ask questions about anything they do not understand about the report.

New technologies offer interesting ways of presenting. Using a computer to punch up charts, diagrams, or outlines can be an impressive addition to the presentation.

Arrange an Exact Sequence

Levinson (1972) describes an excellent arrangement for reporting back to clients. First, he presents the report to the client responsible for bringing him into the organization. They set aside 2 hours for the report. Levinson reads the report aloud while the executive listens and makes notes for later discussion.

> I want [the client] to be sensitive to the way I present matters so that he does not find himself in embarrassing or difficult circumstances because of the way I have phrased things. I make it clear that I cannot change the substance of my findings, but I emphasize my need to have his help in stating what I have to say in the most advantageous way. (p. 497)

The client then takes the report to read overnight. Finally, Levinson meets with the client in a 2-hour session on the next day for further discussion. After this process is completed, the auditor is ready to present the results to other groups in the organization.

Use a Process-Oriented Discussion

Our preferred consulting style is process-oriented in that we collaborate with managers throughout the audit process. This extends even into the feedback phase. The oral report may often be more of a discussion than a formal presentation. It is a good idea to use an exploratory approach rather than a selling approach. Be receptive to questions and do not rush through your points. Even at this late stage, you should ask the managers questions to facilitate discussion. Each group may offer suggestions about presenting the materials to other groups. The discussion of the recommendations is of particular importance.

When auditors identify problems and make recommendations, they give their best thoughts. Nevertheless, there may be alternative ways of solving perceived problems. The auditors' recommendations may stimulate discussion of new possibilities. Above all, the auditors should avoid trying to tell the managers how to run their organization. Their job is to collect the data, summarize it in a meaningful fashion, offer tentative recommendations, and facilitate a discussion so that the best organizational action can be determined.

Involve the Full Audit Team

The director of the audit may handle the entire presentation. However, another option is to assign team members leadership roles in the presentation and discussion. Both methods can be effective. The latter has an advantage of bringing out different orientations while "rewarding" or recognizing the team members for their efforts.

Adapt to the Clients

Throughout the audit process, auditors should have been able to gauge certain characteristics about the managers hearing the report. It is important to consider variables such as education, degree of interest in the project, levels of understanding, and observer biases.

An important aspect of adaptation includes focusing on what is happening emotionally to the clients during the presentation of the report. Certain stages are quite predictable. Initially there may be some tension, because people do not know quite what to expect or may fear the worst. There can also be resistance to the negative information in the report. Scapegoating, rationalizing, and even attacking the auditor are common in this phase. After a while people tend to relax and become more attentive if they find the substance of the report helpful.

Finally, productive discussions will lead to consolidation behind the report and the desire to plan future action around its implications. The following specific behaviors are useful ways of adapting to clients.

Give Assurances

Even some highly skilled managers are nervous when it comes time to hear the results. People fear embarrassment when it comes time to discuss the organization's shortcomings. For that reason, we always take the time to review the entire process that we used and set a very nonthreatening tone. A graduate student from Japan kept one 2003 audit team on track by continually referring to the need to let a certain manager save face in the oral report even though the written report mentioned him specifically.

Answer Questions

Regardless of how well prepared you are, it is important that you take the time to answer the managers' questions. There have been times when we have moved from one point to a second, only to find that someone has been thinking all the time about a previous point and has a question. One must be flexible and take the time to develop each point to the clients' satisfaction.

Deal Gently with Resistance

Most of the time, managers are receptive to the audit reports. They believe that they will learn from the process and are willing to listen enthusiastically. However, there are people who overtly or covertly resist what they hear. This is not so surprising when one considers the evaluation content of the report. Academic auditors, accustomed to being detached from their research data, must realize that because an audit report can have important ramifications for the managers' work lives and careers they cannot be detached about them. Therefore, expect some resistance and respond with genuine consideration. There is nothing to gain by setting up the report time as a confrontation to prove who's right. Some actual forms of resistance are pinpointed in the following paragraphs.

- *"Your data are not valid."* One president kept referring to "your" data throughout the report as if we had somehow manufactured the data out of thin air. He seemed to be trying to separate the organization from the report. Ironically, this happened during what was perhaps the most comprehensive audit in which we have been engaged. Without being defensive, we made careful allusions to the findings and how they had been obtained from "his employees."

- *"I already knew that."* This response can be an accurate affirmation, or it may be a way of belittling the report. Obviously, no audit will discover only things that the managers did not know; the best managers ought to have a feel for their own organizations. These people usually are happy to have their own perceptions reinforced.

- *"I'm under attack."* There are times when the report has negative implications for the managers listening to it. They sometimes begin to consider the report—and perhaps the reporter—as a personal affront. When these cues begin to appear, maintain a supportive climate and provide an opportunity for these feelings to be ventilated. Do not minimize the results, but make certain that the discussion stays on a factual basis. In 2003 we made a report to an organization that had gone down in eight significant factors, and the team was worried that the CEO would feel attacked. They were pleasantly surprised when he expressed appreciation for the report and discussed specific ways he could use it.

- *"What do all these numbers mean?"* This question is often legitimate, but one way to resist the report is to deliberately avoid understanding it. On occasion, respondents can protest too much. The auditors must never lose their patience in giving explanations.

- *"I disagree."* Be open to disagreements. One young auditor had just made a stock recommendation for organizational communication, when the CEO thanked him for the recommendation but explained that the recommendation would not work. Where does one go from there? A diagnosis of what was happening is interesting. After exploring his reaction in a polite way, ultimately the auditors reduced their emphasis on that recommendation and without any intimidation moved to other recommendations that would have more possibilities for implementation.

Demonstrate Appropriate Modeling Behavior

The audit presentation is, in itself, an important communication vehicle. It is a challenge to the auditor to demonstrate how effective communication is accomplished. His or her own activity can become a model that people in the organization can emulate. According to Levinson (1972),

> The behavior of the consultant should be a model for how he wants the organization to go about its problem-solving activity: by joint engagement with authoritative leadership around open examination of mutual problems for collective solutions toward more effective organizational-functioning. He must demonstrate that he does not fear hostility; that he stands confidently for his findings despite differences; that he is willing to be cross-examined about what he has learned and how he has learned it, together with the assumptions he has made;

that he is willing to be appropriately corrected and to have conclusions modified by new data. (p. 501)

Distribute a Separate Brief Report Throughout the Organization

One of the greatest inhibitors to participation in audits is the fact the employees rarely hear the results of the surveys in which they participate. Frequently, they feel cheated out of information. To overcome this problem, employees should be told from the outset that they will get a report, and it should be distributed. The following are useful guidelines for preparing a report:

1. Keep the report to one or two pages.
2. Highlight the basic findings.
3. Keep it simple, because most people are not interested in great detail.
4. Have management screen it.
5. Thank the employees for participating.

In designing this mass report, auditors are not in the business of creating communication problems, and sometimes they learn things that management would not want publicized for various reasons. It may be a matter of timing, or we have had some cases where management knew the report would be leaked to the newspaper so they were very careful what was reported in writing. We do not bend our integrity in reporting results at any time; nevertheless, we do understand managerial prerogatives about when and where things are discussed. Most managers have wanted to be very forthright with the workforce, and we have never been asked to lie.

CONCLUSION

This chapter has emphasized basic considerations for presenting acceptable audit report to the client organization. The entire book has been oriented toward that end. With the conclusion of the presentation of the audit report, the audit project is completed. Somehow it seems an oversimplification to say the process is ended because the auditor has received two challenges. First, although the auditing phase may be completed, the consulting phase may not be over. As we pointed out, managements usually have some rational for conducting a communication audit, and that rationale generally includes a desire for improvement or change. Conducting a successful audit provides such great insights into the organization that the auditors are uniquely equipped to become important consultants for introducing changes for improvement. This task can be even more demanding than conducting an audit.

Second, in conducting an audit, auditors are not only analyzing organization, they are also analyzing their own theories and thinking patterns. In other words, they get challenged mentally, and their knowledge is tested in very practical ways. For us, this has been one of the greatest benefits of conducting audits. We learn something new from each one, and we never end the learning process.

Note. Presenting a full report would take too much space here and would also potentially violate client confidentiality. Therefore, over the following pages we have elected to present abbreviated aspects to offer some examples from several reports of what a final report might include.

EXECUTIVE SUMMARY

1. Participation in the audit was superb: 150 employees returned their questionnaires and 25 employees were interviewed.

2. Levels of job satisfaction and commitment were both high. Furthermore, most people say they enjoy working in a competitive chaotic atmosphere that represents their industry.

3. The communication news is good throughout ABC. The averages for all factors were on the satisfactory side of the 7-point scale, and modest gains have been made in six categories since 1998.

4. The two areas that decreased slightly from 1998 are Communication Climate and Organizational Integration. Both are viewed positively, but these are the areas that have the greatest dissatisfactions.

   In 1998 Personal Feedback and Interunit Communication were the factors needing most attention. Significant progress was made on Personal Feedback, but Interunit Communication is at the same level as 1998. In fact, it is the area in which people are still most dissatisfied.

5. All departments show a great deal of satisfaction. There were no negative averages in any department.

6. Seven of the eight departments are satisfied with the quality of work life at ABC.

7.

8.

9.

FIGURE 14.1. Sample final report.

Historical Perspective

- ABC continues to improve as an organization. It has improved its scores on six of the communication factors since 1998.

- It has maintained the same scores on Corporate Perspective and Interdepartmental Communication as in 1998.

- The scores went down slightly on only two factors: Communication Climate and Communication with Top Management, but both were still in the somewhat satisfied category. Each of these is explored in depth in the following discussion.

- There was also improvement in both the Job Satisfaction and Commitment scores.

Factor	1999	1998	1997
Communication Climate	3.1	2.9	3.8
Corporate Perspective	2.9	2.9	3.6
Horizontal Communication	2.6	2.8	3.0
Interdepartmental Communication	3.3	3.3	3.9
Media Quality	2.7	2.8	3.2
Organizational Integration	2.6	3.0	3.1
Personal Feedback	2.9	3.5	3.5
Relation with Subordinate	2.5	2.6	2.2
Relation with Superior	2.0	2.7	2.6
Communication Top Management	2.8	2.7	3.7
Job Satisfaction	2.4	2.7	3.6
Commitment	2.3	2.7	3.0

1 = High Satisfaction
7 = High Dissatisfaction

[Discussion]

JOB SATISFACTION

Basically, it would appear that ABC is a happy place to work. An overwhelming number (84%) of employees say they are satisfied. Only 15% indicated that they are not satisfied, and that is an unusually low percentage for most organizations and 2% lower than 1998. It is also significant that 31% say that their level of satisfaction has gone up in the last year.

CURRENT LEVELS OF SATISFACTION

Question	VS	S	SS	I	SD	D	VD	Mean
1. How satisfied are you with your job?	39	57	28	1	15	2	6	2.5

Demographic Trends

Managers and nonmanagers were significantly different in 1999. Both groups tended to be satisfied, but managers had a score of 2.2 while nonmanagers had a score of 2.7. This difference is often predictable because of the different natures of the jobs.

COMMUNICATION WITH TOP MANAGEMENT

- Communication with Top Management surfaced as the most important dimension in the 1999 audit. It was a predictor of Job Satisfaction, Perceptions of Effectiveness, Quality of Work Life, and Commitment to the Organization.

- With an average of 2.6, Communication with Top Management still falls generally in the somewhat satisfied category. Nevertheless, it is significant that there was a slight decrease in the ratings of it from 1998.

Historical Comparison of Communication with Top Management

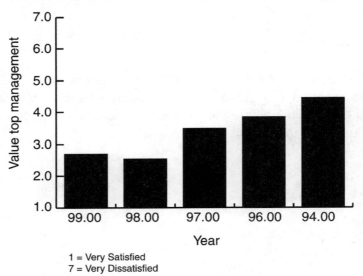

1 = Very Satisfied
7 = Very Dissatisfied

- The dip can be highlighted by looking at other questions.

   A. Only 55% feel that there is a high level of trust between employees and top managers (#79). And only 48% feel that ABC is staffed with enough managerial talent (#76). There is a perception that some managers are stretched so thin that they cannot be around as needed.

   B. There were a number of comments in interviews about upper management trying to micromanage in ways that inhibited good work. This could be a partial explanation for the lack of trust.

- In terms of positive management practices, the qualitative data revealed that:

  A. Many employees feel strongly that ABC and top management really care about employees, and they listed specific ways in which this was demonstrated. One person said, "ABC cares about employees more than any place else I have worked." Similarly there was much admiration for the organization's apparent willingness to change and to try new things to make things better.
  B. The flexibility and autonomy offered here were much appreciated.
  C. Managers are seen as following through on their commitments by 82% of the employees (#83).
  D.

COMMUNICATION ABOUT JOB SECURITY

A. About half (51%) say they are worried about their job security. They know the economy is troubling, but they are also worried that despite their best efforts, ABC may lose some business in the current economy and cannot keep them on.

B. Perceptions vary a great deal in terms of what affects their job security most, and they see it as a combination of factors. However, Leadership at ABC ranks as the thing most influencing their job security. This is followed by Industry Trends and US Economic Trends. It is perhaps significant that there is a real dichotomy involving the area ranked 4th overall: Your personal behavior. Remember that some people are quite certain of their security and 29 people said that this was the thing that influenced their security most.

PERSONAL FEEDBACK

Focuses on the adequacy of giving workers information about recognition of good work, evaluation of their performances, and the criteria by which they are judged.

Personal Feedback is one of the lowest rated factors ($M = 3.9$). This rating has remained fairly constant over time. Despite formal recognition programs, some respondents would like to receive more informal positive feedback. Throughout the interviews and survey, we heard that too much emphasis is placed on negative points, while less is placed on positive aspects.

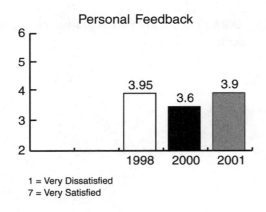

Personal Feedback

1 = Very Dissatisfied
7 = Very Satisfied

Review the Performance Appraisal Process

A performance appraisal can be an effective method of communicating personal feedback. An evaluation provides the opportunity to discuss strengths and weaknesses, to state personal goals, and to discuss plans for the future. Yet, when respondents were asked to rate the usefulness of different types of communication on a 5-point scale (1 = not useful at all; 5 = extremely useful), performance appraisals rate as the least useful form of communication ($M = 3.05$). The grapevine was rated as more useful than performance appraisals.

Enact "More Positive Recognition"

The greatest concern within feedback is the question concerning "Recognition for my efforts" ($M = 3.6$). The ratings were low across all of the divisions, with the Support and Uniform divisions lower than the Administration division. The following quotations exemplify the concerns:

"Not a lot of positive recognition."

"We use face-to-face communication, but only when the discussion is about something negative, not positive."

"Not enough recognition comes from above."

"Problems that arise with one employee need to be dealt with individually, not a blanket reprimand for the department."

"If a problem can be addressed to the individual(s) who are creating the problem, it should be done."

COMMUNICATION WITH SUPERIORS
2ND-HIGHEST-RATED FACTOR

Includes both upward and downward aspects of communicating with managers and supervisors. Is the amount of supervision satisfactory? Are superiors open? Do they listen and trust subordinates?

Communication with Superiors: A Positive Source of Satisfaction

This area elicited the second-highest mean score in the audit, demonstrating a relatively high level of satisfaction with respect to superior communication. As can be seen in the chart below, satisfaction with superior communication ($M = 5$) remains high.

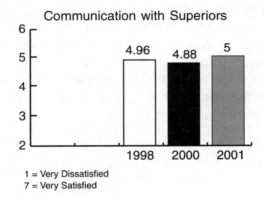

Communication with Superiors

1 = Very Dissatisfied
7 = Very Satisfied

Trust in One's Supervisor Is High

Subordinates were most satisfied with the level of trust offered to them by their supervisors ($M = 5.26$). For example, one interviewee noted that communication in the CID division was "*like a family dynamic, constant communication, lots of verbal, email, phone messages.*" According to the survey, 77% of the respondents are satisfied with the level of trust their immediate supervisor conveys.

Discrepancies among Divisions

Superior Communication Satisfaction

Division	Respondents	Mean
Administration	26	5.7

Service	115	5.4
Manufacturing	282	4.8
Sales	141	4.2
Total	564	5.0

As the above table reflects, divisional differences regarding Superior Communication Satisfaction exist at the ABC. Overall, the Sales department scored much lower on supervisor communication satisfaction ($M = 4.2$) than any other department by more than a half-point. Additionally, the difference in mean score between Sales and Service merits further investigation. The mean score difference between Support ($M = 4.2$) and Service ($M = 5.4$) illustrates the trend of lower satisfaction exhibited by Sales.

Open-ended survey responses elicited how communication between upper and lower levels could be improved at the ABC. Respondents had this to say: "*Treat lower levels better.*" Also, "*They* [upper-level personnel] *need to treat all units the same.*" These quotations indicate some of the dissatisfaction felt by participants in Division X, that they aren't really a valued asset or part of the team. This might explain the lower levels of overall satisfaction with superior communication, since Division X has the highest number of nonmanagement personnel.

Viewing Superior Satisfaction as a "Small Town" versus "Top Down"

"*We are like a small town.*" Quotations such as this capture perceptions of communication satisfaction by subordinates toward their superiors. Many respondents mentioned the effective communication style of their immediate supervisor—a concept best captured by one midlevel manager who stated, "*He is open to new ideas, and gives constructive feedback.*"

"*I only hear from him when things are wrong.*" This statement from an interview highlights the area of superior communication with which respondents were least satisfied—the extent to which supervisors offer guidance for solving job-related problems ($M = 4.59$). Some respondents felt that the level of guidance provided by their supervisor could be improved. As one respondent mentioned in an open-ended survey item, "*Prior to instituting polices that affect our jobs, the uppers need to ask the lowers for ideas on how to make effective changes. . . . Communication starts at the top, period. Upper levels need to treat workers as humans and not numbers.*"

CONCLUSIONS

[Only three conclusions are selected for representation here to indicate how the cases were built to support the conclusions. However, the format might have been more polished in terms of communication.]

Introduction

The communication audit was undertaken to describe the communication process as it presently exists in the Headquarters and to identify some of the major strengths and weaknesses of this process. In order to interpret this data accurately, it is necessary to keep the following items of information in mind.

Nature of the Data

In addition to our observations, we are dealing with perceptual data of employees. Our information was gathered from (1) a Communication Satisfaction Questionnaire, (2) a Communication Experience Questionnaire, and (3) in-depth interviews. Therefore, we describe how employees perceive communication within the organization. Some of their perceptions may or may not be an accurate description of what actually happens within the organization. However, it is important to understand that the way people perceive a situation serves as the basis for their own actions within that situation.

The information came from a large sample of the employees. First-round interviews were conducted with 32 employees from throughout the organization. Upper management, nearly all the managers, and a selection of supervisors and staff members were interviewed.

Following the first-round interviews, questionnaires were distributed to all employees based in the office and to approximately 25 full-time employees. A total of 67 questionnaires were returned, a return rate of over 76%.

The questionnaire was divided into five sections.

The first section was designed to ascertain level of satisfaction with eight facets of communication in the organization: corporate perspective, personal feedback, organizational integration, relation with supervisor, communication climate, horizontal communication, media quality, and relation with subordinates.

The second section addressed satisfaction with communication channels.

The third section asked respondents to rate the importance, quality, accuracy, and timeliness of interdepartmental communication.

The fourth section was concerned with the enactment of company values.

The fifth section solicited a "Communication Experience" from employees. The employees were to describe an instance of a work-related experience in which communication was particularly effective or ineffective. Thirty-four responses were received and analyzed.

Finally, second-round interviews were conducted with 23 employees at various levels of the organization. The interviewer focused on information about company values, day-to-day feedback, yearly appraisals, and the effectiveness of information exchange.

Overview of Communication Concerns

This report focuses on six major areas: (I) Communication with Top Management, (II) Communication Relationships Between Supervisors and Subordinates, (III) Communication Relationships with Coworkers, (IV) Performance Feedback, (V) Coordination Throughout the Organization, and (VI) Overall Satisfaction with Communication.

V. Coordination in the Organization

Orientation

Analysis of the data from the first round of interviews suggested that information flow between departments was sometimes problematic, especially in terms of timeliness. Consequently, this area was probed more specifically in both the questionnaire and the second round of interviews. Questionnaire respondents were asked to rate the information they received from each department on its importance, quality, accuracy, and timeliness. Interviewees were asked to name the other departments whose information was most important to their work, as well as to discuss their satisfaction with the information from those departments. This information, in combination, provided us with a picture of the interdepartmental communication relationships in operation.

In this section we report the results and the implications of our investigation of interdepartmental communication. In most cases, rationale of quality, accuracy, and timeliness are lower than the importance rating. This is probably not too surprising: when we view information as highly important, we may try also to view its quality, accuracy, and timeliness as not quite equal to its importance.

Unclear Job Relationships and Organizational Structure

> Conclusion 6: The organizational structure is not being adequately communicated. A lack of clarity of job functions appears throughout the organization and seems to extend even to top management, with administrators indicating some "fuzziness" and "crossover responsibility."

This problem did not surface in the quantitative data because no question addressed it specifically. Nevertheless, there were many comments about it both in the interviews and on the responses to open-ended questions. The lack of clarity is also reflected in some confusion over the organizational structure. For example, one supervisor mentioned that the company is too big for its once informal ways of communicating. This person felt an understanding of the organization's hierarchy would help persons "get along better." In two departments, there appears to be confusion about the chain of command. Data processing is unsure about Division Y. Consequently, they are unsure about how to interpret apparent "orders." AB employees reveal some uncertainty about who their manager actually is, with some of the employees going to one person and some to another for their concerns. An employee in another department commented that this is a company where one has to feel one's way around; and several staff members identified the need for clearly defined communication channels and an accurate organizational chart.

Conflict Resolution

> Conclusion 7: There is significant dissatisfaction over the handling of conflict at ABC. Establishing a clear organizational structure with transparent job functions may reduce the amount of conflict and actually facilitate better conflict resolution.

Conflict resolution methods appear to be affected by the lack of clarity in organizational structure. On the questionnaire, 38% of the respondents indicated some dissatisfaction with the "extent to which conflicts are handled appropriately through proper communication channels" (Question 27). The lack of clear channels may be one cause of this dissatisfaction. In the second round of interviews, we directly addressed this question.

While responses revealed satisfaction with the way conflicts are handled *within* individual departments, much of the conflict in the organization is across different departmental units. There is a strong perception that managers across units do not coordinate well (Question 47, mean 5.8). Particularly, Sales and Service seem to have different expectations about what their relationship should be, with Sales apparently promising more than Service thinks it can reasonably deliver. People in those units are not certain how to resolve this conflict. Comments included: "I am not sure how conflict is solved in the organization because I really only deal with my immediate supervisor." "There is no kind of grievance procedure. No official way to file a complaint. If you dare to go past your immediate supervisor, you're really in trouble." Other comments indicated that the company is taking some positive steps to improve the handling of conflicts, through Supervisory Training and the Employee Attitude Survey.

References

Adrian, A. (1997). *A fuzzy analysis of the relationships between communication satisfaction and organizational commitment in Australian organizations.* Unpublished doctoral dissertation, University of Maryland.

Adrian, A. (2001, May). *To commit or not to commit: Consider communication when answering the question.* Paper presented at the annual meeting of the International Communication Association, Washington, DC.

Adrian, A., & Ticehurst, G. W. (2001, May). *To commit or not to commit: Consider communication when answering the question.* Paper presented at the annual meeting of the International Communication Association, Washington, DC.

Adrian, A., & Ticehurst, G. W. (2001b, August). *Communication and commitment: The role of holistic communication satisfaction.* Paper presented at the annual meeting of the Academy of Management, Washington, DC.

Albrecht, T., & Hall, B. (1991). Facilitating talk about new ideas: The role of personal relationships in organizational innovation. *Communication Monographs, 58,* 273–288.

Alderfer, C. (1968). Organizational diagnosis from initial client reactions to researcher. *Human Organization, 27,* 260–265.

Alum, C. (1982). *A case study of communication satisfaction in Nova De Monterrey.* Unpublished master's thesis, University of Kansas, Lawrence, KS.

Anderson, B., & Nilsson, S. (1964). Studies in the reliability and validity of the critical incident technique. *Journal of Applied Psychology, 48,* 398–403.

Argyris, C. (1970). *Intervention theory and method.* Reading, MA: Addison-Wesley.

Avery, B. (1977). *The relationship between communication and job satisfaction in a government organization.* Unpublished master's thesis, University of Kansas, Lawrence, KS.

Bailey, P. (1974). *Communication in the congregation.* Unpublished master's thesis, University of Kansas, Lawrence, KS.

Bales, R. F. (1950). *Interaction process analysis: A method for studying small groups.* Reading, MA: Addison-Wesley.

Barge, K., & Schlueter, D. (1988). A critical evaluation of four popular measures of organizational commitment. *Management Communication Quarterly, 2,* 116–133.

Barnes, J. (1972). *Social networks.* Boston: Addison-Wesley.

Bednar, D. (1982). Relationships between communicator style and managerial performance in complex organizations. *Journal of Business Communication, 19,* 51–76.

Bennis, W. (1969). *Organizational development.* Reading, MA: Addison-Wesley.

Berlo, D. (1960). *The process of communication.* New York: Holt, Rinehart & Winston.

Bordia, P. (1997). Face-to-face vs. computer mediated communication: A synthesis of experimental literature. *Journal of Business Communication, 34,* 99–120.

Borgatti, S., Everett, M., & Freeman, L. (1995). *UNICET V.* Columbia, SC: Analytic Technologies.

Brache, A. (2002). *How organizations work.* New York: Wiley.

Brass, D. J. (1995). A social network perspective on human resources management. *Research in Personnel and Human Resources Management, 13,* 39–79.

Brooks, K., Callicoat, J., & Siegerdt, G. (1979). The ICA communication audit and perceived communication effectiveness changes in 16 audited organizations. *Human Communication Research, 5*(2), 130–137.

Burkhardt, M. (1994). Social interaction effects following a technological change: A longitudinal investigation. *Academy of Management Journal, 37,* 869–896.

Cameron, K., & Whetten, D. (Eds.). (1983). *Organizational effectiveness.* New York: Academic Press.

Carnegie-Mellon University. (2003). WWW source: *http://www.contrib.andrew.cmu.edu/~krack/*

Christie, T., & Oyster, E. (1973, May). *A communication audit of the Missoula Bank of Montana.* Paper presented at the annual meeting of the International Communication Association, Montreal, Canada.

Clampitt, P. (1983). Communication and productivity. *Dissertation Abstracts International, 44*(11), 3204.

Clampitt, P. (2001). *Communicating for managerial effectiveness* (2nd ed.). Thousand Oaks, CA: Sage.

Clampitt, P., & Berk, L. (2000). A communication audit of a paper mill. In O. Hargie & D. Tourish (Eds.), *Handbook of communication audits for organizations* (pp. 225–238). London: Routledge.

Clampitt, P., & Downs, C. (1993). Employee perceptions of the relationship between communication and productivity: A field study. *Journal of Business Communication, 30,* 5–29.

Clarke, T., & Clegg, S. (1998). *Changing paradigms: The transformation of management knowledge for the 21st century.* New York: HarperCollins Business.

Clegg, S., Hardy, C., & Nord, W. (1996). *Handbook of organization studies.* New York: Sage.

Collins, J. (2001). *Good to great.* New York: HarperCollins.

Contractor, N., Eisenberg, E., & Monge, P. (1996). *Antecedents and outcomes of interpretative diversity.* Unpublished manuscript.

Cook, D., & Downs, C. (1999, November). *Contrasting Chinese and American orientations toward organizational commitment.* Paper presented at the Third Intercultural Conference, Shenzhen, China.

Cook, D., Patterson, J., & Downs, C. (2002). *Comparison of communication and commitment interface in public and private organizations.* Working paper.

Crino, M., & White, M. (1981). Satisfaction in communication: An examination of the Downs–Hazen measure. *Psychological Reports, 49,* 831–838.

Daft, R., & Lengel, R. (1986). Organizational information requirements, media richness, and structural design. *Management Science, 32,* 554–571.

Davis, K. (1953). A method of studying communication patterns in organizations. *Personnel Psychology, 6,* 301–312.

Davis, K. (1964). Management communication and the grapevine. In C. Redding & G. Sanborn (Eds.), *Business and industrial communication* (pp. 111–113). New York: Harper & Row.

Davis, K. (1968). Success of chain of command oral communications in a manufacturing group. *Academy of Management Journal, 11,* 379–387.

Davis, M. (1986). *Employee attitude surveys: A study to discover the use of resulting data.* Unpublished master's thesis, University of Kansas, Lawrence, KS.

Dawson-Shepherd, A., & White, J. (1994, May). Communication: Why UK managers are shooting themselves in the foot. *Business News,* p. 6.

Debus, M. (1992). *Handbook for excellence in focus group research.* Washington, DC: Academy for Educational Development.

Dewey, J. (1930). *Human nature and conduct.* New York: Modern Library.

DeWine, S., James, A., & Walence, W. (1985, May). *Validation of organizational communication audit instruments.* Paper presented at the annual meeting of the International Communication Association, Honolulu, HI.

Doucouliagos, C. (1995). Worker participation and productivity in labor-managed and participatory capitalist forms: A meta-analysis. *Industrial and Labor Relations Review, 49,* 58–77.

Downs, A. (1991). *The relationship between communication satisfaction and organizational commitment in two Australian organizations.* Unpublished master's thesis. University of Kansas, Lawrence, KS.

Downs, C. (1988). *Communication audits.* Glenview, IL: Scott, Foresman.

Downs, C. (1994). *Analysis of hospitals in Scotland.* Unpublished manuscript.

Downs, C. (2000). *Communication Styles Inventory.* Lawrence, KS: Communication Management, Inc.

Downs, C. (2001). [Unpublished results of professional audits.]

Downs, C. (2002). *The impact of culture on religion.* Working paper.

Downs, C., Adrian, A., & Ticehurst, G. W. (1996, May). *Cultural comparisons of the relationships among communication and organizational commitment.* Paper presented at the Pan Pacific Business Conference, Tokyo.

Downs, C., Adrian, A., & Ticehurst, W. (2002, November). *An exploration of the relationship among communication and organizational commitment in three cultures.* Paper presented at the Nordic Intercultural Communication Conference, Riga, Latvia.

Downs, C., & Conrad, C. (1982). Effective subordinancy. *Journal of Business Communication, 14,* 27–38.

Downs, C., DeWine, S., & Greenbaum, H. (1994). Instrumentation in organizational communication. In R. B. Rubin, P. Palmgreen, & H. E. Sypher (Eds.), *Communication research measures* (pp. 57–80). New York: Guilford Press.

Downs, C., & Hazen, M. (1977). A factor analysis of communication satisfaction. *Journal of Business Communication, 14,* 63–74.

Downs, C., Hydeman, A., & Adrian, A. (2000). Auditing the annual business conference of a major beverage company. In O. Hargie & D. Tourish (Eds.), *Handbook of communication audits for organisations* (pp. 272–290) London: Routledge.

Downs, C., Johnson, K., & Barge, K. (1984). Communication feedback and task performance in organizations. *Organizational Communication Abstracts, 23,* 11–48.

Downs, C., & Pickett, T. (1977). An analysis of the effects of nine leadership-group compatibility contingencies upon productivity and member satisfaction. *Communication Monographs, 44,* 220–230.

Downs, C., Smeyak, G., & Martin, E. (1980). *Professional interviewing.* New York: Harper & Row.

Duke, P. (1981). Communication satisfaction of business education teachers in an urban school system. *Dissertation Abstracts International, 42*(11), 4663.

Dunham, R., & Smith, F. (1979). *Organizational surveys.* Glenview, IL: Scott, Foresman.

Falcione, R., McCrosky, J., & Daly, J. S. (1977). Job satisfaction as a function of employee's communication apprehension, self-esteem, and perceptions of their immediate supervisor. In B. Rubin (Ed.), *Communication yearbook.* New Brunswick, NJ: Transaction–International Communication Association.

Farace, V., Monge, P., & Russell, H. (1977). *Communicating and organizing.* Menlo Park, CA: Addison-Wesley.

Filley, A. C. (1978). *The complete manager.* Middleton, WI: Green Briar Press.

Filley, A. C. (1985). *Introductory notes for Business 838.* Unpublished manuscript.

Filley, A. C., & Pace, L. A. (1976). Making judgments descriptive. In J. W. Pfeiffer & J. E. Jones (Eds.), *The 1976 annual handbook for group facilitators* (pp. 121–130). Los Angeles: University Associates.

Finnegan, J. E. (2000). The impact of personal and organizational values on organizational commitment. *Journal of Occupational and Organizational Psychology, 73,* 149–156.

Fivars, G. (1972). *The critical incident technique: A bibliography.* Unpublished bibliography sponsored by American Institute for Research, Palo Alto, CA.

Flanagan, J. C. (1954). The critical incident technique. *Psychological Bulletin, 51,* 327–358.

Ford, J. D., & Ford, L. W. (1995). The role of conversations in producing intentional change in organizations. *Academy of Management Review, 20,* 541–570.

Fulk, J. (1993). Social construction of communication technology. *Academy of Management Journal, 36,* 921–950.

Fulk, J. & Boyd, B. (1991). Emerging theories of communication in organizations. *Journal of Management, 17*(2), 407–446.

Fulk, J., Schmitz, J., & Ryu, D. (1995). Cognitive elements in the social construction of communication technology. *Management Communication Quarterly, 8,* 259–288.

Fulk, J., Schmitz, J., & Steinfield, C. (1990). A social influence model of technology and use. In J. Fulk & C. Steinfield (Eds.), *Organizations and communication technology* (pp. 117–140). New York: Sage.

Glaser, E. M. (1980). Productivity gains through worklife improvement. *Personnel, 57,* 71.

Goldhaber, G. (1979a). *Auditing organizational communication systems.* Dubuque, IA: Kendall-Hunt.

Goldhaber, G. (1979b). *Organizational communication.* Dubuque, IA: Wm. C. Brown.

Goldhaber, G., & Krivonos, P. (1978). The ICA communication audit: Process, status, and critique. *Journal of Business Communication Systems, 15,* 41–55.

Goldhaber, G., & Rogers, D. (1979). *Auditing organizational communication systems.* Dubuque, IA: Kendall-Hunt.

Gopnik, A. (2003). The return of the word. In E. Tribble & A. Trubek (Eds.), *Writing material: Readings from Plato to the digital age.* Upper Saddle River, NJ: Longman.

Gordon, T. (1949). The airline pilot's job. *Journal of Applied Psychology, 33,* 122–131.

Granovetter, M. (1973). The strength of weak ties. *American Journal of Sociology, 78,* 1360–1380.

Greenbaum, H., Hellwegg, S., & Falcione, R. (1983, May). *Evaluation of communication in organizations: Rationale, history and methodologies.* Paper presented at the annual meeting of the International Communication Association, Dallas, TX.

Greiner, L. E. (1972). Evolution and revolution as organizations grow. *Harvard Business Review, 50,* 37–46.

Gribas, J., & Downs, C. (2002). Metaphoric manifestations of talking "team" with team novices. *Communication Theory, 53*(2), 112–128.

Hansen, G. (1987). Determinants of firm performance: An integration of economic and organizational factors. *Dissertation Abstracts International, 48*(2), 434.

Hargie, O., & Tourish, D. (2000). *Handbook of communication audits for organisations.* London: Routledge.

Hartman, R., & Johnson, J. (1989). Social contagion and multiplexity: Communication networks as predictors of commitment and role ambiguity. *Human Communication Research, 15,* 523–548.

Hartman, R., & Johnson, J. (1990). Formal and informal group structures: An examination of their relationship to role ambiguity. *Social Networks, 12,* 127–151.

Hatfield, J. D., & Huseman, R. C. (1982). Perceptional congruence about communication as related to satisfaction. *Academy of Management Journal, 25,* 349–358.

Hawkins, E., & Penley, L. (1978, May). *The relationship of communication to performance and satisfaction.* Paper presented at the annual meeting of the International Communication Association, San Francisco.

Hecht, M. (1978). Measure of communication satisfaction. *Human Communication Research, 4,* 350–368.

Hilgerman, R. (1998). Communication satisfaction, goal setting, job satisfaction, concertive control, and effectiveness in self-managing teams. *Dissertation Abstracts International, 59*(5), 1661.

Hofstede, G. (1980). Motivation, leadership, and organization: Do American theories apply abroad? *Organizational Dynamics, 9,* 42–63.

Holsti, O. (1969). *Content analysis for the social sciences and humanities.* Reading, MA: Addison-Wesley.

Jacobson, E., & Seashore S. E. (1951). Communication processes in complex organizations. *Journal of Social Issues, 7,* 28–40.

Jones, J. (1981). Analysis of communication satisfaction in four rural school systems. *Dissertation Abstracts International, 42*(4), 1578.

Joyce, W. F., & Slocum, J. W. (1984). Collective climate: Agreement as a basis for defining aggregate climates in organizations. *Academy of Management Journal, 27,* 721–742.

Katz, D., & Kahn, R. (1978). *The social psychology of organizations.* New York: Wiley.

Kilduff, M., & Funk, J. (1998). *Enactment and social networks in a Japanese factory.* Working paper. University Park: Pennsylvania State University.

Kilman, R. H. (1984). *Beyond the quick fix.* San Francisco: Jossey-Bass.

Kilmann, R. H., & Mitroff, I. (1977). A new perspective on the consulting/intervention process: Problem defining versus problem solving. In *Proceedings of the Academy of Management Convention* (pp. 1431–1452). Orlando, FL: Academy of Management.

Kio, J. (1979). A descriptive study of communication satisfaction, need satisfaction, and need importance index among Nigerian workers. *Dissertation Abstracts International, 41*(1), 19.

Klauss, R., & Bass, B. M. (1982). *Interpersonal communication in organizations.* New York: Academic Press.

Knippen, J. (1970). *An episodic study of informal communication in a retail chain store.* Unpublished doctoral dissertation, Florida State University.

Kraut, A. (1995). *Organizational surveys.* New York: Jossey-Bass.

Krejcie, R., & Morgan, D. (1970). Determining sample size for research activities. *Educational and Psychological Measurement, 30,* 607–610.

Krippendorff, K. (1980). *Content analysis.* Beverly Hills, CA: Sage.

Krueger, R., & Casey, M. (2000). *Focus groups: A practical guide for applied research* (3rd ed.). Thousand Oaks, CA: Sage.

Laird, A. (1982). Coordinated management of meaning: An empirical investigation of communication and productive action in two organizations. *Dissertation Abstracts International, 43*(12), 3753.

Lasswell, H. D. (1971). The structure and function of communication in society. In W. Schram & D. Roberts (Eds.), *Process and effects of mass communication* (pp. 84–99). Champaign: University of Illinois Press. (Original Lasswell publication published 1948)

Lawson, D., & Downs, C. (1999, May). *The introduction of Lotus Notes as a new technology into a corporation.* Paper presented at the annual meeting of the International Communication Association, San Francisco.

Leavitt, H. (1972). *Managerial psychology.* Chicago: University of Chicago Press.

Lee, J. W. (1971). An episodic study of communication in a geographically centralized banking organization. *Dissertation Abstracts International, 32*(3), 1127.

Lee, K. B. (1983). Communication satisfaction in private church-related schools. *Dissertation Abstracts International, 44*(6), 1648.

Lee, Y., & Chen, C. (1996). *A study of the relationships among perceived leadership styles, employee communication satisfaction, and employee organisational commitment in the petrochemical industry in Taiwan.* Paper presented at the Fourth Annual Conference on Global Business Environment and Strategy, Anchorage, AL.

Levinson, H. (1972). *Organizational diagnosis.* Cambridge, MA: Harvard Press Review.

Lewis, L., & Seibold, D. (1998). Reconceptualising organizational change implementation as a communication problem: A review of literature and research agenda. In M. Roloff & G. Paulson (Eds.), *Communication yearbook* (Vol. 21, pp. 93–152). New York: Sage.

Likert, R. (1967). *The human organization.* New York: McGraw-Hill.

Mackenzie, K. D. (1986). *Organizational design.* New York: Ablex.

Mackintosh, H. (1973). *A critical incident study of communication factors utilized by prison guards.* Unpublished master's thesis, University of Kansas, Lawrence, KS.

Marting, B. (1969). A study of grapevine communication patterns in a manufacturing organization. *Dissertation Abstracts International, 30*(6), 2204.

Merton, R., Fiske, M., & Kendall, P. (1961). *The focused interview.* New York: Free Press.

Mitchell, T., Holtom, B., Lee, T., Sablynski, C., & Erez, M. (2001). Why people stay: Using job embeddedness to predict voluntary turnover. *Academy of Management Journal, 44,* 1102–1121.

Monge, P., & Contractor, N. (2001). Emergence of communication networks. In F. Jablin & L. Putnam (Eds.), *The new handbook of organizational communication* (pp. 440–502). Thousand Oaks, CA: Sage.

Monge, P., & Day, P. (1976). Multivariate analysis in communication research. *Human Communication Research, 2,* 207–220.

Monge, P., & Eisenberg, E. (1987). Emergent communication networks. In F. Jablin, L. Putnam, K. Roberts, & L. Porter (Eds.), *Handbook of organizational communication* (pp. 304–342). Newbury Park, CA: Sage.

Moreno, J. L. (1934). *Who shall survive?: A new approach to the problem of human interrelations.* New York: Beacon Press.

Nadler, D. A. (1979). The effects of feedback on task group behavior: A review of experimental literature. *Organizational Performance and Human Performance, 23,* 309–338.

Nicholson, J. (1980). Analysis of communication satisfaction in an urban school system. *Dissertation Abstracts International, 41*(9), 3815.

Nie, N., Hull, C., Jenkins, J., Steinbrennler, K., & Bent, D. (1975). *SPSS: Statistical package for the social sciences* (2nd ed.). New York: McGraw-Hill.

Norton, R. W. (1980). Nonmetric multidimensional scaling in communication research: Smallest space analysis. In P. R. Monge & N. Cappella (Eds.), *Multivariate techniques in human communication research* (pp. 309–331). New York: Academic Press.

O'Reilly, C. A., & Roberts, K. (1974). Information filtration in organizations: Three experiments. *Organizational Behavior and Human Performance, 11,* 253–265.

Orpen, C. (1997). The interactive effects of communication quality and job involvement on managerial job satisfaction and work motivation. *Journal of Psychology, 131,* 519–522.

Osgood, C., Suci, G., & Tannenbaum, P. (1967). *The measurement of meaning.* Urbana: University of Illinois Press.

Pacilio, J., & Rudolph, E. (1973, May). *An overview of ECCO methodology.* Paper presented at the annual meeting of the International Communication Association, Montreal, Canada.

Page, P. (1973). Critical requirements for the oral communication of state trial judges. *Dissertation Abstracts International, 34*(12), 7913.

Papa, M. (1990). Communication network patterns and employee performance with new technology. *Communication Research, 17,* 344–368.

Pearce, W., & Cronen, V. E. (1980). *Communication action and meaning: The creation of social realities.* New York: Praeger.

Peters, T., & Waterman, R. (1988). *In search of excellence.* New York: Warner Books.

Pincus, J. D. (1984). The impact of communication satisfaction on job satisfaction and job performance. *Dissertation Abstracts International, 46*(3), 554.

Pincus, D. (1986). Communication satisfaction, job satisfaction, and job performance. *Human Communication Research, 12,* 395–419.

Pollock, T., Whitbred, R., & Contractor, N. (1996, February). *Social information processing, job characteristics and disposition: A test and integration of competing theories of job satisfaction.* Paper presented at the Sunbelt XVI International Social Network Conference, Charleston, SC.

Porter, D. T. (1978). Reliability made simpler: Program PIAS. *CEDR Quarterly, 8,* 711.

Porter, D. T. (1979, May). *The ICA communication audit: Organizational norm.* Paper presented at the annual meeting of the International Communication Association, Chicago.

Porter, D. T. (1985). The validity of communication needs assessment. *Journal of Applied Communication Research, 13,* 59–69.

Porter, D. T. (1986, May). *Contributions of systems theory to the study of organizational communication.* Paper presented at the annual meeting of the International Communication Association, Chicago.

Porter, D. T. (1988). Network analysis. In C. Downs (Ed.), *Communication audits.* Glenview, IL: Scott, Foresman.

Porter, M. (1996). What is strategy? *Harvard Business Review, 74*(6), 61–78.

Potvin, T. (1991). Employee organizational commitment: An examination of its relationship to communication satisfaction and an evaluation of questionnaires designed to measure the construct. *Dissertation Abstracts International, 52*(12), 4147.

Putnam, L., & Cheney, G. (1995). Organizational communication: Historical development and future. In S. Corman, S. Banks, C. Bantz, & M. Mayer (Eds.), *Foundations of organizational communication* (pp. 10–27). New York: Longman Press.

Putnam, L., Phillips, N., & Chapman, P. (1996). Metaphors of communication and organization. In S. Clegg, C. Hardy, & W. Nord (Eds.), *The handbook of organization studies* (pp. 375–408). Thousand Oaks, CA: Sage.

Putti, J. M., Aryee, S., & Phua, J. (1990). Communication relationship satisfaction and organizational commitment. *Group and Organization Studies, 15,* 44–52.

Quirke, B. (1995). Internal communication. In N. Hart (Ed), *Strategic public relations.* Basingstoke, UK: Macmillan.

Read, W. (1962). Upward communication in industrial hierarchies. *Human Relations, 15,* 3–15.

Redding, W. C. (1972). *Communication within the organization.* New York: Industrial Communication Council.

Rice, R., & Aydin, C. (1991). Attitudes toward new organizational technology: Network proximity as a mechanism for social information processing. *Administrative Science Quarterly, 36,* 219–244.

Richmond, V. P., McCrosky, J. C., & Davis, L. M. (1982). Individual differences among employees, management, communication styles, and employee satisfaction. *Human Communication Research, 8,* 170–188.

Rogers, E. (1995). *Diffusion of innovations* (4th ed.). New York: Free Press.

Rosenau, P. (1992). *Post-modernism and the social sciences: Insights, inroads, and intrusions.* Princeton, NJ: Princeton University Press.

Ruben, B. (1972). General system theory: An approach to human communication. In R. Budd & B. Ruben (Eds). *Approaches to human communication* (pp. 120–144). Rochelle Park, NJ: Hayden Book.

Rubin, R. B., Palmgreen, P., & Sypher, H. E. (1994). *Communication research measures.* New York: Guilford Press.

Rudolph, E. (1972, May). *An evaluation of ECCO analysis as a communication audit methodology.* Paper presented at the annual meeting of the International Communication Association Convention, Atlanta, GA.

Ruppel, C. P., & Harrington, S. J. (2000). The relationship of communication, ethical work climate, and trust to commitment and innovation. *Journal of Business Ethics, 25,* 313–329.

Sanders, J. (1976). Utilization of lines of communication within the administration of the University of Kansas described by ECCO analysis. *Dissertation Abstracts International, 37*(8), 4705.

Scott, J. (1991). *Social network analysis: A handbook.* London: Sage.

Semler, R. (1993). *Maverick.* London: Century.

Shannon, C., & Weaver, W. (1949). *The mathematical theory of communication.* Urbana: University of Illinois Press.

Shaw, M. E. (1964). Communication networks. In L. Berkowitz (Ed.), *Advances in experimental social psychology* (Vol. 1, pp. 111–149). New York: Academic Press.

Shelby, A. (1991). Applying the strategic choice model to motivational appeals: A theoretical approach. *Journal of Business Communication, 28,* 187–212.

Smidts, A., Pruyn, A., & van Riel, C. (2001). The impact of employee communication and perceived external prestige on organizational identification. *Academy of Management Journal, 44,* 1051–1062.

Smith, D. (1972, August). Communication research and the idea of process. *Speech Monographs, 39,* 174–182.

Smith, D. K. (1996). *Taking charge of change.* New York: Addison Wesley.

Smith, P., Kendall, L., & Hulin, C. L. (1969). *The measurement of satisfaction in work and retirement.* Chicago: Rand McNally.

Stetler, C. B. (1972). *An exploratory study of the area nurse role.* Unpublished master's thesis, University of Kansas.

Stewart, W. (1982, May). *ECCO analysis program.* Paper presented at the annual meeting of the International Communication Association, Boston.

Stohl, C. (1995). *Organizational communication: Connectedness in action.* Thousand Oaks, CA: Sage.

Sundstrom, E., Burt, R. E., & Kamp, D. (1980). Privacy at work: Architectural correlates of job satisfaction and job performance. *Academy of Management Journal, 23,* 101–117.

Susskind, A., Schwartz, D., Richard, W., & Johnson, J. (2002). *A pair of book ends: Thirty years of organizational communication network research at Michigan State University, 1968–1998.* Unpublished paper.

Thayer, L. (1968). *Communication and communication systems.* Homewood, IL: Irwin.

Thiry, R. (1977). Relationship of communication satisfaction to need fulfillment among Kansas nurses. *Dissertation Abstracts International B, 38*(7), 3131.

Ticehurst, G. W., & Ross-Smith, A. (1992). Communication satisfaction, commitment and job satisfaction in Australian organizations. *Australian Journal of Communication, 19*(1), 130–144.

Tompkins, P. (1977). Management qua communication in rocket research and development. *Communication Monographs, 44,* 1–26.

Tourish, D., & Hargie, C. (1996). Internal communication: Key steps in evaluation and improving performance. *Corporate Communication, 1,* 11–16.

Trevino, L., Lengel, R., & Daft, R. (1987). Media symbolism, media richness, and media choice in organizations: A symbolic interactionist perspective. *Communication Research, 14,* 553–574.

Tubbs, S., & Hain, T. (1979). *Managerial communication and its relationship to total organizational effectiveness.* Paper presented at the annual meeting of the Academy of Management, Atlanta, GA.

Tubbs, S., & Widgery, R. (1978). When productivity lags are key managers really communicating? *Management Review, 67,* 20–25.

Turnbull, P., & Wass, V. (1998). Marksist management: Sophisticated human relations in a high street retail store. *Industrial Relations Journal, 29,* 98–111.

Varona, F. (1996). Relationship between communication satisfaction and organizational commitment in three Guatemalan organizations. *Journal of Business Communication, 33,* 111–131.

Wanous, J. P., & Lawler, E. E. (1972). Measurement and meaning of job satisfaction. *Journal of Applied Psychology, 50,* 95–105.

Weick, K. (1969). *The social psychology of organizing.* Reading, MA: Addison-Wesley.

Weick, K., & Daft, R. (1983). The effectiveness of enterpretation systems. In K. Cameron & D. Whetten (Eds.), *Organizational effectiveness.* New York: Academic Press.

Weiss, D., Davis, R., England, G., & Lofquist, L. (1979). *Manual for the Minnesota Satisfaction Questionnaire.* Minnesota Studies in Vocational Relations Center, Work Adjustment Project, 1967.

Wiio, O. (1976, May). *Organizational communication: Interfacing systems in different contingencies.* Paper presented at the annual meeting of the International Communication Association, Portland, OR.

Wippich, M. L. (1983). *Communication satisfaction, communication style, and perceived organizational effectiveness in an educational setting.* Unpublished doctoral dissertation, University of Kansas.

Author Index

Subject Index

About the Authors

Cal W. Downs, PhD, is Professor of Organizational Communication at the University of Kansas and has held professorships at Northwestern University and the University of Maryland. Additionally, he has been a visiting professor at universities in Finland, Australia, Austria, Holland, and Scotland. Dr. Downs has combined his professorships with an active consulting practice as president of Communication Management, Inc. For many years, he offered in-house training programs for a wide range of organizations, including the University of Michigan Executive Training Center, the University of California, Los Angeles (in their Engineering Management course), and the Agency for International Development. He recently conducted training programs for the top management of OPEC and for companies in China. His expertise focuses on the analysis of organizational communication, intercultural development, and leadership and performance management.

Allyson D. Adrian, PhD, is Adjunct Assistant Professor of Management at the McDonough School of Business at Georgetown University in Washington, DC. Her doctoral research on communication processes in Australian organizations earned her a nomination for the prestigious Redding Award for the best dissertation in communication research. Her research in intercultural communication has led to pioneering work presenting U.S. intellectual culture to non-U.S. Americans. She focuses her current research on culturally strategic communication in the context of global business and education.